T0194244

IN SICKNESS AND IN HEALTH

A wife/caregiver reflects on the words before "I Do"

Deanna Hurtubise

WESTBOW
PRESS®
A DIVISION OF THOMAS NELSON
& ZONDERVAN

WestBow Press books may be ordered through booksellers or by contacting:

WestBow Press
A Division of Thomas Nelson & Zondervan
1663 Liberty Drive
Bloomington, IN 47403
www.westbowpress.com
1 (866) 928-1240

ISBN: 978-1-9736-3078-4 (sc)
ISBN: 978-1-9736-3077-7 (hc)
ISBN: 978-1-9736-3079-1 (e)

Library of Congress Control Number: 2018906886

Print information available on the last page.

WestBow Press rev. date: 06/18/2018

CONTENTS

Dedicated to Tracy
and to Bonnie and the other Hospice angels
for the love and guidance

PREFACE

The words we speak as we gaze into the eyes of our soon-to-be spouses are some of the most important words we will ever utter in our lifetime, or at least they should be. All the year-long preparations have been completed, the families involved have hopefully become friends, and everyone is anxious to celebrate the newly wedded couple. All eyes are on the bride as she walks down the aisle, usually on her father's arm, tears may be shed as he turns his baby girl over to another man to care for her for the rest of her life. Are those tears shed because of the end of an era in the family history, or because as an older and wiser parent, he knows the road ahead will not always be easy for his baby girl.

True married love is made up of three components: passion, intimacy and commitment. The passion is easy to understand; it is probably what attracted us to each other in the first place. It's the glue that makes our sex lives worth looking forward to. Intimacy in this sense refers to verbal sharing and caring, revealing our most private self with another person and being that person's other half, the person who knows you like no other and who shares your most private dreams and fears, the person to whom you can let it all out and know it's okay. It's the part of marriage that provides the shoulder to cry on as well as the fan who is your most ardent supporter, your biggest cheerleader. And then there is commitment, the desire to stick it out through good and bad, the part of the equation that holds you together as a couple when one of the other two components isn't doing so well. But what has happened to this third factor in the marriage equation in this era, the beginning decades of the twenty-first century? When at least fifty percent of marriages end in divorce, one has to wonder what do the words "till death do us part" really mean. As we age, the passion may dwindle but the intimacy and hopefully the commitment should get stronger. When that happens, the marriage lasts.

When we are young and uttering those vows as we gaze lovingly at our partner, love that we are sure will last forever, are we realizing exactly what we are saying? Does the real significance of the words hit home, or are the words just part of the traditional ceremony that goes with the wedding package? In all fairness, if we **really** understood the consequences of "worse", "poorer" "sickness" and "death" instead of hearing in our hearts only "better", "richer", and "health" we'd all probably run for the door and forget the whole thing. If we **really** understood the seriousness of the vows, we'd be scared to death to enter into such a commitment for the rest of our lives. These are pretty serious promises. But for those of us who took the vows, believed in them and took them seriously, be it five years ago or fifty, the understanding of how difficult the promises can be to keep is a reality worth discussing. As a Catholic whose marriage is considered a sacrament, I accept that the vows spoken before "I do" have to mean more than "I do till it's not fun any longer".

In Sickness and in Health is a personal account of one marriage that stood the test of time, not perfectly, but which lasted thanks to those three components of the marriage equation, passion, intimacy and commitment. It is an honest story of a "health journey" through life with one partner with the joys and the sorrows, the pitfalls and the promises and, most importantly, the faith that helped manage it all.

CHAPTER 1

February, 1962: Paul and I met on a blind date arranged by my sister and soon to be brother-in-law. She was interning in microbiology at Good Samaritan Hospital where she met Paul who was teaching her techniques used in the blood bank where he worked to put himself through school. I was dating someone else at the time that my family didn't like very much but with whom I was quite smitten. I thought Paul was cute in a leprechaun kind of way with his red hair and impish smile and a rather corny sense of humor. We dated only four times, and then he stopped calling me as he pursued dating most of the nursing students at the hospital. I wondered what I had done to put him off but since I was still dating someone else that question remained only a curiosity. I found out later that Paul had been feeling some pressure by my family and didn't want to succumb to that kind of pressure. I admit I did find myself thinking about him quite a bit over the summer.

October, 1962 to June, 1967: We didn't see each other again until my sister's wedding. Paul didn't come to the wedding but did come to the reception. When I saw him approach the receiving line, I had no clue what I would say to him after all those months and apparently he didn't either. Instead he just grabbed me by the shoulders and kissed me! We had a few dances later in the evening, and he took me home after the reception. We dated exclusively every weekend for the next five years. However, I knew after only two months that I would probably spend the rest of my life with him, have his babies and live happily ever after.

The December of 1962 we went to my college Christmas Ball. Unfortunately, I became violently ill afterwards with food poisoning and was bed ridden for four days until Paul came over on New Year's

Eve. Still not feeling great, we didn't want to go out anywhere to party, but he asked me if I wanted to see where he worked. Then he asked me if I knew my blood type! *What a really crazy question!* I thought. Since I really didn't know it, he suggested he draw my blood to find out. These were the days when knowing your Rh factor was important. After drawing my blood, Paul told me I had type A, Rh negative blood and without thinking first I blurted out, "Oh no! What type are you?" I don't think he understood where my thought process of having his babies was going after only two months of dating, and I didn't tell him. As it turned out, he was also Rh positive!

Paul was four years older than I, and my mother thought he was too old for me, but I readily reminded her that she was six years younger than my dad! That was the end of that discussion. I felt I had really met my soul mate; we hardly ever disagreed on anything, and our deep conversations lasted into the wee hours. He was a deeply spiritual man who had spent several years in Holy Cross Seminary at Notre Dame, Indiana before realizing the priesthood was not for him. Their loss was my gain.

1963: I've always loved Valentine's Day. As a child, I used to write a poem to my mom and dad every year to let them know how much I loved them. My parents never forgot Valentine's Day, and they gave each other wonderful cards that my mother kept in a big box for years. On Valentine's Day, 1963, I was still juggling dating Paul and a few others, seeing one on Friday another on Saturday and usually Paul on Sunday when he ate a free meal cooked by my mother. I found this arrangement stressful, dating several guys at the same time, and it lasted for six months. No one else acknowledged Valentine's Day at all, but Paul sent me a beautiful bouquet. I made the decision to end my relationship with the others right then and there and the rest was history! Consequently, I have always felt that Valentine's Day was a personal anniversary for me.

In November, Paul was going to drive back to South Bend, Indiana to be with his family for Thanksgiving. I was shocked when he invited me to go with him for the weekend to meet his parents and siblings. My mother wasn't at all in favor of my traveling with him over a weekend, but I assured her I would be staying at his family's home, and all would be on the up and up. I loved his entire family immediately with maybe the exception of his dad who was a bit intimidating. He was terribly overweight and looked very unhealthy. This was a little off-putting for me because I wondered if Paul would end up like his father, and that thought was definitely not appealing, but at that moment I couldn't imagine this thin, healthy, red head looking anything but wonderful. His three younger brothers and his sister were delightful and his mother most inviting and welcoming.

Summer, 1966: Somehow, my four years of college ended in what felt like a blink of an eye. They were some of the most wonderful years of my life up to that time. I found my calling to teach high school French and had enjoyed dancing in the college theater productions and, of course, had loved those four years of dating Paul. We became engaged during my senior year, but we hadn't planned on marrying until summer of 1967.

We had gone out on a date one Saturday night in August, 1966, and Paul hadn't left to go back to his apartment until after one o'clock in the morning. So I was surprised to get a phone call from him around four thirty early Sunday morning telling me his dad had died during the night of a massive heart attack. He was going to leave shortly to drive to South Bend to be with his family, and he was obviously distraught. My parents had heard the phone ring and wondered what was going on. When I told them, my dad told Paul to come to our house first, get some coffee and something to eat before making the four hour drive. Then he told Paul not to make any important decisions during such an emotional time. This was before the era of cell phones, but he managed to call me long distance every day to let me know what the funeral arrangements were going to be. My parents and I drove to South Bend to attend the services. We stayed in a motel nearby, and I was so frustrated at not being able to be with Paul at his mother's house.

The funeral lasted three days; the visitation went on for two days since there were relatives who had to come from out of town. The funeral Mass was the third day after which his body was transported to Chicago where he was interred. I remember how awful it was, how distraught Paul was and how pitiful his mother was. She didn't even drive a car, have a job or know how to support herself and her three children who were still at home. And to make it worse, his dad had been an insurance salesman but didn't have life insurance of his own! His sister was just starting high school that September. I remember sitting on the front porch with her when she said it was so sad that he had to die just when they were starting to be friends! My heart broke for all of them, and I told my parents when we all got back to South Bend from Chicago, I was not driving back with them. I wanted to stay with Paul's family and help in any way I could. Paul and I would drive back together later. They didn't like the idea, but I wasn't exactly asking permission.

Paul's father was only fifty-eight years old when he died, but he had lived a very unhealthy lifestyle. He was the same age as Paul's grandfather when he, too, died of a massive heart attack. It was at that moment I thought about my future with Paul and hoped his life would turn out differently. Would he be able to break the cycle of death at age fifty-eight?

CHAPTER 2

June, 1967: Our wedding was beautiful, and I remember every moment of the day. My sister was living a private nightmare as her husband was in Vietnam, and as I was walking down the aisle to take a husband, she didn't know if hers was dead or alive. She never told me at that time that a news story had just broken that her husband's unit had come under attack, and she was terrified that as I was becoming a new bride, she was becoming a new widow! The eve of the wedding she told me to make a mental note to try and remember every single aspect of the day which I did. I gladly repeated those vows, for better or worse, for richer or poorer, in sickness and health until death do us part. Then we began our life journey together. I was twenty-three and Paul was twenty-seven.

No one ever knew, however, that in the back of my mind was the ominous fear that he would follow in the footsteps of his father and grandfather at age fifty-eight. I thought back to that first time I had met his unhealthy father and was privately concerned. After all, I knew he had a family history of heart disease and to make matters worse, Paul smoked a pack of cigarettes a day, which I hated. I calculated that I had thirty-one years of wedded bliss to look forward to before I'd have to face the "till death do us part" possibility.

Three children blessed us with their arrivals during the first five and half years of our marriage, our first daughter, Jennie in 1968, our son, Jamie in 1971 and another daughter, Julie in 1973. I gave up my teaching career to be a stay at home mom until they were all in school, a decision I have never regretted even though it took twelve years to get back to a classroom. Paul continued his education first with a master's degree and then a doctorate at Ohio State University in a new field of science at the time called Immunohematology.

Those lean years were definitely the "for richer or poorer" years, emphasis on poorer. It still amazes me when I think back to how I managed the money as well as I did. I wasn't working outside the home, and Paul made a paltry stipend as a student. I panicked if I spent more than $20.00 a week at the grocery, I learned to sew little sun dresses for our daughter and made all our Christmas gifts for family on a shoestring budget. When our son was born, my dad paid the hospital bill since students had no medical insurance. In retrospect, they were very lean years but some of the happiest I can remember. The "poorer" wasn't so bad, and the "for better or worse" was leaning heavily toward the better!

1976: Well established as a scientist, Paul had stayed on at Ohio State University Hospital for a short time but had been invited to move our family from Columbus to follow his mentor who had left the previous year. It was a very difficult decision for him to make, and he changed his mind over and over. One week he wanted to move, and I would begin the mental process of thinking about selling the house, finding a new house, finding a school for our oldest daughter, a pre-school for our son, a pediatrician, and a vet for the dog. And just when my mental list was formulated, Paul would change his mind and decide to stay. Then I would rethink all the positive reasons to stay in Columbus. Then he would change his mind again. This went on and on for nine months until intense stomach pain landed me in the emergency room. After many tests and finding no explanation, the doctor asked me what was going on at home. When I described our state of indecision, he diagnosed me with a severe stomach spasm from stress, gave me a prescription for the pain and told Paul to make a final decision that night…and stick with it! That diagnosis would continue to plague me over the years as it seemed my stomach was definitely my "stress center".

I was thrilled when Paul finally decided to follow his mentor and return to my home town, my parents and my sister and her husband who had returned in one piece from Vietnam. I remember the night well since I went to bed relieved but also wary of all the work that needed to be done to accomplish the transition, work that would inevitably fall onto me since Paul was always busy at the hospital. It was the night I had a very personal, spiritual dream in which Jesus told me not to worry, and that He was with me and would always be with me.

I woke up wanting the wonderful and powerful dream to continue, but He was gone. Apparently He was with me because everything fell into place more easily than I could have ever predicted. Our children were two, four and seven when we said goodbye to Columbus, and I was a busy mom with a new house we had built next door to my sister's family. It was a wonderful community for a growing family with a pool, tennis courts, club house, and a lake with ducks to feed in the summer and to ice skate on in winter. And to make it even better, the following year my parents moved into a townhome in the same community allowing our children to literally walk "over the creek and through the woods to grandmother's house". They loved it, and so did my parents. However, the children and I didn't see much of Paul as he was very busy building a brand new immunology lab at University Hospital, establishing himself in the hospital community and traveling to every medical conference he could. It was a lonely time for me in the marriage, and though the "for richer or poorer" was getting richer, the "for better or worse" felt a bit worse for a while.

There was, however, one perk with his job in that I was able to pursue my master's degree in French language and civilization tuition free as the spouse of a faculty member, who apparently felt I needed to improve myself instead of being just a stay at home mom, an attitude about which I had mixed feelings at the time. I experienced many a tearful day trying to resume study habits, taking exams and continuing to be a homemaker and full time mom to three little kids. I was pretty worn down by January of the second year into the program when I became ill with pneumonia, and it took all I had to rebound since Paul was rarely around to help me much. It seemed the "for better or worse" kept getting worse and gnawing at my soul. "In sickness and in health" became very real since I had never felt that bad before or as incapable of doing all I had to do. I don't know how I would have made it through that time without my mother living so close, and she helped me with the children and the housework. I knew I had been really sick when during my recovery I couldn't vacuum a room without feeling faint.

August, 1980: Having finally acquired my advanced degree going part time over three years, I did eventually appreciate Paul's urging me to go back to school, and I found the perfect part time job teaching in a small high school close to home when our youngest was in first grade. I loved my new job and income! Paul and I were both working hard, earning more money than either of us had before. Suddenly the "for richer or poorer" was promising a brighter future, and I felt I had the best of both worlds. I could be home to get the kids on the bus in the morning, and I returned home from school before they did. I loved using the French language again, bringing home a paycheck and still having the luxury of my time with the kids after school. But I never lost track of the fact that now Paul would reach age fifty-eight in only seventeen years. He continued to smoke heavily which he knew I hated but he was hopelessly addicted and quite honestly, very unpleasant to be around when he tried to quit.

We were both enjoying successful careers, and I built my part time job into full time over the next four years. We traveled with our children every summer providing them with the same kind of quality vacations my sister and I had enjoyed growing up. We had bought a Volkswagon pop up top camper bus which served as my car and provided us with the ability to travel on a budget. Our family became quite enamored with camping; traveling from Ohio to California and back also proved how well we could all get along in a small space for three weeks. Between 1984 and 1999, Paul and I were also fortunate to travel for free to France with my students on seven different occasions seeing cosmopolitan cities and charming villages I had only dreamed of visiting and which transformed my Irish leprechaun into a true Francophile. Our life was definitely better than worse and richer than poorer.

Spring, 1984: I am happy to say that I have not had many health issues to deal with during my life with the exception of the stomach spasms from time to time. Other than for the births of our three children, I had never been hospitalized. But that was about to change. During my annual physical, the doctor found a painfully cystic ovary that had to come out. Surgery was scheduled for the week of spring break. Paul was working in the field of Pathology and didn't let me know how worried he was. I'm glad he didn't since I was scared enough already! The actual surgery went well with no malignancies, much to my husband's relief. The only complication was that I couldn't urinate on my own. I had to have a catheter multiple times a day, and there didn't seem to be a solution. They began by giving me a pill to stimulate the bladder, but it didn't work. They changed it to an injection, but that wasn't working either. Then one morning at the shift change, the night nurse gave me the pill and the day nurse gave me the injection and I overdosed on the medication. I remember salivating so much I couldn't swallow fast enough, and I thought I was going to drown. Somehow, I managed to get out of bed and walk down the hall holding on to the wall since I was so faint. I remember yelling every curse word I knew until someone came running to put me back to bed and shut me up. Only after they took my blood pressure and found I was going into shock did they realize what had happened. Convinced they were going to kill me, I called Paul and told him to come and take me home immediately. The only problem was that I still couldn't urinate. To my surprise, the surgeon allowed me to leave with multiple catheter packages to use at home. He felt once I could relax at home, nature would take its course. I hoped he was right; how was I going to go to France with students in six weeks and have to use a catheter all through the trip? Fortunately, he was right, and I only had to use the catheter once!

I was supposed to take off work for six weeks, but our first student trip to France was six weeks away, and I had to return after only two weeks of rest to get everything done in time. The doctor was not happy but made me promise to teach sitting down. I discovered how difficult it was to be a patient. By the time school was out for the summer, I had lost weight and was very tired. But out first student trip to Europe was ready to roll, and I just had to get my act together. The first foreign travel experience with a group of fifteen teenagers went without incident, and we had a fabulous time. I was very relieved and very tired after we returned home but also most grateful for having been physically capable of completing the task. We would do it six more times over the course of my career.

CHAPTER 3

1997: During the thirteen years that followed my surgery, our lives were good. I was enjoying my career; we traveled to France with my students a few more times, and we had marvelous family vacations every summer. Paul continued to smoke despite all my objections, and I continued to worry. He was going to be fifty-eight years old in eighteen months. Thirty years after our wedding, I could see Paul's health deteriorating. The tell-tale signs of heart disease were there. He was always exhausted, had very little energy to give to the family, his complexion looked ashy and unhealthy, and he continued to smoke a pack a day despite my pleas for him to quit. Even his best friend and colleague asked me one night if he was alright. Our first born was getting married in September, and I was keenly aware that age fifty-eight was getting dangerously close. I prayed he would live long enough to walk her down the aisle. I had a recurring nightmare that he died in our home leaving me and the children alone, just like his dad had done to his mom, and I would wake up crying. If he asked me what I had dreamed, I would tell him honestly, but that only seemed to irritate him.

March, 1998: Fortunately, he did walk our daughter down the aisle, but six months after the wedding, Paul continued to look worse and worse. When his best friend expressed concern to me again wondering what was wrong, on a cold day in February I threatened to leave my husband if he refused to go to the doctor. Thankfully, he agreed and didn't make me have to decide to follow through with my ultimatum! After a hopelessly failed stress test, the doctor told him he needed an angiogram immediately. Paul's response was that it would have to wait till the following week since he had a business trip to Colorado that weekend. I never knew until much later that for quite some time he had been short of breath and having chest pains even walking around the hospital complex. Had I known, I never would have allowed him to travel especially to a place where the altitude would be a factor. The angiogram was scheduled for the Monday after his trip, and the doctor advised him not to do anything stressful until then! I have never prayed so hard to see him return safely from a business trip!

I took off work to be with him for the test, and when I met him at the hospital he said his lab techs were worried about him, but he had reassured them saying, "It's not like I am having a heart attack or anything!" I remember vividly sitting in the waiting area when the doctor came out and told me they were admitting him immediately. I was not shocked to hear that he needed five bypasses the next day, or he could die. His fifty-eighth birthday was three months away! Suddenly the "till death do us part" thing was looming as a real possibility. Over the years we had proven that having very little money was doable, and that stressful periods in our marriage were surmountable, that caring for each other during minor illnesses was not difficult. But I don't think there is any way to prepare for the reality of the "till death" part when it hits. There's really no training for this possibility. I remember feeling very calm, almost as though I knew this was the inevitable, it was going to be the result thirty years after our wedding that I had always feared, but at the same time I was not able to fully comprehend that it was actually our reality at that moment. I was too terrified to cry for the first time in my life. After getting him settled in his room, I left the hospital to go home to tell the family. I stopped first at the marina where we had our boat docked and looked out at the Ohio River, the wonderful river overlook where we had spent so much time and where we had planned to spend our retirement years, and I prayed. "Dear Lord, please let him survive to enjoy this place again." I went back to the hospital later that night and watched him smoke his last cigarette.

In the pre-op room the following day, my inability to cry was resolved when one of my former students who had gone with us to France in 1984 appeared at his bedside. She was now a critical care nurse and had seen his name on the roster and asked to be on his case. She said she wanted to take care of the man who had taken such good care of her in Europe. My tears finally flowed freely as he was wheeled away to the operating room. There is no more gut wrenching experience than holding your loved one's warm hand and wondering if it is the last time it will feel like that.

My sister came to sit with me for part of the time he was in surgery. She brought me something to eat, but there was no way I could even look at food. There were other family members awaiting the appearance of their loved one's doctor, many of them pacing back and forth. Something happens to me when I am that terrified. I become like stone and remain nearly motionless, as though if I move, something bad will happen. I don't want to talk; I don't want to eat; I don't want to move. The only thing I can do is pray.

After an interminable day, Paul survived the gruesome procedure of cracking open his chest, hours on the heart/lung machine and five bypasses reconstructed from an artery taken from his left arm. The surgeon emerged to tell me that he didn't understand how Paul was even alive after what he had to repair. Honestly, after all he told me, I wasn't sure why either. I went back to the recovery room and hardly recognized the man I married. He had tubes and wires coming out from everywhere and the gas they blew into his body during the surgery puffed him out resembling the Michelin Man. I couldn't believe my eyes, and it was difficult to even stay in the same room with him looking like that. The surgeon had tried to prepare me for how he would look, but the reality was worse than I had anticipated. But at least he survived and "till death do us part" would just have to wait! His fifty-eighth birthday was a joyous celebration three months later, and no one but me understood the real significance of it. Ignorance truly is bliss when shortly after the surgery he developed a slight tremor in his left hand due, we thought, to some nerve damage after removal of the artery from that arm. But, unfortunately, that was not to be the case.

CHAPTER 4

O ctober, 2000: After the cardiac surgery, Paul slipped into a mild depression, a fact that I learned is predictable after this procedure. It is due in part to the brain chemistry being altered while on the heart/lung machine. He stopped going to church, seemed to withdraw into some inner place and refused to do most of the therapies necessary during his recovery.

The tremor in his left hand continued, and eighteen months later, he felt his left foot drag slightly. It was so slight that I never noticed it at all. But he knew something was definitely wrong. I asked him what he thought it was, and he screamed, "I think I have Parkinson's disease!"

"What?" I asked. "Why in the world would you think something like that?" He walked out of the room and never answered me. It wasn't until much later that I learned his aunt and uncle also had the disease and that there is a genetic component involved.

I went with him to his first visit to the neurologist who diagnosed him with early stage Parkinson's based on the rigidity in some of his joints, the hand tremor, the foot drag and the absence of a sense of smell. This last symptom, we discovered, is the first sign of the disease years before any other symptom shows up. I knew he had lost the sense of smell years earlier, but he attributed it to a chemical accident in the lab. I will never forget the moment when the doctor pronounced the diagnosis because I really didn't see this coming. The heartbreaking image of my husband in tears asking the doctor if someday his grandchildren would be afraid of him is seared into my mind forever. Suddenly, "in sickness and health" reared its ugly head again after I had thought the successful cardiac surgery had put that fear to rest.

With no scientific proof at the time to back up my personal theory, I felt convinced that Parkinson's disease is a two sided gamble, one genetic and one environmental. The aunt and the uncle with the disease were on his mother's side, adding credence to the genetic. When Paul was on the heart/lung machine, we now know that the process affects the neurons in the brain. Since his hand tremor started just days after the surgery, I felt certain that the surgery exacerbated the problem within the altered brain environment triggering the onset of the symptoms. Of course, we will never know if the disease would have ever manifested itself without the cardiac surgery to trigger it or at least put it off until a much later age. The following month, the reality of the disease hit me, and I realized I had not yet given in to my emotions. I stopped at my parents' home after work and sobbed for an hour at the realization that our golden years were going to be so compromised instead of as wonderful as my parents' had been. I was beyond devastated, and it felt like a death to be grieved. I sat in their bedroom and let out all that emotion.

Our youngest daughter was scheduled to be married on St. Patrick's Day, 2001. Her future in-laws organized a wonderful patio party the summer before for all the members of both families to get acquainted. It was a lovely, sunny day, and I was a bit nervous, not because of meeting the other family because we had already met some of them on other occasions, but because I had discovered that my future son-in-law's Godfather was none other than one of the guys whom I had dated in the sixty's! Who could have ever predicted that? Now there was no way he and Paul wouldn't meet each other for the first time in nearly forty years! I had to admit he didn't look so good to me when he walked in, and it was really sweet that Paul looked very nervous.

Five months into his diagnosed disease, our daughter did get married on St. Patrick's Day leaving us with an empty nest. No one at the wedding reception had any clue that the parents of the bride were facing such an uncertain future. Adding to my stress level was the fact that Paul didn't want anyone to know his diagnosis. He forbade me to share this information with anyone but our children and my parents. What he didn't realize was that by so doing, he was denying me any kind of support system. He didn't even share it with his own four siblings or his mother. Even my only sister was kept in the dark which eventually blew up in my face. One of her best friends worked with Paul at the hospital and noticed changes in his demeanor so she asked my sister if there was something wrong with him. When my sister called to ask me, Paul was sitting across the kitchen table from me so I couldn't speak freely. She was getting angry at my hesitancy to answer her which I could easily understand. Finally, he gave me permission to share this unpleasant information with her.

April, 2001: When I thought my heart could break no more, life delivered another crushing blow. My dear ninety-six year old father died suddenly of a ruptured abdominal aorta aneurism. It seemed life was falling apart all around me. Those early weeks after his funeral are now a blur, but I do know I stuffed my grief way down as I began caring for and hurting with my ninety year old mother. They had been married sixty-eight years, and she had never lived alone, having gone from her parents' home to her husband's. It became evident that living alone was so foreign to her, and she was not thriving. My heart broke for her as the "till death do us part" was her new normal.

Two months later, Paul and I were scheduled to go to Colorado for a niece's wedding, and Paul's three brothers would be there. It coincided with Father's Day, a particularly difficult day for me that year. Our daughters were on the trip with us and presented Paul with a gift of a sizeable donation in his name to the Michael J. Fox foundation. He was so shocked and moved that he began to cry. It was a defining moment for him and one I will always remember because he had just publicly come face to face with the reality from which he could no longer hide. He cried for almost an hour which was cathartic for him, and he decided right then to finally share his diagnosis with his three brothers. He still didn't want to tell his mother because it would upset her. But at least now we both had a broader support system to lean on.

April. 2002: With the approaching first anniversary of my dad's death, my stifled emotions caught up with me. I actually had to call in sick to work one morning because I could not stop crying. I had never had an emotional meltdown like that before, and I frightened myself. It was like all the tears that had been bottled up inside for so long finally were released. I knew I needed help, and for the first time, I called a psychologist, a former Psychology professor who had a private practice. I had always been able to counsel my own children, and I had spent countless hours counseling my students over the course of my career, but at this moment I was incapable of helping myself. The tears continued with the psychologist as I related the emotional events since October, 2000, beginning with Paul's devastating diagnosis, our empty nest and my father's death. I told him I felt like I was losing my mind since in the year caring for my mother, it felt like I had been inside her head and heart, always knowing what she was thinking, always feeling what she was feeling, piled on top of my own grief. Sympathy had morphed into an empathy I could not sustain any longer. He assured me I was not losing my mind but simply giving in to all that I should have processed a year earlier. He explained that empathy is a very real and devastating emotion, and I had been empathizing with my mother for the entire year. He provided some tools to help me cope, and with time, they did.

June, 2002: It was apparent that my mother was not thriving, and finally after a year of prodding her to move in with us, she decided to take us up on it. Paul was totally on board with this decision, and I was most grateful to him for his compassion. It was not an easy transition for either of us, but no longer alone, she began living again, not completely since she admitted she felt like half a person, but at least she was eating and sleeping and occasionally laughing again. This was also the beginning of my last year of teaching, and I was emotionally and physically exhausted. My mother felt she was needed and had a purpose again keeping my house clean so I could come home every day with very little to do. We shared some of the chores and meal preparation, and it was a win-win for both of us.

February, 2003: The year started off joyfully as our oldest daughter had twins in February, and our youngest daughter announced she was pregnant. Three new babies in one year made 2003 a year of more positive emotions. Meanwhile, Paul's disease continued to respond to the prescribed medications, and the ugly diagnosis of Parkinson's disease didn't impact our lives too much yet. He continued to work full time at the hospital, and I set about loving my new role of grandmother. I retired in June, and that August, as my former colleagues were going back to school, Paul and I stepped onto a very luxurious cruise ship to explore the inside passage of Alaska. Life was definitely returning to the "for better". Although he was three years into the disease, it didn't stop him from hiking on glaciers, canoeing on pristine lakes and touring this incredibly beautiful part of the world. It was our first experience cruising, and we were hooked!

Paul continued to work for three more years, and we traveled extensively every summer spending money like never before. Our lives were definitely richer and our bank account poorer, but I knew there would come a day when he would not be able to travel at all so it didn't matter. We spent the summer of 2004 in Florida with my mother and our children and four grandchildren to celebrate my sixtieth birthday, and his disease still did not hamper him in any way. He continued to walk the beach daily although he did tire more easily, and his medications were keeping the symptoms at bay. In 2005, we went to California to visit his mother, and though she knew nothing of his diagnosis, she would never have guessed from Paul's outward appearance. He did, however, finally share it with his sister. Then in March, 2006, Paul finally retired after thirty years at the hospital. We immediately set out to plan his dream retirement trip, a Mediterranean cruise to Italy, France, Spain, Majorca, Tunis, Sicily, The Amalfi Coast and the Isle of Capri with the trip ending in Pompeii. For better or worse was looking a whole lot better. I had heard friends say they dreaded when their husbands retired and were under foot all day, but I genuinely loved having him around all the time. And then everything changed for the worse.

CHAPTER 5

March, 2006: Only weeks after Paul retired and four years after moving in with us, my ninety-five year old mother became totally disabled with severe rheumatoid arthritis. Overnight she went from taking daily walks to not being able to move any joint in her body without incredible pain! It was like she had been hit by a two ton truck. We took care of her as well as we could, Paul arranging for her to see his friend, a renowned rheumatologist, who prescribed some pretty heavy duty drugs. She never liked taking medication, and she never took more than one Tylenol at a time, never two! The symptoms were somewhat relieved, but she was a very sick lady. I honestly don't know what I would have done if Paul had not been home with me during this time. Eventually, all the drugs lowered her immune system, and she developed double pneumonia over the Fourth of July weekend. We got her into the emergency room, and the attending physician admitted her immediately. He told me there was a good chance she would not leave! The pneumonia was necrotizing, literally destroying her lung tissue on both sides. She remained there for twenty-one days with a member of our family at her bedside 24/7. On the eighteenth day, she couldn't even hold her head up, eat or stay awake. The staff suggested we call Hospice, and we were all devastated. We also called her priest who was going to meet us there the next morning. On the nineteenth day in the hospital, we entered her room with heavy hearts dreading what was to come, only to find her sitting up in the chair, cheerfully eating breakfast and wondering why her priest and Hospice were there. I'll never forget the look on the Hospice worker's face as she asked why in the world she had been called. It was like an overnight miracle. I had been making a novena to my patron saint, St. Anne, whose feast day is July 26. I prayed that she intercede and help my mother get well or have a peaceful death. On the twentieth day in the hospital, she had a pacemaker implanted to regulate an irregular heartbeat, and she left for rehab on the twenty-first day! It was July 26, St. Ann's feast day! No one on the staff could believe that she had beaten such a serious case of pneumonia, especially at age ninety-five.

My sister and I took turns visiting her every day at the nursing home where she had to get intense physical therapy to regain her strength, and daily we could note her progress. She absolutely amazed everyone there. Paul and I felt certain our late August Mediterranean cruise would still be possible. My sister was going to live in our house with her if she were able to come home during our vacation. But two weeks before our departure date, she developed a terrible bacterial infection called C-difficile which is notorious for killing people much younger than she. I wanted to cancel the trip, but she would not hear of it, and she made me promise that we would still go. She was so excited that at the end of our itinerary we were going to see Pompeii, and she had even given me a book that she and my dad bought there years before. The night before our departure, we visited her, and she was noticeably failing. My heart was breaking at the thought of leaving her, but she looked at me and said, "No tears!" Paul gave her a hug, and he told me later that she said, "Paul, thanks for everything." She also told my sister how much she was going to miss me. I am convinced she knew we would never see each other again. I will never forget the intense sadness I felt leaving her room that night.

Paul's dream retirement trip quickly became a nightmare. It began with the loss of our two carry-on bags which somehow never made it on to the ship. Consequently, I had no shoes except the sandals on my feet, but even worse, Paul's bag contained all his medications. This was a serious setback. He went to the ship's doctor to inquire how to remedy the situation who told him he would have to wait until our first port in Monaco. He would call ahead and give them the list of all his Parkinson's medications. The only problem with that was the length of time in between his last dose and his next dose. In addition, the European dosages were different from those in the United States, but at least he got the meds! To make things even worse, the statins he had been taking for his cholesterol suddenly began creating unbearable leg pain, and he had a terrible time keeping up with all the tour guides on the excursions. And then the unthinkable happened.

September 3, 2006: I checked my email on the ship daily, and when we got back from the beautiful island of Majorca, where ironically, I had bought my mother a music box playing Chopin, there was an email from my sister saying that our mother had died during the night. When I figured the time difference, she had probably died while I was buying her gift. The music box played Chopin's *Tristesse,* which means "sadness" in French. I sat in front of the computer screen and just yelled "NO" and took off running back to our cabin. I remember opening the door, and Paul was sitting on the bed as I screamed, "she died!" His response was just as mine had been as he kept saying "Oh no, no." I was in such a state that I couldn't even cry. I just kept pacing around the room wondering what to do. We decided we were going to fly home immediately, but when we talked to our daughter, Julie, on the phone, she had us rethink the plan. Apparently, she had visited her grandmother the evening before she died, so she was the last family member to see her alive. My mother had asked her if she could get a message to me. She said, "Tell your mother to remember Pompeii," our final stop on the trip. Then Julie said, "Mom, I think she knew she was going to die, and she wanted you to finish the trip." After talking with my sister, she said she would handle all the funeral details, and it would take place upon our return. She reiterated that we should not cut the trip short. That was the hardest thing I have ever done. We did make it to Pompeii, and I got chills when our tour guide told us his name was Angelo, "you know, like the angels", he added.

Unfortunately, Paul's leg pain continued to be a serious problem, and he was forced to give up taking all statins. I knew this would be a complication since it was the statins that were controlling his heart disease. But at least the Parkinson's wasn't causing him any further problems. We came home on schedule with very heavy hearts and laid my mother to rest. It was the most devastating day of my life.

2007: That Christmas, we decided to go to San Francisco again to visit Paul's mother, brother and sister before we left for our trip of a lifetime to Antarctica in January with my sister and her husband. It was indeed our favorite voyage ever and even the crew called it a miracle trip since of the ten ports that were possible, we made nine of them thanks to unusually good weather for January in Antarctica. But we called it our miracle trip for another reason.

During our first excursion in a tender boat passing the first of many icebergs, I spotted something different on one of them that didn't appear anywhere else. Plain as day in brown letters on the white surface were an O, an M and an A. The guide could not explain it and had never seen it before. But my sister and I knew what it was. My mother's name to all her grandchildren was "Oma" and we figured since it was the gift of our inheritance from her that paid for the trip, she was just signing the card! It still gives me chills to remember that moment.

Later in the trip, as we were about to be in the middle of nowhere, we received a phone call from our son who said, "Mom, I can't believe I am telling you this again, but grandma died today in San Francisco!" Not again! The following day we were going to be sailing into a part of the south pole where there would be no available communication, no way to make plans with our family, and certainly no way to leave the trip early. Finally, the ship's captain allowed us to use his ship-to-shore emergency equipment to try and contact Paul's brother in California and also the airlines to get us there upon our return from Antarctica. We couldn't believe this was happening to us again, and it felt very surreal. It is truly unsettling to realize you are about to go to a place where there are no other human beings except those on the ship with you, and that there is absolutely no way anyone from home can contact you. Under any other circumstances, that thought would be a bit exciting, almost romantic. But under these circumstances, it felt dangerous to be so out of touch at such a terrible time. Though we felt like our emotional life was unraveling, at least Paul's Parkinson's symptoms were still under control.

We managed to get home just long enough to unpack our luggage, throw clothes into the washer and dryer and repack for a departure the following day to California. Paul wasn't saying much about his mother's unexpected death but I knew he was thinking about what he would say for her eulogy. The flight was uneventful; our youngest daughter came with us to represent her siblings, and it was so good to have her there, too. As we deplaned, it was hard to believe that just days before, we were communing with thousands of penguins and enjoying another continent. The morning of the funeral, Paul awoke early to attempt putting words to paper for his mother's eulogy, but nothing came. So in a moment of panic for him, I volunteered to relieve him of this burden, and I wrote it. The service was beautiful, and the family enjoyed a reunion as we all said our goodbyes to a wonderful lady.

CHAPTER 6

We were almost afraid to travel again for fear we'd lose someone else, but we pushed those fears away and continued to travel twice more in 2007 with no further drama or crisis. That summer we took another outstanding vacation, a Baltic cruise, which sent us to England and the white cliffs of Dover, Germany, Russia, Estonia, Finland, Sweden and Denmark. This proved to be an amazing time and a real high point in our travel memories. Paul was beginning to show signs of some dystonia, the unnecessary upper body movements similar to those of Michael J. Fox, and also some bladder incontinence. These were definitely new symptoms for which we were not prepared. Other than his usual travel-related constipation (we thought) and more fatigue than usual, he did well. Later we learned that the severe constipation is another symptom of Parkinson's and would cause much bigger problems down the road.

October, 2007: We had celebrated our fortieth anniversary in June, and we decided to take a cruise through the Hawaiian Islands where we would renew our vows. Forty years! It didn't seem possible that so much time had passed since we said those words before "I do" for the first time. I had had him by my side for nine years longer than I thought I would on our wedding day, and I was incredibly grateful. There is nothing but beauty in this part of the world, and it felt like a dream as the wedding ceremony unfolded aboard ship with the Hawaiian sunset for a back drop. One of the crew played the ukulele and sang the Hawaiian Wedding Song in the native language. Neither Paul nor I was prepared for how emotional this moment was going to be, even more so than the first time we had repeated those words after the priest in 1967. So much living had occurred since then, so much shared joy, so much shared grief. We had experienced the better and the worse, the richer and the poorer, the sickness and the health. We cried as we repeated the familiar vows for the second time as they seemed to mean even more now than forty years earlier.

Summer, 2008: Paul continued to do well managing the disease as long as he was faithful to the medication regimen. There were little things that were more annoyances than real problems, like the bladder incontinence from time to time and the chronic constipation. At this point, I was not keeping track of how many days he would go without a bowel movement nor was I in charge of refilling or organizing his medications into the twenty-eight little weekly boxes. But that would soon change.

We continued to make travel plans, and the adventure that year was a Danube River cruise with my sister and her husband. We had decided that if we were going to spend money on travel, we would try to get as many countries into one trip as we could, and this cruise did just that. We were able to visit Hungary, the Czech Republic, Austria, Slovakia and Germany. We were proud of ourselves for having gotten the most for our money by visiting twelve countries in only the last two trips! The only problem that occurred on the Danube trip was that Paul picked up a stomach virus and spent an entire night and the next day vomiting. This was a real wakeup call for me since he hadn't been able to keep anything down including his medications, and the Parkinson's symptoms were worse than I had ever seen. After so many hours without meds, he could hardly move much less walk to the bathroom. His feet were just stuck, a symptom known as freezing which I had not witnessed before. The time frame without the drugs was nearly identical to the time in France when he lost his carry-on bag, but after two more years of the disease progressing, the consequences were noticeably worse. There was no doubt that the disease was getting worse and his dependency on drugs more important than ever. Fortunately, the virus passed quickly, he got better and then gave it to me. "In sickness and in health" I thought to myself as I heaved over the toilet.

September, 2008: Every year the Parkinson's Foundation holds a day long symposium with guest speakers, most of whom are physicians from Paul's neurology doctors' group. These talks are always very informative with information on the latest research, etc. One of the presenters was a young man with the disease whom we had heard several years before. He had been an athlete, a cyclist, when he was diagnosed at a very young age with Parkinson's, but this year he returned to the group after having had the deep brain stimulation surgery, a relatively new procedure. Previously, he had demonstrated much dyskinesia and was an obvious Parkinson's sufferer. This time he made his entrance by running down the center aisle and leaping onto the stage! In addition, he had gotten off all medication as a result of the surgery. I was nearly in tears when I saw this and felt for the first time that there was hope for Paul to improve. Granted he was a younger man than Paul and a former athlete, which Paul wasn't. I asked the question if getting off all meds was a given result after this surgery, and unfortunately the answer was no.

January, 2009: As the New Year began, we had some tough decisions to make regarding this surgical procedure. We had to learn everything we could about it and weigh the pros and cons as it was extremely dangerous surgery. But first, he had to pass a screening process to determine whether or not he was a good candidate for this elective surgery. After undergoing many motor and cognitive tests, he was determined to be a good candidate. Now the decision was in his hands. The entire process terrified me, and I was most reluctant to see him undergo the gruesome details of the procedure. He would be awake throughout the three to four hours of surgery, his head firmly locked into a cage-like box to keep it immobile. Then holes would be drilled into his skull and the surgeon would carefully probe into his brain locating the bundle of motor neurons that are affected by Parkinson's. This would be repeated on both hemispheres of his brain. When the neurons were located, the probes would be inserted there, and wires attached to the probes would be placed under the skin of his neck and eventually be connected to two batteries placed in his chest, much like pace makers. The batteries would be activated two weeks later. Incredibly, he would be able to go home twenty-four hours after the surgery! Once the batteries were activated, they would continuously stimulate those motor neurons, and though it was not a cure, it would slow the progress of the disease. It sounded almost too good to be true, but we had seen for ourselves the amazing results at the fall symposium. After much discussion, Paul decided to go for it! There was a window of opportunity to have this done before he would no longer be a suitable candidate so we had to make the decision final and commit to it! The night before the surgery, neither one of us got much sleep, but I'll never forget what he said as we lay in bed. "I hope this isn't the beginning of the end."

"Don't be silly," I replied optimistically. "It'll be the beginning of a new and better you." But in my heart, I was so unsure of my words. Unfortunately, it was indeed the beginning of a new Paul, but one who didn't deserve the outcome.

CHAPTER 7

March, 2009: We arrived very early at the hospital to begin the gruesome preparations for the actual surgery. For me, these procedures were actually more frightening and uncomfortable to witness than the surgery itself since once they got into his brain, he wouldn't feel any pain. They proceeded to give him numbing injections in his skull and began fastening his head into the box which would make it impossible for him to move during the surgery. I found it terribly difficult to watch the surgeon do this part of the ordeal but tried to keep my facial expressions positive so as not to scare Paul any more than he already was. I admit I cried like a baby when they wheeled him into the operating room. This was the bravest decision my husband could have made, and I prayed it was the right one. I hadn't been this scared since his open heart surgery.

The hours in the waiting room dragged on longer than what the doctor had told me he needed to complete this procedure, and I was getting more and more nervous. During those five hours of anxiety it is amazing how many thoughts can go through your head. Did I tell him I loved him before he went in to surgery? Did I apologize after that stupid disagreement we had last week? What would have happened if I hadn't urged him to see the cardiologist years ago before his fifty-eighth birthday? Would he have been better off dying quickly from a heart attack and never to have found out he had Parkinson's? But if he had died then, he would never have known his grandchildren, who, by the way, were not afraid of him as he had expressed. The wheels kept on spinning until I thought my head would explode into tiny pieces and bits of my brain would be all over the floor! "Clean up in the family waiting room!" The surgeon finally emerged to tell me it took longer than usual because he had needed additional time to locate the cluster of neurons on the right hemisphere, and it had been necessary to probe several times before he found the right spot. Once that hemisphere had been successfully implanted with the tiny probe, it was easier to locate the neuron cluster on the other side. This additional time consuming process didn't register anything in particular at the time other than I was glad the whole thing was finished. He was in recovery, and I could go back to see him in a little while.

I began weeping tears of relief and couldn't wait to see him, imagining him being able to run again like the symposium speaker had done. Maybe our golden years would be better than I had thought they would be. Eventually they allowed me back into recovery, and he was wide awake and waiting for me. I hugged him as he said through the tears streaming down his face, "We did it."

"No," I answered. "You did it! I am so proud of you!"

They said his room was not available yet, but I would be able to pick him up the following day in the neurology wing. He and I were both so exhausted from the ordeal of the day, and he was falling asleep before I left. So I drove home to get some much needed sleep, too. As I drove I thanked God for this technology and for getting him through it, and I found myself with renewed hope and a positive outlook....for better or worse. He would be better, and he would be healthier. I knew this was no cure for the disease, but it would definitely slow its progress.

I phoned the following morning to check on him before going to the hospital and was connected to the nurse station. My heart sank as she said that he was a little confused. "Confused about what?" I asked in a panic. "What do you mean?" She really didn't give me any information that I could understand so I left immediately to find out for myself.

In retrospect, there were so many mistakes made that all could have been avoided. The first was that they had taken him to the orthopedic wing instead of neurology because they were told there was no bed waiting for him there. There was, in fact, a bed waiting for him in neurology, and they wondered why he had not been brought up to them, but no one bothered to check to see where he had been taken! If he had been where he was supposed to be, those nurses trained in neurology would have acted with more immediacy when the confusion began by alerting the surgeon. But precious time had been lost. The man in the bed was not the man I had spoken to and cried with in recovery the night before. His face was the same but the words coming out of his mouth were gibberish. Incredulously, the nurse who had told me on the phone that he was a little confused indicated that his clothes were in the closet if I wanted to dress him to go home! WHAT?! A little confused? He was more than a little confused. He was speaking in tongues, for God's sake. What was she thinking? I remember the moment well: my insides were in a panic, my words were controlled. "I cannot take him home like this. Get his surgeon, NOW".

At that very moment, the first of many graced moments, Linda, one of Paul's former colleagues who had seen his name on the patient roster, appeared at his door. Her role was no longer in the lab but as a patient advocate. God does work in strange ways. She could see the problem and immediately went into action getting the surgeon there STAT. Paul had moments of verbal clarity when he would say, "I'm in here; I'm just not out there." My heart was breaking for him; he had no clue what was happening to him and neither did I. Was this the beginning of the end that Paul had feared?

The surgeon and his assistant in the operating room showed up in minutes and ordered a CAT scan. Meanwhile, Linda went to find out why Paul was not in the neurology wing. I have never prayed as hard as I did while he was gone to X-ray. I begged God to help him move through this setback quickly, but unfortunately, He said no. The scan showed a slow seepage of blood in the brain, not an outright stroke but a brain bleed around the right probe and swelling around the left. He was taken to neurology intensive care where we discovered a bed had been waiting all night. I was beyond livid when the nurse said, "We wondered why he hadn't arrived." I had to ask, "Did anyone think to ask where he was?" I have come to detest the pat response of 'confusion during shift changes'. It seems to explain a multitude of errors and oversights.

The ten days that followed are a kind of blur. Our children and I were at his bedside more than we were not. I remember my emotional state more than my physical activities. Anger took turns with terror; rage replaced tears. Every time I remembered that this surgery was elective and not a requirement, I lost it. Eventually, he needed to be sedated and intubated, and I was really not prepared to see him in that state: A large tube down his throat, oxygen in his nose, a catheter in his bladder and IV's and wires coming out of everywhere. This was the picture of the man who twenty-four hours earlier had cried, "We did it." At that moment I thought, yes, we did it alright, and we made a huge mistake. Yet no one had discovered why this bleed had occurred. They tested him for an allergic reaction to the metal in the probes and for anything else they could think of. What could possibly have happened? And then the answer came.

At some point during those first days in ICU, I was leaning against the wall in his room next to the door, and I overheard the two surgeons talking outside his room. "It seems his brain was more brittle than we had known." The other replied, "Yes, it looks like we may have nicked a blood vessel." I think that is the moment when my rage hit a peak I didn't even know I possessed. I wanted to scream at them, rip their eyes out and watch them writhe in pain knowing they would never again be able to perform surgery on anyone who trusted them with their lives. And then I remembered the consent form Paul had signed stating that they would not be held responsible for the one percent chance of a complication. My very brave husband had been the one percent.

I mentioned that there had been more than one mistake made in his case. The first, of course, was the doctor's causing the brain to bleed. Apparently, it occurred when they had to repeatedly go in with the probe to find the cluster of neurons on the first side. The second mistake was moving him from recovery to the orthopedic floor. The third was not having inquired why he hadn't arrived in the neurology wing. But unfortunately, that was not to be the end of the fiasco. The physician who intubated Paul damaged a vocal cord, but we wouldn't actually know that until later. Meanwhile, as he was fighting for his life, he developed a severe bladder infection that went untreated for days. This was a serious complication that almost ended his life. To add insult to injury, one morning I went into his room and for a moment I thought I was in the wrong room. I didn't recognize the man in the bed. A nurse's aide had decided to shave off his beard completely, the beard he had had for thirty years! I have no idea what possessed her to do that, but when I went on my latest rampage with the staff, they acknowledged the mistake and deeply apologized!

After those ten days of stress and fear, we had to make a decision where to take him for rehabilitation, and he wanted to go to a hospital, a thirty minute harrowing drive from home on Interstate 75 which was a route I usually avoided. It would not have been my first choice, but it was his, and it was a good thing I listened to him. Eight weeks later, I had successfully overcome my nerves on I-75! And the physician in charge there saved his life!

Every day for eight weeks, I faithfully made the trek on I-75 to spend three to four hours with Paul. I never knew what I was going to find when I got there. My anxiety levels were at an all -time high. The day after he had been admitted, I arrived early to find the doctor waiting by his room. "The news," he said with a grim look on his face, "is not good." His untreated urinary infection was so bad, he was urinating blood, and he was severely dehydrated. And the worst news of all was that his kidneys were beginning to fail, which I knew could quickly lead to death. He said he would do the best he could to save his life! Was this the …until death do us part?

I was overwhelmed, confused, terrified beyond words. How could all this have happened, all the mistakes, all the complications with no one held responsible? If this was the end, he didn't deserve to go this way. It was not fair! I have never felt more alone in my life. I wanted to run to my mother and cry on her shoulder, and I missed her at that moment more than I had thought possible. Ever since we got married, when anyone had a medical question, a hospital crisis, they went to Paul for advice and his professional input. Even my dad said that when he was in the hospital for bleeding ulcers, when Paul entered his room he felt immediate relief, and he could relax. But now, Paul was the patient, and he needed an advocate in the worst way. At that moment, I didn't feel qualified to handle all the responsibility. I felt like I had to be one step ahead of everyone on the staff, to look out for the slightest slip-up in his care so there would be no repeat of the mistakes made at the hospital. It was overwhelming. Our children joked later that the hospital staff scattered in all directions when they saw me coming! And I had to wonder what people do who have no one to advocate for them.

Over the course of the eight weeks at the hospital, he had to have a feeding tube inserted into his stomach because the vocal cord damaged in the intubation procedure was so weak and stretched, they were afraid he would aspirate. He lost twenty pounds during this period. Finally, on Easter Sunday at the Mass held at the hospital, the first food he took was the host at communion. "Please, God," I prayed, "Don't let him choke on You."

May, 2009: Finally on May 15, 2009, after eight weeks of intensive physical therapy, occupational therapy, swallow therapy and intense medical treatment, the feeding tube was quickly and painfully removed, and he was discharged from the hospital. We had to go straight to the surgeon's office to be checked out before going home, and I was not looking forward to seeing that man's face again. We had forty-five minutes in the waiting room for me to seethe and build on the hatred I had for this physician who had ruined Paul's life...and mine. When he finally called us back to his office, the overly friendly smile on his face made me physically sick. How could he behave as though everything had gone so well? How could he look so happy with the results of his handy work? It had been ten weeks since the surgery, and the batteries placed in his chest, which should have been activated two weeks later, were still not turned on. We made the appointment then to see the programmer in a few days. We had no idea what to expect or how it would feel once they activated the probes, but at that point, there wasn't much left that could go wrong! The good news was that Paul said he really could feel a difference when they "turned him on." There was an immediate tingling in his hands and he knew something was different.

August, 2009: Before the brain surgery, we had arranged to travel in August to France with our good friends. The plan was to spend a few days in Paris while they spent a few days in London and meet up on the third day in Paris. Then we would all take the train to Nice. Through a mutual acquaintance, we had reserved an apartment in the tiny town of Menton, the last village next to the Italian border. When Paul was discharged in May, we were still hoping to accomplish this.

He began recuperating at home and we knew he had three months to regain his strength before our trip. He seemed to get better every day. When we celebrated his sixty-ninth birthday in June, his brother and his wife came from Colorado for the joyous and emotional occasion, and I couldn't believe he had cheated death again. It was unbelievable that he would be able to travel internationally in August when only a few months earlier we didn't think he would survive.

CHAPTER 8

Two days before our anticipated departure for Europe, Paul fell in the kitchen. I was in a different room and didn't actually see him fall, but when I got to him, he said he had just gotten dizzy for a second and fell. He was trying to get up as he said, "I just got a little dizzy and lost my balance." I asked him if he felt up to the French trip, and of course he said yes. But my alarm bells were going off once again.

One thing I had not counted on was the effect the six hour time difference would have on Paul. He can always sleep on an overnight flight, something I have yet to accomplish. But even with the sleep, his schedule for taking his medications would be affected by the time difference. We found that going through airport security was going to be a new and interesting experience now that he had probes in his brain, and it took longer than usual, even with a card from the neurosurgeon explaining his situation. By the time we got through the airport hassles, got a taxi and drove through the incredibly harrowing Paris traffic to our hotel in the delightful St. Germaine des Près district, we were both exhausted. We grabbed a quick nap and began planning our time alone in the City of Light. This was the first time we had ever been there without my students, and we were ready to have a new Parisian experience. I had been there alone with other teachers many years before, and I knew of several places I wanted him to see.

After surviving our jet lag, all was going well, and by the evening of the second day, we had walked who knows how many kilometers. I was feeling optimistic that he was enduring the pace and enjoying our time together. That evening, we crossed one of the many beautiful bridges to the other side of the Seine and strolled along the *quais* before settling on an outdoor café for dinner. We were relaxed and enjoying our wine as we "people watched", always a great past time in Paris. As we were contemplating what to have for dessert, a woman with a large parrot on her shoulder walked by and stopped at the café next to ours. I couldn't help but wonder if the Parisian bird said "Hello" or "*Bonjour*" so I left our table for a moment and walked over to see her. Our table was located right next to an ice cream freezer which separated the two cafes. Paul had decided to raid it for his dessert while I was meeting the bird and its owner. I was away from Paul less than two minutes, but when I returned, I found him leaning over the closed freezer, eyes wide open but obviously unconscious. Puzzled, I called his name several times getting no response. As I was processing what to do next he came back to life and wondered why I was yelling at him. He looked fine again and just said he had felt a little dizzy. I thought back to the day before we left when he fell in the kitchen and had said he had felt dizzy and lost his balance. Was that another incident like this? Had he blacked out but came to before I could get to him then? My alarm bells were getting louder.

Our friends arrived the next day, and we enjoyed a delightful evening at the famous café, *Les Deux Magots,* and planned our next few days in the south. I was very concerned about Paul but mentioned nothing to our friends at that time. The train ride to the Riviera was most enjoyable; Paul and I have always enjoyed train travel, and it was relaxing and fun to share with friends. We arrived in Nice, found the rental car agency and began to set out for the tiny village of Menton and our apartment for the next few days in the glorious south of France. What we didn't know ahead of time was that August is peak season in Menton, and it was bumper to bumper traffic. In addition, the directions to the apartment were vague, and we drove around for over an hour trying to find it. When we finally did, we were all frustrated, hot and tired and then discovered that the only available parking was on the street, and there was nothing even remotely close to the apartment. So we parked illegally and hauled our luggage up two narrow flights of stairs to our home away from home. It was indeed a lovely place overlooking the Mediterranean Sea, but it was really better suited to two people, not four. There was no air conditioning, and Menton was having an unseasonable heat wave. Our bedroom did not have a window, only a transom open to the master bedroom which had the only window. Occasionally we felt a slight breeze. We finally found a legal parking place, but because of the crazy situation, once you found one, you didn't give it up so we decided to walk everywhere.

Paul actually did well the first full day of sightseeing and we walked till we dropped. But the second day we reluctantly relinquished our coveted parking space to drive up into the mountain overlooking Menton to find a tourist attraction that was definitely worth the tense drive over multiple switchbacks and narrow roads. Paul did well relating later that it was his favorite day of touring. And when we returned, of course, our coveted parking spot was gone. Our friend, who was our chauffeur for the time there, was not a happy camper as he searched again for a spot. After he returned and a few glasses of wine later, we discussed where to go within walking distance for dinner.

One thing about traveling with friends, and especially friends who have no health issues to deal with, is that compromise must be a part of the day's activities, and this particular evening, unfortunately we didn't make that happen. Paul needed to take his medications with food within a certain time frame. Our friends were used to having dinner at a much later hour than we were accustomed to, and it was already late when we started to walk to find the best restaurant. There were several that I thought looked pleasant with a good menu, but our friends wanted to keep going until we found the right ambiance. We walked for what seemed like forever until we reached the westernmost edge of Menton and were forced to choose the last place in the village. By this time Paul and I were both exhausted and would have eaten anything anywhere. We were shown to an outdoor table, the only seats left by this time of night. Paul was unusually quiet all through dinner which I chalked up to fatigue after a long day and more walking than he was used to. It was after ten P.M. when we got up to begin the very long trek back to the apartment which was on the opposite, easternmost edge of the village. Before we made it off the restaurant premises, Paul folded into a heap on the ground, again with eyes wide open but unconscious. That was the third time in less than a week, and I knew something was terribly wrong. After a few seconds, he came back to us and wondered why he was on the ground with everyone standing over him! Joe ran all the way back to the parked car so we wouldn't have to walk that far again, and we all drove back together. I finally felt forced to relate to them what had happened in Paris, and I feared we were going to have to leave our friends and go home early. What was wrong? Was he having small strokes like he had had after the brain surgery? Was his heart acting up ten years after the bypass? Or were we facing yet another medical problem? …..in sickness and in health!

The owners of our apartment had left the name of their doctor in case of emergency, and I wanted him to evaluate Paul before I called home to Paul's neurologist and cardiologist. Fortunately, we could get in the next day. The only experience I had had with the French medical system was on one of our student trips. One of our more illustrious senior boys got drunk in Nice, stepped barefoot on broken glass and landed in the emergency room and needed stitches. I had been impressed with their system and would continue to be with Paul.

We drove to the office and found the doctor's suite easily. As we sat in the waiting room, my mind raced over all the vocabulary I had taught in a French II class regarding hospitals, doctors and ER's just in case this physician didn't speak much English. It was a good thing that I did because not only did he not speak much English, he spoke no English. I was shocked when he personally came out to the waiting room instead of a nurse and invited us back into his examining room. It became evident quickly that I was going to have to explain Paul's very complicated medical history completely in French with the hope that he would understand me and get an accurate picture. In retrospect, I think a Divine Translator was helping me through it because the words, phrases, sentences and long descriptions of Paul's past history flowed effortlessly from my mouth. And the doctor actually understood me! He took Paul's vital signs and found absolutely nothing wrong; in fact he was probably healthier at that moment than I was, given my stress level. But at least I had numbers to relate to Paul's doctors back home. One thing he said was when someone faints and his eyes remain open, he is in a state of profound unconsciousness. His use of that word scared me a little, and I would remember to tell our doctors what he had said. Then he presented us with a very small bill for his services which we paid to him right there in his office in euros. Quite a different experience!

When we returned to the apartment, I phoned his neurologist and his cardiologist. The latter said he thought we should cut the trip short and come home immediately. Then he set an appointment to see Paul the day after we were to get home. Reluctantly, we packed our bags, and I phoned the airlines in tears explaining the medical emergency requiring us to change flights. After an uncomfortable verbal hassle, the airlines allowed us to change the flight at no additional charge. We were so upset and so were our friends, but I knew if we continued our stay with them, it would have caused them to worry and not enjoy their remaining time in France. They had truly been terrified when he had fainted at the restaurant. Even if the doctor had not advised us to come home, it wouldn't have been fair to them to stress them any further on their vacation.

We did get home safely and saw our doctor the following day. Fortunately, the solution was a simple one and had we known, we could have stayed in France. Paul had been taking blood pressure medication since his open heart surgery ten years earlier, but now as a Parkinson's patient, he no longer needed it and should not have been taking it at all since Parkinson's disease tends to lower the blood pressure naturally. So when he stood up quickly, his pressure plummeted and caused him to faint. After removing that pill from his daily regimen, the fainting disappeared! Lesson learned!

In September, he had been asked to go back to U.C. to give a lecture on Understanding Disease to retirees for the Osher Lifelong Learning Institute. It was the first time since his brain surgery that he had appeared in public to speak, and I was very nervous for him. When he entered the room, the audience stood and applauded him; apparently the moderator had informed them of his brain surgery and all he had been through. I sat in a chair in the back of the room and overheard two women in front of me whisper, "He's too smart for me!" Granted, he was speaking over their heads, but I didn't care. I had never been more proud of him.

CHAPTER 9

May-October, 2010: From the time of our return from France until May of the following year, Paul was doing pretty well. His driving ability had been compromised, I noticed frequently as I practically put my foot through the floor of the passenger seat trying to press on non-existent brakes! What I was observing was that because of the brain bleed, he was losing peripheral vision, and also his motor response time seemed slower causing me no end of stress in the passenger seat. It got so bad that I finally refused to drive with him and insisted that any time we had to go anywhere together, I would drive. That infuriated him to say the least and caused many arguments and moments of tense silence, but I held firm. But every time he went out alone, I prayed him out and back. If I heard a siren, I said a quick prayer that he had not been in an accident.

That May, our dog had to be euthanized and we were both devastated beyond words. Out of sheer grief, we packed our bags and made a weekend trip to the Smokey Mountains to escape our empty, dog-less house. Hiking in those mountains was something we had done for years with our kids as well as later by ourselves. The mountains were a place where Paul always found his peace, and it just felt like the right place to go. Paul insisted he begin the driving, but after several other drivers let us know that he was a hazard on the road with honking horns and angry gestures, we stopped for lunch, and then I took the wheel. I could see that his driving ability was even worse than it had been. We found a room in a motel overlooking a small creek. It was a good idea to get away, but it didn't take long to realize that Paul's ability to hike had also been compromised since the last time we had been there. We had to limit ourselves to the easiest hikes available, and it saddened me to remember all the strenuous hikes we had taken in the past and would no longer be able to enjoy. What was supposed to be a relaxing weekend getaway became for me, at least, another reminder that our lives were changing in sad ways. Going home to a house with no dog wagging to greet us was like an additional stab in the heart.

Paul's seventieth birthday was in June, and it was a joyous occasion. He was one of the only males in his family to live past the age of fifty-eight, and though he had some serious medical issues, he was doing great after all he had been through. One thing I had noticed after his brain surgery was his inability to read as well as before, and also that he struggled at times to find the right word he wanted to say. This was particularly frustrating for him since he had always been a voracious reader and an excellent lecturer. After the brain surgery, he spent countless hours in voice therapy due to the botched intubation, and at times his volume was reduced to a whisper. Adding another complication to the vocal issue, his life-long asthma returned limiting the amount of air intake to make it possible for him to complete a sentence without fading out altogether. He would start out fine but his voice and air were gone before the end of the sentence. We spent countless hours driving to the hospital for vocal exercises and therapies. Now we could add a pulmonologist to his list of physicians. In addition to all these, he needed to see an ENT specialist. His Ear, Nose, Throat doctor wanted him to undergo a surgical procedure that would implant a substance permanently to his vocal cord thereby allowing the two cords to vibrate against each other and produce volume again. Paul told him in the office that day that he agreed to do it, but my gut kept telling me NO! I don't know if it was because I feared him going through more surgery after all he had been through already or if my instincts told me it was the wrong decision. All I knew was that when I objected and began to cry, the doctor looked at me like I was crazy. He stormed out of the room saying, "Maybe the two of you should talk about this first." I cried all the way home and begged Paul to reconsider. Meanwhile, since the asthma had returned we had to see the pulmonologist. After Paul completed the breathing tests prescribed and failed them, the doctor said that having the procedure suggested by the ENT would have been disastrous, based on where the air flow problem existed. I began to trust my gut more than ever. If we had to live with a whisper, so be it!

We decided to celebrate Paul's seventieth birthday later in October with a trip to Colorado. His brother was going to organize a sibling reunion for the weekend. We timed this to coincide with the rutting season of the elk in Rocky Mountain National Park, an event they said we needed to experience! Three of his four siblings made the trip, and it was truly a joyous reunion. Paul and his sister and two brothers sat for hours on the deck reminiscing. We spent time driving around the park taking in the wondrous elk and their trumpeting mating rituals! I hadn't seen Paul look this happy in a very long time. The downside was that the altitude and the cold temperatures played havoc with his asthma and necessitated using his inhaler after the least strenuous exercise. Even putting on his seatbelt in the car caused his breathing to be labored enough that his brother was alarmed. But, oddly enough, the Parkinson's didn't seem to bother him. The "better" overruled the "worse" for five wonderful days. We ended the week with a visit to some friends in Broomfield, Colorado, but by this time he was getting tired. He asked for a cocktail which he shouldn't have had due to all his medications, but he would not be swayed despite my objections. The alcohol hit him like a ton of bricks, and I was truly embarrassed when he said, "I just want to go home" in front of our friends. It was all I could do to get him up the stairs and into bed. I knew after that incident that alcohol would never be a part of his life again.

CHAPTER 10

January, 2011: I'm not sure why we decided to take a cruise in January to the Bahamas, Jamaica and the Grand Caymans other than to escape winter in Ohio. It was a terrible experience. The leg pain he had experienced on the Mediterranean cruise returned as well as the asthma attacks. As luck would have it, our stateroom was the last room farthest from the elevators, and he had such a difficult time just walking and pulling his suitcase, hobbling and doubled over, I was terrified. When the steward unlocked our cabin door, Paul literally fell into the room and on to the bed. The steward looked at me with great concern, wanting to know if he was okay. I honestly didn't know, but told him he would be fine. I knew immediately we had made a huge mistake traveling, and I concluded if anything else happened, we would never travel again. That one more thing did happen after a fun day in Jamaica swimming with the dolphins.

It had long been a dream of mine to do this, and it was really the only reason I wanted to take this trip. Paul has never been a great swimmer, but we had life vests on, and all we had to do was paddle ourselves to wherever the dolphin trainer told us to go. But Paul even had a difficult time getting from one place to another in the water, and I had to practically pull him along with me as I swam. It seemed he had no core strength to tread water upright and I was concerned. Even the dolphin trainer could see my dilemma trying to get him out of the water so he helped us accomplish that. Despite all Paul's inabilities, the dolphin swim was everything I hoped it would be, almost a religious experience being up close and personal with this amazing creature, riding on its back and feeling it's snout giving me a kiss. That afternoon, I had to leave the ship again to go back and

41

pay for the "must have" photos of us with the dolphin. I wanted to go alone because I could go faster without Paul, but he was afraid to let me alone on the island and insisted to come along. I did leave him to sit and wait for me at one point and ran to the shop to pay for our photos. It took a bit longer than I had anticipated, and he became worried that something had happened to me, so he set out on the trail to find me. By the time we met up, he could barely walk again, and a very worried and sympathetic Jamaican man helped us by getting a wheelchair which was the only way I could get him back to the ship. When we finally managed to return to our stateroom, again no easy feat being so far away from the elevators, I was angrier than words can say. I realized it was sweet of him to worry about my safety, but I really could take care of myself, and he created a much bigger problem for me by coming to find me. I honestly felt like this trip couldn't be finished fast enough.

When we did return home, I told him that I had had it being responsible for him on vacations, and it was getting much too stressful for me. I hated having to say this especially when he said with tears streaming down his face, "If I can't travel any longer, it will kill me. I'd rather be dead." Shortly after this conversation, we bought a cane which helped him a little with his walking.

May, 2011: Four months later, our friends invited us to spend a week with them at their house in Hilton Head, South Carolina. We had done this before driving the two days to get there, but this time we decided to fly to Savannah where they would meet us and drive the hour back to Hilton Head. The airport security was beyond ridiculous with all the hardware Paul had in his body by this time: brain probes in his head, wires under the skin in his neck connecting them to the two battery packs in his chest, and clamps reconnecting his ribs from the heart surgery! Even with the identification card provided by the medical staff explaining all the hardware, the security staff had him practically stripped down to his underwear before they cleared him. It took forty-five minutes from the time he went through the scanner until we were on our way to the plane. One other problem with airport security that I had forgotten about was the fact that all that scanning could turn off his chest batteries. When we were leaving home for the airport, I had remembered at the very last minute to pick up his handheld battery checking device, another graced moment. He had forgotten to pack it, and I was lucky to have seen it on the dresser. I don't know what we would have done if I had not picked it up because the security scanners did "turn him off". It isn't a sensation that he is immediately aware of, and I never thought to check the status of the batteries after we had finally been cleared.

Our friends met us in Savannah and we began the long drive to their home. It had been a very long day of travel, and we were both tired, so the fatigue Paul exhibited didn't alarm me. But the next morning after a good night sleep, he could hardly keep his head up and his eyes open at breakfast. Our friends looked concerned, and it was then that the light bulb went off for me. Check his batteries! I ran upstairs to get the checker, and indeed the batteries had been turned off. One zap on each side of his chest and he was like a different person. This was a real eye opener for me and for our friends and a moment I will never forget. It had been only two years since the deep brain surgery, and I could see how the disease had progressed in that short amount of time. To see how unresponsive he was without the stimulation from his chest batteries was truly alarming; the picture wasn't pretty, and for the first time, I was glad he had chosen to have the grueling surgery done. It is truly amazing technology but frightening to witness the "off/on" difference.

We discovered during our stay in Hilton Head that biking was a particularly wonderful activity. Neither of us had biked in so many years, but as the saying goes, it does come back...like riding a bike. The bike paths were beautiful as we passed little lagoons, egrets standing like statues, heron and even a few alligators. Spanish moss draped from tree branches, and the abundance of tropical flowers filled the air with incredible scents, at least for me. I felt bad that Paul's sense of smell failed him in this amazing environment. We became so enamored with cycling there with our friends that we bought bikes when we got home. Needless to say, the scenery left much to be desired in comparison, but it was, none the less, a new activity to be enjoyed together. However, in time, even this became a problem after Paul fell several times. His balance was getting worse, and that took the stress free fun out of yet another activity.

August, 2011: Our daughter, Julie, and her family were planning a Michigan vacation in August and invited us to go along. She insisted that we follow them in our car and that I do all the driving, or they didn't want us to join them! Both she and her husband had witnessed Paul's compromised ability to drive safely after the brain surgery. He fought me on this and was still convinced that he was not a hazard on the road, but Julie was insistent, and that stopped the argument. I had to admit it felt good to have some back up on the subject. I had also been noticing for a while a new symptom of Parkinson's called *festination*. It was a term the neurologist explained as a postural shift forward of the upper body but the feet not catching up resulting in falling forward. It's frightening to see, and it was also why the cane was so important since it kept the festination in check fairly well. However, Paul had also figured out a way to fall even with the cane several times when he positioned it to his front instead of to his side and he tripped over it. That had happened when we went out one evening to a play, and the staff had to call the EMT's to come and check him out. They determined that he hadn't needed to go to the hospital and asked him if he wanted a refund for the play. "No," he shot back. "I want to see this play!"

After we got to Michigan, I realized I had forgotten to put his cane in the car. He and Julie drove to a fruit stand to buy some fresh cherries, and while they were gone she witnessed the festination, and it scared her to death. When they returned she said, "Mom, I know what you mean now about how frightening it is if Dad doesn't walk with a cane. I had to keep him from falling on his face!" She bought him a new cane the next day. The physical changes were becoming evident more and more to everyone.

Another problem symptom that was worsening was REM sleep disorder. When most people dream in the REM stage, their bodies become paralyzed, but Parkinson's patients do just the opposite. When Paul dreamt, he flailed about, yelled out loud and made it impossible to sleep with him. I couldn't count the number of times I had been hit during his dreaming or awakened out of a deep sleep in a panic when he yelled. And we had a king sized bed at home. In Michigan, we had a small double bed, and after two nights of fighting with him, I had to sleep on the couch for the rest of the vacation. I knew I had to address this problem with the neurologist when we got home.

This week spent with family, swimming, boating and fishing with our three grandchildren was a fantastic time. Paul had never been a fisherman like our son-in-law, but when our granddaughter offered her pink, Barbie fishing pole to him, he couldn't refuse. The photo of him holding up his first little fish on that girlie pole was hilarious. I couldn't remember when I had had so much fun; I realized it had been way too long since I had relaxed, laughed and played, and it felt good again. A call to the neurologist when we returned home resulted in yet another prescription to control the REM sleep disorder. Maybe I could get a good night sleep now!

September, 2011: As I wrote in 1984, hospitalization was a rarity for me, thank goodness. But twenty-seven years later, it was necessary to say "uncle" to the hip pain caused by arthritis. All those years of ballet training in my youth, age eight to twenty-four, had done a number on the left hip joint, and I needed a full hip replacement. I was terrified to go through this procedure after hearing all the gruesome details, and after talking to others who had done it, I knew the recovery wasn't going to be easy. I could either go to a rehab facility for a while afterwards or go home and have "in-home physical therapy". I opted for the latter since Paul was able to take care of me. He said he was up to the task, and I just hoped he was right. After four days in the hospital that I really don't remember very well due to the powerful pain medication, I came home. In retrospect, I don't know why anyone would want to keep taking Oxycodone because I couldn't wait to get off it.

Paul did the best he could to care for me, helping me in and out of bed, preparing my meals, some which were edible, and keeping me company. The first three weeks were impossibly difficult, and I was so disappointed in myself for not recovering faster. But it did get better, and the six weeks of physical therapy really did help. When insurance ran out for that service, I was able to drive again and continue the therapy in the orthopedic facility. This was an eye opening time for me because I was not used to being cared for; I took care of others. I didn't like it at all! Later, our daughter told me I was a terrible patient!

CHAPTER 11

April, 2012: Nothing too terrible had happened to Paul, no drama, no medical crisis between August, 2011 and April, 2012, but then things began to change for the worse. I had been babysitting for our son's two daughters one day, and as I drove up the hill approaching our house, I thought I saw Paul on the front porch on all fours. I drove up to see what was going on instead of pulling into the garage and was horrified to see him bleeding badly from his forehead. He had gone to get the mail and tripped up the porch step, cracking his head on the edge of the concrete step. I tried to see from where the injury originated. I ran into the house to get towels to clean him up. When I found the deep wound, I ran inside to call 911. Then I called our daughter, Jennie, to come over to help me. We had been dog sitting for our other daughter's dog while they were away for spring break, and I needed some back up with that and help cleaning up the porch. Fortunately, Jennie had just arrived home moments before my phone call, and she came right over. The expression on her face when she saw her dad mirrored what mine must have looked like. I followed the ambulance to the hospital and prayed all the way. When the doctor saw the injury, he asked Paul if he had lost consciousness when he fell. Paul answered that he hadn't which amazed the doctor. I'll never know for sure whether that was actually true or not. It is difficult to believe that anyone could have hit his head that hard and not lost consciousness. It was a deep wound that required multiple layers of stitching. They did a CT scan to check for internal bleeding, and I held my breath until the results came back. What he didn't need was another brain bleed! Fortunately, the results were negative, but my biggest fear was that even though he did not have a concussion, I wondered if the tremendous jolt to his head could have shifted the probes in his brain. The doctor was amazed that he did not have a concussion, and I was overjoyed that my husband had such a hard head. Later, the neurologist reassured us that those probes are securely positioned so deep inside the brain they would not have been affected by such a blow.

June, 2012. Since the head blow in April, we had purchased an expensive, three wheeled walker with hand brakes like the ones on bikes. It wasn't easy for him to remember to use it when he could also get around with a cane, but I wanted to have it for times when we had to walk greater distances. By now he owned three canes, and I used to sing a parody to Three Coins in a Fountain. "Three canes and a walker, to help you get around, three canes and a walker so your head won't hit the ground," I would bellow out for my own amusement more than his.

We decided to celebrate our forty-fifth wedding anniversary by taking a short road trip to Ste. Genevieve, Missouri, where their French Cultural Heritage Festival coincided with our big day. It was also the first time we took the walker to try it out, and it did come in handy. The weekend was sweet and uneventful for the most part except when he discovered he couldn't even drink a few sips of wine because of all his medications. After stopping at the local vineyard winery, it was all I could do to get him back to the car even with the walker. I don't know what I would have done without it.

Toward the end of the month on a Saturday evening, Paul drove to Mass alone. I had planned to go, but the puppy our children had given us for Christmas was sick, and I had to stay home to keep an eye on her. At six PM, I received a phone call from the hospital telling me they had my husband in the emergency room. He had fallen again and needed stitches. Apparently, he had arrived late to church and had to park a good distance from the entry. He left his cane in the car, as well as his identification, and was hurrying without any support. I could picture him festinating and falling outside the church door. He was transported by ambulance so his car was still in the church lot. The hospital didn't need his identification since he had been there so many times already; by this time they were practically on a first name basis. Our son had to pick me up and drive me to the church to retrieve his car, but I couldn't find his spare key. Finally, after locating it in the trouser pocket that he had put in the laundry hamper the previous day, I made my way to church to retrieve his car and on to the hospital where I found him again waiting to be stitched up. I was getting angry with him now because it was becoming clearly evident that so many of his accidents had been unnecessary if only he had used his cane or his walker for support, but getting him to make use of these items when I wasn't around to remind him continued to be a problem. It seemed like we were experiencing more of "the worse" instead of "the better" and more of the "sickness" instead of "the health".

July, 2012: Paul was still driving much to the dismay of our children, and I continued to pray every time he ventured out. He simply refused to acknowledge that he had any problems behind the wheel although it was apparent that his response time was slowing and his peripheral vision wasn't as complete as it should have been. I remember when my mother had to take the keys away from my father after he began his macular degeneration, and it nearly killed him to give up driving. But that was such a no-brainer in as much as his vision was so terribly compromised. Paul's problems were not as obvious from a physical point of view but very real none the less. No one could convince him to relinquish the keys.

One hot day in July, I was babysitting our son's daughters at the new house where they were living at the time. Paul had gone to his cardio-pulmonary exercise class. Our son was due home in about an hour when the doorbell rang. A young woman asked me if I was Mrs. Hurtubise. I said that I was but not the Mrs. Hurtubise who lived there. She said she knew that and wanted to tell me that she lived two streets over across the way from where my husband had crashed his car! When she saw the look on my face she said, "He's okay; I called the police, and they are going to drive him here in a moment because his car isn't drivable." He had tried to surprise me by coming to the house, but since it was a new residence for our son, Paul couldn't remember how to find it, and he was driving all around this maze of a neighborhood looking for my car. Apparently, he had cut a right turn too close and took out a mailbox and a fire plug, evidence of his failing peripheral vision. His car was going to have to be towed, and she had to go back to tell the police where I was. I was shaking like a leaf when she left and trying to keep it together in front of my grandchildren. I phoned my son and told him to get home as fast as he could. Fortunately he was only ten minutes away.

The police arrived, and I helped him out of the car just as our son got home and took him to get a cold drink. The policeman started asking me questions that I was dreading.

"Do you think your husband should be driving?"

"No," I said, "but I can't convince him of that."

"Does he suffer from dementia?"

"What? No!" I answered emphatically. "Why do you ask that?"

"We asked him where he was trying to go, and he said he didn't know."

"Of course not. He knew where he was trying to go, but he didn't know the address. He's never driven here by himself," I said realizing that I was probably making things worse for him.

"We asked him if he had a cell phone, and he said he forgot it at home."

"Yes, he never remembers to take it with him," I replied.

"We told him we would call you for him, and we asked for your cell phone number, but he couldn't remember it." I knew by this time he was probably so befuddled and upset, he wouldn't even remember my name much less my phone number. He has always had a terrible memory for phone numbers. Besides, he had always had either me or his secretary to remember details like that, so this wasn't anything alarming to me. But I was sure the policeman was convinced he was suffering from dementia. I couldn't blame him for the impression he had, but I knew better. Then he asked me a question I was not prepared to hear. "Would you like me to inform the Bureau of Motor Vehicles to cancel his license?" Oh, was that tempting, but my heart was breaking for Paul. I didn't want him to be any more humiliated than he already was. So I said, "No, I appreciate that, but I want him to come to that decision on his own, not like a child who is being punished. Maybe this accident will help him come to that conclusion." I could only hope!

We had a long talk later that evening after we had both settled down. After finishing my first glass of wine, I told him everything the policeman had asked me. Unfortunately, this difficult conversation had done nothing to sway his opinion to quit driving. How could he be so mulish? I realized he was not only the most stubborn man I had ever known but also completely in denial. I was successful, however, in convincing him to be tested by an Occupational Therapist to determine his driving ability. At first he wasn't for it, but I told him that if he passed it, I would drop the subject. This was his opportunity to prove to the kids and me that we were wrong. He agreed readily. Fortunately, we were down to one car as his was being repaired, and I could do all the driving!

October, 2012: We drove to Mercy Hospital where the therapist was waiting for him to take the two part test. The first hour was cognitive testing and the second hour was the actual driving in a part of town totally unfamiliar to him. I held my breath waiting for the results. When they returned, the therapist said, "Well, you passed but just barely! There is going to be a time when you can no longer drive, but it's not today!" I couldn't believe it. I had just lost a most important battle, and there was nothing I could do about it. My only recourse was to stick to my guns and insist that I drive whenever we were together, but he could still drive himself whenever he needed to go somewhere alone. Obviously, it would be a while before the knots in my stomach would relax.

CHAPTER 12

April, 2013: Thirteen years after the original diagnosis of Parkinson's and four years after the deep brain surgery, Paul's disease was noticeably progressing. The "for better or worse, in sickness and in health" was definitely getting worse and sicker. He was falling more often due to not remembering to use his cane. He was also forgetting to take his meds with the regularity that is so important for Parkinson's patients and even neglecting to have them refilled on time. Up till that time, I had nothing to do with his medications since he had always been in charge of them. Suddenly I was seeing serious changes in his demeanor and his alertness, and I was afraid things were getting worse so I called his neurologist office. The physician assistant who always treated him and checked or programmed his chest batteries told me to have him checked for a urinary tract infection before anything else since that could explain all that I was seeing, but upon checking at the nearby clinic, there was no evidence of a UTI. I called her back and made an appointment for her to see him the following morning. Later that same evening, I happened to see his medication box open in the bathroom and noticed that there were many pills from earlier in the week that had not been taken. He admitted that he had "not been complying with the program." To say I was furious with him for his negligence is an understatement, and I was completely incredulous that he would knowingly allow this to happen. It was his negligence rather than the disease progressing that was causing the changes I had seen and which had caused me so much worry. The appointment the following morning wasn't pretty, and I actually lost it when I told her what I had discovered. The angry tears flowed freely, and I felt completely defeated at that moment. It was the first time I actually felt like running away from home and letting someone else be responsible for him. She was calmer with him than I, but just as firm in her admonishment of what he had done. She suggested that perhaps he needed to talk to a psychiatrist to find out why he wasn't complying. She also suggested that I take over the administering of the medications as well as making sure they were refilled on time. This was no easy task since he took so many different pills for so many issues; asthma, heart disease, Parkinson's, REM sleep disorder and bladder issues. Now adding to his regimen was an antidepressant which the psychiatrist said he needed. Almost all Parkinson's patients end up suffering with depression, and it was time for him to add this additional pill to his daily meds. I approached this responsibility with some trepidation, to say the least. It took me hours to figure out the directions for all his different medications, some taken once a day, some twice, some three times and others four times. I finally got a system organized which made it easier, and I only had to refill the box with the twenty-eight little compartments once a week with a phone call to the pharmacy at the same time for any refills needed. I felt like I had just passed a test in pharmaceuticals. Eventually, I could recite the name of each one, how many times a day he needed it, what it was treating and even its generic name. The difference in his overall demeanor improved almost immediately, and we slowly returned from worse to better and from sickness to improved health. My stress level went down once I was in control of what went into his body.

May, 2013: One of the chronic problems with Parkinson's disease is the tendency to become severely constipated. Paul had always had this problem whenever we traveled, but we always thought it was due to prolonged sitting in airplanes, tour busses etc. He had struggled with this off and on for quite a while, but suddenly, out of nowhere, it seemed he had no control over his bowels at all, and he soiled himself multiple times a day with runny diarrhea. I was stumped after two weeks of this and took him back to the neurologist who was no help at all and told me to take him to his primary care doctor. He told Paul to collect a stool sample to be tested and told him that since the results wouldn't be back before the Memorial Day weekend, to take an anti-diarrheal for relief until then. I bought a box and gave him one after dinner, and he immediately threw up twice in the kitchen sink. His pallor was terrible, and I decided to take him to the emergency room. They did a CT scan of his belly and found that what we thought was diarrhea was actually a dangerously severe case of bowel impaction. Half of his bowel was impacted; that added up to twelve feet of impacted bowel, and the watery diarrhea was actually just fluid intake working its way around the impaction. He had to be admitted that night, and they were going to keep him until he emptied everything inside. It was during this hospital visit when we made the acquaintance of yet another doctor who would be instrumental in Paul's health. When I returned home I began thinking about the neurologist who missed this possibility and who should have known better, given the fact that impaction is a serious risk for Parkinson's patients. When I returned to the hospital the following morning, the gastroenterologist who treated Paul told me how alarmed he had been when he saw the CT scan. He had never seen that much impaction before, and it was very serious. Their treatment worked, and he was able to come home later that day. I was wishing I had weighed him before and after because I know he must have lost 5-10 pounds! I also made sure the neurologist knew my feelings on this subject!

The doctor determined that one of the things Paul had been doing that may have contributed to the severe constipation was drinking a lot of the diet supplement, Boost, which contains iron, and iron is constipating. He suggested Paul discontinue drinking it altogether. There were still several bottles in the refrigerator, and it didn't occur to me to throw them away since I just assumed he would comply with the doctor's advice. Then one evening when all was going well, I noticed an empty Boost bottle in the trash. When I confronted him with it, he lied and said it was the only one he had taken. But after searching the other waste baskets in the house, I continued to find several more empty bottles. Once again I was incredulous that this intelligent man would be so irresponsible after all he and I had been through. After getting over the initial shock, I knew I had to get away from him and leave the house before I broke something over his hard head!

First I walked outside to our patio to get some fresh air, clear my head and think for a minute. I had been afraid to leave him alone for such a long time that the thought of going anywhere seemed impossible at first. But all my responsible care for him seemed to be a waste of time and energy after what I had just seen, and my anger grew. Just then a rabbit hopped across the patio just feet away from where I was standing. I hadn't seen any rabbits that entire spring or summer, but it didn't necessarily seem strange to see this brown, long-eared bunny hanging around. Then I decided to get in the car and leave, leave this man alone for the first time in weeks and go somewhere, anywhere, to try and think clearly or at least have a good cry by myself. Whatever would happen to him in my absence would happen. I honestly didn't care at that moment, but I didn't know where to go. Going to our children's houses wasn't an option because I didn't want to fall apart in front of the grandchildren. So I drove to the park a few miles away to just sit in the parking lot and cry it out. But as luck would have it there were soccer games going on, and the lot was filled with cars and parents coming and going. After a few moments of increased anger and frustration, I banged the steering wheel with my hand since there didn't seem to be any way to get away from people who could observe my meltdown. Just then, in a crowded, concrete parking lot, a rabbit hopped right in front of my car and sat there looking back at me. I was so shocked to see a second rabbit, the twin of the first one in our yard. He just sat there, looking at me, not moving at all. A co-incidence, I thought, and I decided to go somewhere else. The car seemed to drive itself out of the park and to the parking lot of my church about a mile down the road. No one would be there on a Tuesday evening, and I would be able to give in to my tears in private and have a long, unfriendly talk with God while I sat there. As the tears ran down my cheeks, I lay my head down on the steering wheel. "God," I cried "help me to know what to do for this man and for myself. You know how tired and angry, scared and overwhelmed with responsibility I am. Help me please." I pleaded out loud knowing no one was around to hear me. After a few moments of venting all my emotions, I lifted my head to blow my nose and there sat a third rabbit in front of my car, again just sitting there and looking at me! It was so bizarre I had to laugh. Just what was going on here? It had to mean something.

I returned home, still too angry to talk to my husband and went right to the computer to search for any symbolism of rabbits. I honestly didn't expect to find anything, but what I found gave me chills. One anonymous source said that in many cultures, the rabbit symbolizes fear and reminds us that fearful thoughts bring on the very thing we fear. Rabbit people are afraid of illness, and multiple sightings may be telling us to stop worrying and re-evaluate what we are undergoing.

I reread the passage several times, still incredulous at how on the mark it was, and I was overwhelmed with gratitude to God for sending me this message, not once, but three times and for whispering in my ear to look up what it meant. And I felt calm for the first time in months. I have to admit there were other moments of weakness after that when I gave in to anger and self-pity and momentarily forgot the message. But on one of those occasions as I was driving home and feeling reluctant to resume my responsibilities, another rabbit hopped across the street in front of my car. "Okay, Lord," I said out loud. "I hear You."

June, 2013: Two weeks after the impaction episode, it was June 15, Paul's seventy-second birthday, and we had been planning to go to our daughter's house that night for a big party. But he awoke with a terrible head and chest cold, and I had to call off the festivities. He came out to breakfast pushing his walker, but he was completely naked, something he had certainly never done before. He was acting very bizarre and "out of it" to the extent that I was becoming nervous again. When he picked up an imaginary coffee cup and put his fingers to his mouth as if to drink, I told him to go back to bed and get more rest while I called off the party. He got up around eleven o'clock, but by then he couldn't function at all. He couldn't get himself dressed, could hardly talk intelligibly and was frozen, unable to walk. I was aware that infections can really mess with Parkinson's patients like this, but his symptoms were so severe I had to call 911. Again, he was admitted and treated for pneumonia like symptoms although the X-ray didn't really show it. But he had a fever and serious congestion so they treated him with a pneumonia protocol. They also checked him for sepsis, and it came back a few days later as positive! I had noticed a poster in the emergency room that said to check for sepsis if the patient presents with a fever and had been recently hospitalized, which he had two weeks earlier for the impaction, but I hadn't given it much thought then. The following morning, once again I thought we were going to lose him.

The phone rang at six A.M. and it was his nurse telling me to come right away; he was worsening, incoherent, combative and having trouble breathing. I immediately called our three children and my sister and told them I was really afraid that something terrible was happening to him. My sister joined me at seven in his room and I kept the kids posted by phone. We were all sure he was going to die that day since the sepsis tests had come back positive. I called for our priest to come and suddenly, the "till death do us part" seemed like a real possibility. Could this really be his time to go? It seemed so unfair. Did he become septic due to an infection he had contracted two weeks before in the hospital? Could I have done something differently to avoid all this? Should I have known to take him to the primary care doctor sooner and possibly prevented the impaction in the first place? All I had were questions with no answers, and I was in a panic. The kids called sitters and came to the hospital prepared to say goodbye to their dad. That whole day we prayed like never before, trying to get answers when there were none to have. Once again, somehow, he survived that twenty-four hour period and eventually began to show signs of improvement. Three days later, we celebrated both my birthday and his in the hospital room, and he came home on the twentieth. How he survived this, no one really knew because he had been a very sick man. I had to admit that the pattern of having questions with no answers was becoming most irritating.

June, 2013: The following day, care givers from Care Connection came to the house to get him scheduled for home physical and occupational therapy. The nurse had just left our house, her car not even out of the driveway, and Paul was sitting in the living room when the phone rang. I left to answer it in the next room, and a few seconds later I heard an awful crash. I screamed into the phone that I had to hang up. I found him lying on the hardwood floor on his back with his walker on top of him. Once again, his eyes were open but he was totally unresponsive. I called 911 and the same men who had transported him two weeks earlier with pneumonia returned. By this time he was responsive and talking coherently. They couldn't believe that this was the same man they had transported earlier with the pneumonia and freezing Parkinson's. I asked him what happened, but he honestly didn't know. He didn't think he had fainted this time, and he had no explanation. I determined that one of his shoe laces was open. When he stood up and walked with the walker, he probably tripped and landed on his back, the walker on top of him. He went to the hospital again for X-rays and needed no stitches this time, but he had a nasty contusion on the back of his head. Once again his hard head had paid off! I was beginning to get very tired of all the drama and critical moments, and my stomach felt the same way!

CHAPTER 13

July, 2013: We were overdue to retest Paul's driving ability, and to prove to him that I had his best interest at heart, I made the appointment with the tester to come to our home for the cognitive tests, and then he could drive around our area familiar to him, which I thought, would give him every benefit of the doubt. He was absolutely sure that he would pass again and once again prove us all wrong. The cognitive tests did show a small decline in function, and then they left for the test drive. Thirty minutes later, they arrived back home. I checked out his facial expression and body language for any signs of self-doubt and found none. But then we heard the results; he had failed miserably despite driving in his own familiar neck of the woods. I will never forget the look of surprise and devastation on his face as she relayed all the things he had done wrong, things that compromised not only his safety but the safety of other drivers around him. Even though I was relieved to know he would no longer be behind the wheel, my heart broke for him. It was like someone had just cut off one of his limbs, taking away his independence, and I knew he was angry. When the tester left, he turned to me with a look I had never seen on his face before and with tears in his eyes snapped, "Well, are you happy now? You got what you wanted." I couldn't help but cry with him. "It isn't what the kids and I wanted for you, but we knew it had to happen. I hurt for you, but at least you're still alive." He lost his license that day and also a part of his self-esteem. As our son said when I told him, "Well, Mom, today dad was castrated!" It was an interesting comment coming from another man who could understand his dad's perspective. Years later, he still believed he was unfairly tested that day and should have been able to keep his license. There was no way to convince him otherwise. And he actually told me that he was going to draft a letter to the Motor Vehicles Bureau to get his license back!

2014: The following five months were relatively free of crisis and drama. I was doing all the driving which I never minded, and I was more relaxed knowing he could no longer cause an accident, hurt someone else or take out more fire plugs! But the Parkinson's changes were becoming much more evident. His posture was terrible as he became crooked and always leaned his torso to the right, something the neurologist called truncal dystonia. Consequently, his back always hurt, and he was getting weekly chiropractic adjustments to relieve the pain. We began going to a fitness studio nearby which specialized in programs designed for Parkinson's patients. He would hobble in with his cane and work with the trainer for thirty minutes three times a week. It was expensive since insurance wouldn't cover it, but I could see that he was getting stronger core muscles and more flexibility. So it was worth every cent. But I could also see that his cognition was getting worse. Because he couldn't remember to use support when walking he fell multiple times at home resulting in several black eyes, cuts and bruises but nothing that required stitches or trips to the hospital. At his spring checkup at the neurologist, I told her that I was getting terribly frustrated with him because of this, and I just didn't know what to do any more. She was firm with him and explained that he had been lucky up to this point to not have broken any bones. But then her next words were more ominous.

"You know, Paul, if you do fall and break a bone, you will not recover like a non-PD patient. An injury like that will take its toll on you and you will end up either in a wheelchair or a nursing home!" I was hoping that she was just being dramatic to scare him into being more careful, but unfortunately, that was not the case.

August 8, 2014: A good friend was in town from Michigan and wanted to get caught up. She realized that I was not comfortable going out for any length of time like we used to do since I was afraid to leave Paul home alone. She offered to come to our house and we planned a happy hour on the patio followed by a casual dinner. Usually August in Ohio is sweltering, but we enjoyed a warm, pleasant evening and great conversation before heading up to the kitchen for dinner. Realizing that she and I wanted some girls' alone time, Paul offered to do the dishes while we went to the living room to continue our visit. And then it happened, the moment that decidedly changed our lives. We were looking at the tapestries I had brought back from France when a loud crash came from the kitchen. I yelled and ran to find Paul on the floor, one of the kitchen chairs on its side. Once again he had turned to walk to the pantry without using support and fell onto his right side. He was having a tough time getting up, and if my friend had not been there, I'm not sure that I could have lifted him. But we got him standing and checked him out; there was no blood, no obvious injury, but he was limping a bit as we got him seated in the family room. I turned on the TV for him, and she and I continued our visit, but honestly, my heart was no longer in it. When it was time for her to leave, we hugged in the driveway, and I literally broke down, my tears soaking her shoulder. I will never forget the moment because deep down I think I knew our lives were about to change, and change they did! After she left, I tried to get him up to get ready for bed. It was obvious that he was in some major discomfort walking. I asked him, "On a scale of one to ten, how bad does it hurt?" He said maybe a four. Then I suggested we go for x-rays, and his response floored me. "If anything is broken, it will still be broken in the morning. Let's go to bed!" I couldn't believe it. But an hour later, when he tried to get up to go to the bathroom, he could barely walk at all. So, at midnight I called 911, and we left for x-rays.

The initial x-ray showed no obvious reason for his pain or inability to walk, and I was shocked. At three o'clock they took a CT scan which showed the upper shelf of his femur was cracked as it was rammed up into the ball joint of his hip, and he would need surgery. At that point we didn't know if he would need total hip replacement or not. As it turned out, the good news was that he needed three pins put into the area to secure it from movement, and he would need weeks and weeks of therapy. The procedure went well, but the neurologist's words came back to haunt me. How well would he recover? The bad news was the fact that he would not be permitted to put any weight on that leg for six weeks! How, I thought, will he be able to do physical therapy without putting any weight on his right leg? That would be tough for someone without Parkinson's disease. But first we had to get him through his hospital stay.

Everyone who knew Paul knew what a gentle, kind soul he was. So when I received a phone call at five o'clock in the morning telling me to come right away, I knew we had a problem. He had been awake all night, had gotten violent with the nurse, pulled out his catheter, took off his gown, ripped off his heart monitors and worst of all, he had torn out two IV's with blood going everywhere. I arrived fifteen minutes after getting the call and calmed him as best I could, trying to reassure him he was safe. Because of the narcotic he had received, it had not been advisable to also give him his Parkinson's sleep medication which controls the REM sleep disorder. Fortunately, the medication had solved the problem of yelling and hitting at home, but he had not been able to take it in the hospital that night. So not only was he flailing about and screaming at everyone, he was forcing the staff to call code violet, meaning a violent patient. The treatment was a shot of Halidol to calm him but which also kept him asleep most of the next day, thereby missing his Parkinson's meds entirely. I was surprised when the nurse handed me his wedding ring because he hadn't been able to get it off for years, but apparently he got it off somehow and threw it across the room. His sleep was wild and fitful and frightening to witness, and it was five hours before he slept calmly. Fortunately, he did not have a roommate yet to have to put up with all this ranting and raving! He was in and out of sleep by afternoon, and I really needed the nurses to give him his meds as he was already several doses behind, and it is very difficult to play catch up. They refused since they were afraid he would choke on them as he wasn't fully "with it". Finally, I remembered how I crushed our dog's Heartworm pill in her food and suggested they crush his pills and bring me some pudding, and I would get them in him. I still cannot figure out why they couldn't have thought of this remedy themselves. At least that problem was finally solved.

Later that night, he did get a roommate, a retired, career army veteran who proved to be a different kind of challenge. Marcus was in the other bed when I arrived on Monday morning with the curtain drawn between the beds. I couldn't see him but he was a very vocal man with a domineering voice that made it known that he was not a happy guy. When I thought I heard him snoring, I peeked around to see him. He was twice the size of Paul with a full, bushy grey beard and wild hair sticking out everywhere. He snored as loud as he talked, and I nearly jumped out of my skin when from behind the curtain came a booming stream of profanity. If Paul had been asleep before he wasn't then. Marcus was forever dropping the nurse call device and couldn't retrieve it because he had a broken arm. I peeked around and asked him if I could help. He just continued to yell, **"I can't hear anything you're saying!"** I picked up his call device for him and went back to my kind and gentle husband. This was going to be an interesting few days.

Eventually, I met his wife, a tiny German woman he had met while he was in the army in Frankfort, Germany. She seemed to have the ability to calm him down and was used to speaking very loudly to him. The nurses took a while to realize that they had to speak up, and every time he couldn't hear them, his language got more and more colorful. By the time we had two TV's going, Marcus' and Paul's, on two different stations, his nurses and his wife screaming at him to be heard, and all the bells and whistles that hospitals are known for, the din was unreal. I felt very sorry for his wife who was dealing with her very difficult husband in this hospital as well as her daughter who was in another hospital thirty minutes away with a brain aneurysm! She was running back and forth from one to the other. She was also trying to find a rehab facility that would accept him through the Veterans Administration. That took her nearly three days, but eventually she learned of one rehab facility that would accept him. Since I had spent fifty-six days driving to the same one for Paul in 2009, I could give her directions which she found daunting...as did I the first few days. I still think about the two of them and wonder how their family is doing.

Eventually I asked Paul why he took off his wedding ring and how he had accomplished it. He had been so paranoid, convinced he had been captured by kidnappers who were going to take his jewelry, and he was going to make sure they weren't going to get his wedding ring! So he kept sucking his finger until it was so wet it finally came off. This confusion continued all the way up to the time of discharge, but at least they were happy delusions. He was convinced he was in a comfortable bed on a yacht and he thanked me for putting together the wonderful trip! At one point he had tried to get out of bed again to walk out in the hall, which he thought was the boat railing. When I asked him why, he said he wanted to jump out onto the pier! I hated to tell him the trip I'd arranged was really a "working vacation" in rehab!

When it was time to discharge him, I had to find a facility where he could do his rehabilitation. Several people had recommended a newer care center close to home, and I went to see it. It was quite impressive, and they held a private room available for him. It would be his home, we thought, for the next six weeks. But we were misled with that prediction. He was actually there for thirteen weeks; the first six was just for non-weight bearing exercise. By the seventh week he was permitted to put fifty percent weight on the leg, and by the eighth week, as much weight as he could tolerate. It was very difficult for him, and at one point he thought I was putting him there for the rest of his life and just not telling him. He had tears in his eyes when he asked me that. It was all I could do not to cry when I reassured him that I was definitely not putting him in there for good. How terrified he must have been!

The night I checked him in, despite the fact that the two year old facility was only fifteen minutes from home, I was dreading the moment when I had to say good bye to him. But there was at least one moment of levity to help me keep my tears in check. We were getting settled into his private room at the very end of the hall where there would be no back and forth traffic. It was sparse but clean, uncluttered and more than adequate with a small fridge and microwave! Thank goodness there would be no roommate, no sharing a bathroom and only one TV going. It was so quiet!

I was worried that being in yet another new place would trigger the state of confusion that Paul suffers in hospitals but fortunately that didn't happen. He was in his wheelchair watching me unpack his clothes when a little, white haired lady in a wheelchair showed up outside his door. She just sat there watching everything I did, saw each piece of clothing as it went from suitcase to closet. She never said a word, never waved hello or acknowledged us in any way, but she never took her eyes off Paul and me. I joked later that maybe she was thinking, "Oh goodie, fresh meat!" I watched where she went as she wheeled herself into the room right next to Paul's. His neighbor's name on the door was Nellie.

After everything was accomplished getting him settled in, he was obviously tired and reluctantly, I had to leave him in the care of total strangers. Would they make sure he didn't try to get up? Would they make sure his food was cut up into the bite size pieces he required? Would they give him his meds on time? Would I get another frightening phone call at five in the morning telling me to come and calm him? I expressed my concerns to the night shift nurse, Josh, who assured me that for this first night, he would station someone outside his door all night, and I could call him first thing in the morning to see how it went. I had done everything I could think of to ensure his safety. I had made photocopies of the business cards of each of his physicians, a detailed list of his medications and when to administer them. The staff was amazed at how thorough and complete my notes to them were, and they actually appreciated the input. Despite all that, I had to put my trust in them and in God to keep my husband safe. I admit I cried all the way home.

Thankfully, I received no distressing phone call and when I called Josh in the morning, he told me Paul had slept soundly all night long. Later Paul said it was the best night sleep he had in a long time! The relief was overwhelming. I stayed with him that entire morning, and we ate lunch together in his room. He didn't feel ready yet to tackle the dining room, and neither did I. Suddenly, I heard the voice of one of the nurses yelling, "Nellie, no! What are you doing, dear? Come back here. You don't have any underwear on!" Then she called for help, and another nurse came to get Nellie dressed and back in her wheelchair. I couldn't help but laugh when I saw the look on Paul's face when I asked him, "Do you think she was on her way in to visit the fresh meat?" Oh, did I mention that Naked Nellie was 104 years old?

CHAPTER 14

Although he had speech therapy, physical and occupational therapies every day with staff that were dedicated and thorough, he spent most of his time in a wheelchair, and the neurologist's words were coming true. I spent hours there every day with him, missing only one day in thirteen weeks. I had one meal a day with him during this time, and we both enjoyed meeting the other patients and getting to know more about their lives. Nonetheless, his days were long, and he was asleep before eight o'clock every night.

After several days of taking all his meals in his room, Paul was finally feeling like perhaps it would be more fun to go to the dining room for a change of scenery. I saw this as a positive sign, and I wanted to be with him for that first dinner with other patients. The facility had a beautiful dining room decorated in colors of purple and green with lots of windows and light. Normally five or six people could fit at one table but with most of the patients in wheelchairs, four were all that could fit. We chose a table with two other gentlemen already seated in their wheelchairs and made our introductions.

Paul was hesitant to open conversation because he wasn't comfortable yet with his voice being heard in a setting with so much background noise, a problem we had encountered in many restaurants. Actually it wouldn't have mattered since both of these men were hard of hearing! Neither was very forthcoming with conversation, and I could quickly see that it would be up to me to get the ball rolling. Realizing that most people enjoy talking about themselves, I asked the man across from me what he had done for a living, always a good conversation starter with men. Unfortunately, Lou was just as soft spoken as Paul and appeared shy. He was sweet looking, slim and probably good looking in his day. He didn't offer much other than he had worked for the Gas & Electric Company for thirty-six years. When I could see that he wasn't completely comfortable talking, I tried the gentleman to my left, George.

George was a very pleasant looking guy, had no teeth but a smile from here to the next room. He was much more loquacious, twinkled when he laughed and seemed to enjoy talking about himself. I found myself truly fascinated by this chubby man whose face reminded me a little bit of the comedy mask in the theatrical tragedy/comedy portraits. He had worked for the Keebler Cookie Company for thirty-one years as a machinist who built and serviced the equipment that turned out all those delicious treats. After he retired from there, he worked for five more years for a cookie company building, servicing and maintaining the machines that iced the cupcakes and cookies. He prided himself on knowing how to get all the machines to work most efficiently. It wasn't until the meal was finished and he moved his wheelchair out from under the table that I got a huge surprise. Jovial, easy talking, and quick to smile his toothless grin, George had no legs below the knees! Eventually, many meals later, I asked him how he came to be in that situation. He was very matter of fact and told me he had lost one in an accident and the other years later from an infection. His attitude was so incredibly positive I knew that he was a very special man.

He was also an interesting character who had been born in the hills of West Virginia and had the twang in his speech to prove it. He was one of eight children with only one sibling still alive. At some point in time his family moved from there to the eastern edge of Kentucky on a tract of land that his father bought. He called his home a plantation house with six bedrooms upstairs, a grand stairway and six rooms downstairs. His father traveled for his job and was away much of the time leaving his mother to care for her children. At lunch one day, he began telling stories from his childhood.

His favorite was an account of a time when his father was gone and his mother heard someone knock on the front door. They had no electricity, and his mother took the oil lamp with all the children huddled around her as she opened the door only to find no one there. But they all heard the distinct sound of footsteps entering the house.

"There was no doubt about it," he said. "It was the sound of maybe the heels of cowboy boots or ladies' high heels. We followed the sound all the way down the hallway, where they turned around and made their way back to the door. Then the footsteps went up the stairs and came back down," he continued, his voice getting quieter. "We were all frozen with fear as the footsteps just walked right back out the front door!" I asked him what his mother did or what she said.

"She just stood there afraid to move. She closed and locked the door and never said a word about it to any of us. But I remember it as if it were yesterday."

George had eventually married his school sweetheart from West Virginia and fathered children of his own. He proudly mentioned several times over the course of our meals together that he was never out of work, put in six days a week for thirty-six years and did what he had to do to support his family. He had just a few visitors at the rehab facility, but his positive outlook continued to inspire me and Paul. Physical therapy with only one good leg to stand on was definitely better than having no legs to stand on. We both looked forward to dining with George each day; his sunny personality always made everyone feel better. When he passed away years later, I 'm sure he died with a smile on his face!

This facility offered Happy Hour from every Thursday. They actually had a cocktail lounge open to patients, their families and friends. Anyone can have as many as two alcoholic drinks at no charge as well as appetizers to rival any restaurant, and there was always live music playing in the back corner. It's an amenity I had never seen in a rehab facility before! It certainly was one way to attract visitors. By quarter to three, patient after patient came wheeling in either by their own efforts or by being pushed by a nurse or family member. The first time Paul and I attended this amicable gathering, we were surprised to hear live music. The three piece combo was comprised of a young flutist, a middle aged bassoonist and a more senior clarinetist who were quite good. They played all the oldies that patients and guests would enjoy. Many sang along making the most of a truly happy hour. Even though Paul was not into singing, he usually tried to join in. It was very uplifting to see how hard the staff worked to make the patients' stay as enjoyable as possible.

There are many rehab facilities in our city, and I have only been in three of them during my lifetime. The first two were not pleasant experiences with all the depressing sights, disgusting smells and unhappy faces everywhere. But this third facility probably shouldn't even have been listed under the same category because of all its uplifting qualities. Not only was the building itself remarkably clean, cheerful and downright unbelievable, the staff was just as amazing. For a relatively small place, they had an abundance of employees. After you learned the system, you could easily recognize what department someone worked in based on the color of their uniform. Nurses wore light tan, nurse aides wore burgundy, therapists wore blue, food service varied depending on whether you worked in the kitchen or in the dining room. Unbelievably, after eleven weeks of visiting Paul every day, I had not met anyone who wasn't kind, caring and hard working. And after ninety-one days, I have to admit there were only two days when I had an issue with Paul's care.

Paul and I talked on the phone every morning and every night before he went to bed. One morning after not hearing from him the previous night, I asked him why he hadn't phoned. I thought I detected caution in his voice when he replied that he couldn't call me because he was serving a disciplinary punishment! At first I thought he was joking, but he was totally serious; then I began hearing anger in his voice. My next thought was that his paranoia was returning, and I was going to have to deal with another problem. This incident occurred early on in his rehab when he could not put any weight on his right foot and consequently was not allowed to get out of bed or the wheelchair alone without setting off an alarm at the nurse station. For some reason, he just didn't remember that very important rule and set off the alarm twice while Patty was on duty.

Patty was a middle aged woman with an odd speech defect that sometimes made it difficult to understand what she was saying. In time I got tuned in to this irregularity of speech without having to ask her to repeat. She was a joker with the patients, especially the men, and she usually got a smile out of the patient with whom she was kidding around. I asked Paul what he had done to be punished, and he told me that Patty sat him in his wheelchair next to the nurse's station which put him on display to everyone who walked by. So he was not by his phone to call me. My first reaction was that it was just her sense of humor that I had witnessed so often with the men and not really a punishment, but he was adamant that she was not joking around but very serious and upset with him. He was convinced she put him on display to punish him. He was terribly humiliated and felt like maybe he didn't belong at this place. My heart broke for him, and then the patient advocate in me got angry!

Upon my arrival that day, I went straight to the nurse's station and asked a nurse aide about the incident. "Excuse me, but could you tell me if it is a common practice to punish someone by sitting him out here on display?"

"I don't know what you are talking about," she replied a bit flustered. Just then, a tall, thin woman whom I had never seen before, wearing a tasteful business suit and three inch heels, emerged from the office behind the nurse's station and asked me to repeat my question. I repeated what I had said and also what my husband had told me on the phone. By this time I was having a difficult time controlling my tears. I discovered that she was the head of the entire nursing staff. We talked for a while, and I found out that Paul had tried to get up by himself twice so I understood that something had to be done to secure his safety, but I emphasized that I would not tolerate anyone berating him or treating him like a naughty child standing in the corner! She asked for the name of the nurse, and I really didn't want to rat out an employee, but she insisted. When I told her, she admitted that Patty joked around a lot with the patients. I told her that I had said the same thing to Paul on the phone, but he insisted that she was definitely not joking. Then she shocked me with her next words.

"Can I go and meet your husband?" This I was not expecting from the head of the nursing staff, and I had no idea why she wanted to meet him. He was sitting in his wheelchair with his head and eyes cast down, and she squatted down to meet his eye level. I couldn't believe when she apologized for the way Patty had made him feel. She recognized that he was going through a very difficult time in his life, and he didn't need one of her nurses to make him feel any more uncomfortable than he already did. She promised she would take care of the problem. We were both impressed. From that moment on, Patty was assigned to other rooms.

Paul seemed relieved, but I noticed from that time on, Patty's attitude and demeanor did a 180 degree turnaround. She wouldn't smile, glared at me in the hall, and the tension was unreal. Then one day Paul told me he was convinced Patty was the gang leader of the night nurses and was turning them all against him. Oh no! Here we go again, I thought. Of course, that was his paranoia kicking in, but I felt I had to do something immediately to better this situation and make him feel safer. He still had many more weeks of rehab ahead of him. On my way out that afternoon, Patty was sitting at the nurse's desk with several other nurse aides, and she gave me her beady eyed glare as I approached. So I stopped and confronted her once and for all.

"Patty, are we alright here?" I asked.

"Well, I'm not allowed in his room anymore!" she practically snarled.

"I am truly sorry for the way this has played out. It was never my intention to get you in any trouble, but I have to be an advocate for my husband, and he was so very humiliated and upset." And then the tears returned, and there was no way I could hold them back, nor could I even speak. She softened a bit, and after we talked it out I truly felt the crisis was over. I made sure that Paul knew everything was alright, and there was no conspiracy against him. The following day she saw that he had turned on the call light, and she was the only one around to answer it. She approached his door and stuck her head in and asked his permission to come in and help him. Of course, he said yes.

The only other incident occurred on a weekend when there was a different staff. Once again, while I was there with him, he had to go to the bathroom. It was against the rules for me to help him so we had to wait for the nurse aide. I was shocked when three girls I had never seen before all came in to help. I don't know what would have happened if I had not been there. None of them had ever met Paul, nor seemed to be aware of his weight-bearing restrictions. It was evident none of them had read his chart or knew anything about his care. They were ready to let him get up and walk into the bathroom by himself! After my unpleasant reprimand, he was wheeled safely into the bathroom. I immediately went to the registered nurse on duty and asked about their system of communication when shifts change or new people come on board. Apparently none of these three newbies had ever consulted any notes on Paul's care or else the nurse whose shift ended hadn't fully explained individual patients' needs. I saw that as a serious flaw in the system, and I wasted no time making it known! After that, all went smoothly, Patty continued to help him, and everyone paid my husband the respect he was due.

No facility is perfect and this particular one was certainly better than most. But I also realized that no matter how professionally run a place is, every patient needs an advocate to look out for potential problems that could compromise his safety. There's a fine line between making sure no harm is done and making too many waves, turning people against you. It's a line I have always found difficult to walk, and I know there had been times during Paul's many hospitalizations that I came across as abrasive. Our children's joke that the nurses scattered when they saw me coming was probably never going to change. That may have been an exaggeration, but if I could help it, no one would hurt my husband's body or his pride, so watch out!

One other patient whom we befriended was a guy named Mike. He was confined to a wheelchair because a mistake in his medication from months before had weakened his legs, and he couldn't walk. He was a very slight man who looked sad most of the time, but when he did smile, it was beautiful to see. Mike and I hit it off right away. He had been a high school teacher, too, and we enjoyed many conversations as we sat outside in the sun and telling funny stories about our careers. We always managed to sit with him in the dining room or found him outside on nice days reading his books. His daughter-in-law lived very close and came almost every day to spend time with him so we got to know her, too. Unfortunately, Mike was not progressing with his therapy; he was losing weight that he couldn't afford to lose and several times sank into a serious depression. He had no appetite and picked at his food so when the staff commented to him that he had to eat, I noticed him hiding his food in his napkin so the staff would see his empty plate and think he had eaten. I was worried about him and managed to pull his daughter-in-law aside and told her what he was doing. The closer Paul came to being discharged, the more depressed Mike became. His insurance was running out, and he knew he couldn't afford to stay at this facility without it. He could not go back to his home since he was widowed and lived alone and really had no choice but to move in with his son and daughter-in-law. The day we left, he cried, and so did we. We exchanged phone numbers and promised to get together sometime soon. This was early November, and he did leave a few weeks after

Paul did. I talked with his family later in the month, and we decided to have a visit as soon as the holidays were over. Unfortunately, Mike didn't last until the end of the year, and when his family phoned us with the news that he had died, Paul and I both wept. We had lost a good friend.

CHAPTER 15

During Paul's time away from home, I had discussed with our son, a realtor, the possibility of looking for a one level home. Earlier in the summer, he and I had decided that if we were ever going to try and sell the house, we needed to do a pre-sale inspection so we would not be blind-sighted by anything should a buyer order such an inspection. So in July, our home underwent a thorough professional inspection and ....failed miserably! I was shocked to say the least, and the dollar signs started adding up in my head! Between the months of July and October, I paid for granite kitchen counter tops, bathroom tile professionally cleaned in three bathrooms, additional insulation in the attic, a new roof, a fireproof door leading to the garage, professional interior painting, new bedroom carpeting, fireplace repair and some plumbing updates to meet code. After all this work was completed and the checks written, all while Paul was in the hospital and rehab center, I found a ranch style house that looked promising, and our son managed to get me inside. I immediately fell in love with it, and our son felt good about it, too. "I can see you and dad living here easily," he said. Getting his endorsement kind of sealed the deal for me. I printed out twenty-five photos that had been online so I could show Paul as much as I could, and he reluctantly agreed to make an offer on the house. He honestly wanted to be able to come home to our present house for a while before moving, but that didn't look like it was going to happen. We came to an agreement with the sellers and then had to pay for an inspection of their home. Meanwhile, a "stager" from the realty company came to our home to instruct me on how to prepare the house for showing. By the time she left I was in tears. There were only two weeks from that day to the day our son wanted to put a sign in our yard. To make life even more amusing, I broke out with Shingles during this time, but there was no way I could let that discomfort get in the way of the task at hand. It didn't seem possible that there could be any way I could get the staging done in that amount of time and still go to spend time with Paul every day. I spent a fortune on packing materials and spent every waking minute packing up anything that looked personal; family photos, which were everywhere and whose removal then necessitated re-painting the walls, removal of anything resembling a collection of something personal which in itself was daunting, removal of all clutter, again daunting after living in a house for 27 years, emptying china cabinets and bookcases, the list went on and on. I was exhausted and sore from lifting heavy boxes and somehow getting them down the stairs and into the garage. By the time I was finished, half the garage was filled with packed boxes. Incredibly, I got it done two days before my schedule said I had to finish! But then something happened that I didn't see coming. The inspection of the seller's house indicated a serious foundation problem. Our son said, "Mom, this is a deal breaker. Get out of the contract." So, we did, but now the down season for selling houses was upon us, and we decided to wait until spring to put a sign in the yard. I had a house so empty that it echoed when I walked through it, and the garage was filled with the contents of everything personal from every room. I was devastated because I had loved the other house and had pictured where all the furniture was going to go, where our three Christmas trees would be and how Paul and I would enjoy sitting on the screened porch overlooking the wooded back yard. But it was not to be.

November, 2014: Finally after thirteen weeks, we were ready for the care conference to discuss his discharge with the therapists. My care giving instructions were daunting and disappointing. He could not be permitted to walk anywhere without his walker, something I always knew from the beginning. But the bad news was that even then, I had to be right with him for every step he took everywhere for the rest of his mobile life! He would need supervision twenty-four hours a day. I don't know why I didn't see this coming, but I didn't, and it was a terrible shock, for him and for me. For the rest of his life, he would need a walker and a wheelchair, and it wasn't going to get any better. I thought back to the neurologist's words and realized she was absolutely correct. He would not recover from this ordeal like a person without Parkinson's disease would. My heart sank. I wanted him home, but I was terrified again to be solely responsible for his physical and mental well-being. I had tried to think of everything he would need at home and prepared the house for the necessary changes; a commode by the bedside which was also equipped with a urinal; a plastic mat under the commode to catch any accidents and spare the new carpeting in the bedroom; a commode in the bathroom downstairs with a separate urinal; a third urinal in the kitchen for quicker, more urgent needs; protective padding for the bedding since incontinence had become a new symptom, and unfortunately, a very expensive chair lift for our steps. Every fear imaginable crept into my head the night before he came home. I was afraid to go to sleep for fear I wouldn't hear him if he had to get up and go to the bathroom. I was afraid to not be within his visual range in case he forgot the rule of not walking without me. And the thought that I would never be able to leave him alone in the house if I had to go somewhere really freaked me out. How was I going to grocery shop, go to my weekly massage, and any of the many things I was used to doing? How would I be able to take the dog for a walk if I couldn't leave him home alone? My mind was spinning. I had made all the necessary plans for his well-being, but I hadn't a clue how to prepare for my own.

His first week home was a total nightmare. I got less than four hours sleep every night as he was awake several times to use the urinal and couldn't seem to get himself up alone or back in bed by himself. He was 195 pounds of dead weight, and it was all I could do to help him. He soaked through the bedding every night, and I was stripping sheets every morning. After that first week when I was beyond exhausted and in tears nearly every day, I realized something that he didn't. He was used to an entire staff of women at the rehab center waiting on him night and day, changing his bedding, changing his soiled clothes, wheeling him around everywhere, taking his order for breakfast, lunch and dinner . They were paid to do all this for only one shift a day. I was only one person doing all that twenty-four hours a day by myself in addition to taking care of the house, shopping, paying the bills, and taking out the garbage until I was ready to drop. Something had to change! To add insult to injury, when I was trying to lift Paul from a sitting to a standing position, I hurt my calf so badly that I screamed. It was more than a pulled muscle, it was torn. The pain was intense, and my leg swelled and bruised. I had to get to a physician quickly. He confirmed my worst fears; the muscle had ripped and needed to be wrapped with minimal weight put on that foot for several weeks. I broke down in tears wondering how I was going to accomplish all that I had to do on a bum leg.

I had been afraid that the stairs in our bi-level home would present a problem so before he came home I researched chair lifts. I was totally deflated by the cost of these less-than-attractive additions to our home, and because of all the other home improvement expenses we had incurred in the months of his hospitalization when I thought we were going to move, I hesitated to make this decision. I was dumbfounded to learn that insurance would not cover this expense since they considered it home improvement rather than a medical necessity. I could think of many more ways to spend $10,000 to improve my home! But I thought since he had been doing stair therapy at the rehab center, I was hoping he would be able to manage ours. Then, out of the blue, we were offered the $10,000 by a "guardian angel" who wished no one ever to know of their generosity, and we accepted. The chair lift was supposed to be installed before Thanksgiving and he was coming home on November 5. Surely, I could help him on the stairs for those few weeks! But until then, getting him down the stairs was painful and slow with my bad leg. Consequently, we limited that activity to once a day!

Taking the stairs entailed giving him a cane in one hand, the bannister in the other, a therapy belt around his body and my gripping the belt behind him to insure he wouldn't fall. It took forever to get him down the stairs, and my vice-like grip on the belt was killing my hands and shoulders. It didn't help that he had gained twenty pounds in the thirteen weeks of rehab, thanks to the free ice cream parlor there! He did better going up the steps, but going down was scary for both of us. In addition, he had developed a new symptom; his left foot kept freezing when he walked and that was supposed to be the good leg! So whenever we went down the stairs, his left foot was like a lifeless limb that just flopped onto each step. It was painfully clear that the $10,000 chair lift was going to be a necessity if we were going to stay in this house. Unfortunately, the day the men came to install it, they discovered that the manufacturer made an error in calculation on one of the rails and they had to re-order that part so we had to wait another three weeks! Instead of having the chair lift before Thanksgiving, it wasn't finished until the day before Christmas.

The home therapies continued twice a week, and I looked forward to the arrivals of the physical therapist, occupational therapist and the nurse with great anticipation. Not only were they moral support as they worked with him and gave me feedback on vital signs and motor progress, but I knew that for forty-five minutes, someone else was responsible for his well-being. That doesn't sound like much, but for someone new to the twenty-four/seven caregiving job, forty-five minutes off duty was a luxury. I usually used the time to get away and run an errand that I knew I could do in that brief, blessed amount of time; sometimes I just got outside and took the dog for a walk around the neighborhood like we had done every day when Paul was in the care facility. After the end of the first week, I was getting very discouraged. He was just so lethargic and out of it. I called the neurologist and got him in for a check. My daughter accompanied us to the appointment to help me with the wheelchair. The neurologist was obviously shocked to see the decline in Paul since our last visit in the spring. Not only were his motor skills terribly reduced, but his cognition was very strange. She made the decision right then to increase the voltage to his chest batteries, and within ten minutes he was more responsive and more like the Paul she remembered, at least cognitively.

After the first month of home therapy, it felt like the therapists were old friends. They knocked and let themselves in the front door, and the dog would go wild with excitement at seeing them again. The home visits continued into the second month, and by the beginning of January, Paul's constipation issues flared up again. After five days of not having a bowel movement, he began talking bizarrely, so much so that I was afraid of a repeat bowel impaction like he had had in 2013. By noon I became so alarmed that I called 911 and had him evaluated at the hospital. Fortunately, this time his bowels were not impacted, and after an enema or two, he was discharged.

The home therapists informed me at the end of December that it was time to re-evaluate him to see if he needed the therapy to continue. They were going to have to reassess his progress to either justify Medicare continuing to pay for it or discontinue their services.

Inwardly, I panicked at the thought of losing not only their moral support but also my little bit of time to myself. Their reassessment indicated that he no longer needed occupational therapy, but the nurse and the physical therapist decided he needed more time with them. Whew! Along about this time, the biggest problem for me as his caregiver was his memory and illogical thinking. He continued to get up alone and twice took a few steps without his walker. I was livid. He really didn't see why I was so upset. I totally lost it when he showed signs of being deceitful, like thinking I was out of earshot and getting up alone to go to the cookie jar. I caught him, literally, with his hand in the cookie jar and no walker in front of him. What followed was not pretty! He insisted I kept throwing new rules at him. "The only rule you have," I reiterated for the umpteenth time, "is not to get up alone and walk without the walker! Why can't you remember that?" I was growing more and more frustrated with him. It was becoming evident to me that my anger and intense fear were nearly indistinguishable.

Two months into home therapy, he showed frightening cognitive changes. One Sunday night, he claimed to have had a conversation with my mother, who had been dead for eight years. He claimed she had been sitting on the edge of the family room sofa, and he would not be convinced otherwise! He also told me after his nap that he thought his brother in Colorado was out in the family room. His eyes had a different look about them, and I was so alarmed that I called all three of our children and asked them to come over right away for a family meeting. Naturally, they wanted to know what was wrong, but I didn't want to have to repeat things over three different phone calls so I just told them to come as soon as they could. I'm sure they were terrified by the alarm in my voice. This was a first for me, and I'm sure my blood pressure was sky high by the time they all arrived, noticeably concerned that I had felt the need to do this. I realized for the first time that I really needed additional eyes and ears to assess these new symptoms. I hated to admit it, but I was afraid to be alone with my husband for the first time in fifty-three years…for better or worse. The family spent over an hour with him in the kitchen asking him questions and talking gently with him. He admitted that his hallucinations had freaked him out, but the children's visit seemed to have comforted both him and me. It was an emotional time for all of us especially when they asked him what my mother had said to him. "She thanked me for trying," he said. Everyone's eyes were wet when he said that. I had a moment of intense guilt for having been so frustrated with him so often. Maybe he really was trying hard, and this was as good as it was going to get.

The following day, I phoned the neurologist with these new symptoms, and she called in an anti-psychotic medication. I had it filled but held off giving it to him at that time. The home nurse also suggested he be tested for a urinary tract infection which could cause similar symptoms. I wasn't sure what I hoped the results would be. A UTI meant an antibiotic but could explain the hallucinations. No UTI meant the confusion and hallucinations were a new part of Parkinson's, and I hated the thought of giving him such a strong anti-psychotic. The UTI test was negative, but I still held off on giving him the new medication. He exhibited these symptoms off and on but only when he was really tired, so I didn't worry…too much!

CHAPTER 16

January, 2015: Paul enjoyed a few good weeks with no real drama or medical crisis. Christmas had been a busy time, and we entertained family and friends with no repercussions other than fatigue. Then Friday morning, January 9, we walked back to the bedroom after his breakfast. I thought he had been particularly lethargic that previous week, and the physical therapist had also mentioned how out of it he seemed during their sessions. I got him seated on the commode, and within seconds, he arched his body and lunged backwards stiffly, knocking over the lamp sending a picture frame crashing to the floor. His eyes remained open but glassy, and he was totally unresponsive for six or seven seconds. I screamed his name over and over and got no response, and his body remained rigid. My first thought was that he had died perhaps from a stroke or blood clot to the brain or had finally had the heart attack like his father and grandfather had experienced. I had been allowed to have him for sixteen years longer than I thought I would have on our wedding day. Was this until death do us part? Then he finally relaxed and was again responsive but very pale and had no recollection of what had just happened, other than he remembered hearing me scream his name. I called 911 again, and the EMT's took an EKG and his blood pressure. The EKG was inconclusive as they always are due to the chest batteries, but the blood pressure was dangerously low. He was transported to the hospital again and had multiple tests run, but they found nothing but slight dehydration. After an IV fluid bag, his blood pressure was normal and they were ready to discharge him. Because it was an extremely cold day, I told the nurse who was preparing the discharge papers that I was going to leave him and go start the car to warm it up. He had left home in just his pajamas so I left my coat with him since I was at least dressed in layers. She said she was going to get the aid to bring him a wheelchair, and he would bring Paul out to the car. As I left him, I said, "Now don't do anything stupid, OK?" Annoyed, he answered, "Do I ever do anything stupid when I am here?" I nodded and left the room to brave the cold. It seemed to take forever for the car to heat up due to the terribly frigid temperatures outside, and I couldn't understand why he had not been wheeled out. Something had to have gone wrong, so I turned off the car and went in to find him. There he was sitting in the wheelchair with the aid next to him who explained that after the nurse left the room and before he had returned with the wheelchair, Paul had stood up alone and fell, cutting his elbow. The nurse found him and helped him up, but he couldn't leave until the doctor gave him a quick check to make sure he was in fact okay. Of course, the doctor was busy with another emergency, and we had to wait even longer before we could leave. I was furious with him once again for having done something stupid.

We got home too late to phone any of his doctors, and all I wanted to do was get his Parkinson's meds in him. We were already three hours late taking them thanks to his falling and making us even later than we would have been. It was the weekend, and I would have to wait until Monday to call his physicians to report this latest incident. I was admittedly nervous thinking back to the events of that Friday morning. I had never seen him "faint" in this manner before. Previously in Europe, he had just slumped to the floor with his eyes open. This was so different, like a seizure, and I was once again terrified. It was going to be a long weekend.

The remainder of the weekend was uneventful, but Monday I called his cardiologist to make an appointment. Even after I described the events of Friday morning, they said they couldn't fit him in for eight days! I made the appointment, fuming as I hung up the phone. On Tuesday, his home nurse came for the weekly visit, and she was aghast that he had to wait that long. While she was taking Paul's vitals, I couldn't get the image of his stiff body lurching backwards out of my head, and in my gut I knew it wasn't a simple fainting spell. So I called his neurologist thinking that maybe there was something wrong with his DBS batteries or the actual brain stimulators. She assured me that it couldn't be that, but co-incidentally, that very morning, she had seen a patient who did the exact same thing, stiffening, unconscious, and glassy eyed. As it developed, this patient had alarmingly low blood pressure which she explained could trigger a seizure! She suggested I get the cardiologist on the phone again and get him to write a script for a medication to elevate his blood pressure. She could write it, but thought it really should be written by the cardiologist. And so I tried to explain, once again, to the cardiology receptionist that Paul's neurologist suggested the doctor write a prescription for the blood pressure. She told me his nurse would call me back. No one ever did, for the next three days. Finally, I tried again and was told that they could not write a new script without seeing the patient first! That's when I stopped being polite and demanded that they see my husband that very day, even if it was with a different doctor in the practice. Suddenly, they found an opening, and we went that afternoon. After checking Paul, the cardiologist said, "Well, he definitely needs a medication to raise his pressure!" "Yes, he does, and he needed it three days ago!" I replied. The script was written, and I bought a new monitor so I could keep a better check at home. Maybe it was because my estrogen/testosterone levels were shifting at my age, but I was finding it easier than ever to exercise more aggression than I used to, and it wasn't pretty. But I was getting results!

Saturday, Jan.17: Paul began taking the new drug which was written at the lowest dosage possible for the sake of caution. I thought he seemed better, but Saturday morning he had another fainting episode, this time without the seizure, but with the glassy eyes remaining open for over ten seconds this time. He finally responded and again was pale and with an alarmingly low blood pressure. Evidently, the dosage of the new script wasn't strong enough! Why is it that everything always happens on a weekend when the doctor's office is closed? The cardiologist on call agreed that he didn't need to go to the hospital this time but to hydrate him all day and allow him to rest. I had to monitor his pressure all that day and the next. By the end of the weekend, he was better, but I couldn't get two consistently good readings on the monitor in a row. His blood pressure was all over the place. At least, he didn't faint any more. But my stress levels skyrocketed. This was something new to worry about. The worry list kept getting longer and longer. I didn't even want to take my blood pressure!

Sunday, January 18: Sunday night we sat down to dinner around 6:45. As a precaution, it is my habit to always give him his meds before he eats anything in case he were to get food stuck in his esophagus and be unable to swallow, something I learned the hard way earlier. He had begun with his salad, and once again I heard the unmistakable sound of his throat trying to dislodge his food. I couldn't believe it! Not this again! It had happened the previous Thanksgiving when a piece of turkey got stuck and also the previous June in a restaurant and he got a piece of shrimp lodged in his esophagus sending the poor waitress into a fit of panic. He managed to successfully dislodge it that time, and we avoided a trip to the hospital on our anniversary! But I made the decision that night to never go out to eat again if it wasn't completely necessary. So we both knew sometimes it was possible for him to cough the food up, but this time nothing was working, and he was miserable. So off we went to the hospital at seven thirty, and they attended to him quickly. Fifteen minutes later the hospitalist recognized the problem, one they see frequently, and asked me what he had eaten. "It's just a piece of lettuce," I answered, "but he can't seem to clear it this time." She also saw his history of his needing endoscopic relief, and she called the GI doctor on call who refused to come in because it couldn't have just been a piece of lettuce. He said something else had to be wrong. "What?! He's on call, and we know these symptoms", I shouted. The hospitalist knew I was right and indicated as much, but her hands were tied, and she had to follow his orders. He had instructed her to give Paul an IV fluid bag with an esophagus relaxant added to see if it helped him resolve the problem. She admitted she had never seen this actually do any good, but she had to start with that. By this time it was eight thirty and Paul was most uncomfortable not even being able to swallow his own spit. She phoned the doctor again who ordered a CT scan with contrast to see if anything else was lodged in there. It couldn't possibly be lettuce. I could not believe this, and the hospitalist and the nurses were scratching their heads because they had never done this procedure before for a lodged food issue. "How is he going to be able to swallow contrast fluid when he cannot swallow his own spit?" I screamed. I was livid and wanted to rip the phone out of her hands and talk to this sadist doctor myself. Everything takes forever in a hospital, and the technician from X-ray finally arrived well after nine o'clock. Of course they couldn't get a good picture since he couldn't swallow.

Then we had to wait for another doctor to read the CT scan which took another half hour. Finally by ten thirty the hospitalist phoned the doctor on call and said "This patient is in even more distress than he was before and you need to get here to scope him!" The doctor must have suggested that it wait till morning, and that's when I lost it completely.

"No, No! He cannot wait till morning. He needs to be able to swallow his Parkinson's meds tonight or else tomorrow there will be even more issues to deal with. He needs to have this done right now!" She conveyed my message, and finally he ordered his nurses on call to meet him at the hospital to assist him. They arrived promptly to prep Paul for the procedure, and even after that was complete, the doctor still had not arrived. At midnight, he strolled in with a smile on his face. I wanted to kill him right there.

"So," he said casually, "How are we?"

"How are we? I'll tell you how we are," I said, my voice getting louder. "We are not very good at all."

"Well, why not? What's going on?" he asked looking totally incredulous that I should be so upset. I tried to tell him calmly, but not very successfully, that this had happened several times before, and we were not stupid people, we knew the symptoms and what we were doing. Then he completely befuddled me by turning the situation around and asking me in a most condescending tone, "Well, what have **you** been doing in between episodes to keep this from happening again?" as though this was my fault. I was so dumbfounded I stammered like an idiot and just walked out leaving him to do his job. His job only took ten minutes and at twelve fifteen Monday morning, he called me back into the room. "Well, he had a piece of salad stuck in there." he said.

"Really? I think we told you that four hours ago," I said wanting to strangle him on the spot. Then he simply turned and left. It was then I realized what had happened. The staff had been checking the TV all evening because the playoff football game for the Super Bowl had been on. I realized he didn't get to the hospital until the game had ended! Both the nurses and the hospitalist had been documenting all the unbelievable occurrences of the evening and even told me that Paul's regular GI doctor who was in the same practice was not going to be very happy with his colleague. While Paul was trying to come out of the anesthetic, I ran home to get his last meds for the day so the nurse could give them to him before he left. He was three hours late taking them thanks to a football game and what I considered an unethical doctor!

The following morning I called Paul's doctor and told him how terrible our experience had been with his colleague. I left out nothing! His response was interesting. "Oh no, what did he do?" but it was the way he said it that indicated he meant to say what did he do this time? Evidently, this was not the first complaint against his colleague. As the nurse had indicated, Paul's doctor was not happy at all. He apologized profusely, and it was obvious to me that his dismay was genuine. "I'd appreciate it if you would address this matter with him," I requested.

"I will speak with him before the end of the day, believe me." He suggested that we schedule an outpatient procedure in several weeks to scope him again and stretch his esophagus.

February, 2015: We checked in for the endoscopy as planned, and I went with him and the nurse to prep him for the procedure. She looked at his chart and said, "Oh, I see he was just here recently." "Yes," I responded. "For the first time we had a very bad experience." When I mentioned the doctor on call by name, she just rolled her eyes and added, "Oh, I know all about that doctor." She really didn't need to say any more, but then she added under her breath, "Did you lodge a formal complaint in writing?" I told her I had spoken to Paul's doctor on the phone the day after. "Write the letter!" she whispered.

The procedure went flawlessly, and the doctor spoke with me afterwards. I asked him if the matter we had discussed on the phone had been addressed. "Oh yes! On multiple fronts!" he said knowingly. I didn't press for details, but I got the impression he had set the ball in motion to have a serious matter resolved.

By the beginning of February, the process of re-evaluating Paul's progress in physical therapy was repeated, and I felt sure that they would decide he had reached a plateau and could not justify their coming back. But because Paul had experienced those bouts of hypotension and fainting, they decided to give him another month. I knew that time was running out on this in-home care, and I just dreaded it. But at least I had another set of eyes and ears and moral support for a few more weeks.

As the dreary month of February plodded on, grey, cold and snowy, it was time for the cardiologist follow-up to see if the blood pressure meds were working. I was so disappointed when there hadn't been enough of a change to satisfy him. Once again, the doctor doubled the dosage but also explained that sometimes with Parkinson's disease, the adrenal glands become weaker, and they produce less cortisol which can lower blood pressure He wanted Paul to have a three hour blood test to check on this, just to rule it out. During this procedure, blood would be drawn followed by the administering of a medication intravenously followed thirty minutes later by another blood draw and then another one hour later. The doctor called the diagnostic center where we would go to see if there were any special instructions and there didn't appear to be any. A week later, I hauled the wheelchair into the back of my car, and we drove to the hospital for the latest test. We signed in at the registration desk and waited to be called. We waited and we waited, and thirty minutes later a nurse came over to us and said that we could not get the test done that day because the IV medication had to be ordered from the pharmacy. We needed to call ahead and schedule this test. She gave me a phone number and sent us on our way. This was so frustrating because it was no easy task getting Paul in the car, hoisting the wheelchair into the back seat and going out into the very cold winter temperatures which aggravated his asthma. But we had no choice but to go home and make the phone call. When I reached the person on the other end, she had no idea what kind of test this was and said that they didn't do this test there. "Let me put you through to a special testing department," she said. The nurse who answered the call said, "Hello, x-ray." I didn't think this was an x-ray test, but what did I know? I told her the name of the test and her response was, "Like I said, this is x-ray. We don't do that test here." By now, I was fuming at the ridiculous communication breakdown so I called the cardiologist office and relayed the sequence of events. The doctor called me back and said he would take care of it. Someone would call me to schedule it. What happened next was something I could not believe. They told him that someone from there had called me to schedule the test, but that I had told them that my husband had back problems and had to undergo some procedure before we could have this test! What? No one had called, and my husband does not have back problems. I'd love to know just to whom they had really spoken! Eventually, we did get the test scheduled to be done in the infusion laboratory which was one door down from where we had started earlier.

As it turned out, February proved to be one of the coldest months in the city's history. The day we finally were scheduled for the adrenal test, the temperature had dropped below zero. I decided not to take Paul's transport chair since at the previous visit there had been wheelchairs available at the valet parking. But of course, this time, there were none! We had to wait in the car until the attendant could go into the hospital to find a chair. I turned over my car keys and slipped the valet ticket into my purse and off we went. Nearly three hours later, we returned to the valet station. A different attendant was working there now and I gave him my ticket. We huddled together shivering in the arctic temperatures as he searched everywhere and finally said, "I can't find your keys." Meanwhile, other people were exiting the hospital and waiting for their turn to get their cars. The attendant was working alone and looked quite befuddled with this situation. Should he help the others whose keys were readily available and leave us freezing in the frigid temperature, or should he help us since we were there first and keep all the others waiting? Unfortunately for us, he chose the former. I was incredulous, and he could see I was really losing patience. He phoned the first attendant who had taken our keys and asked him where he had put them "They should be right there," he said. "I'll come back if you can't find them." I could actually see in the distance where our car was parked, and I did have the spare key in my purse. "Do you think he may have locked the keys in the car? If so, I could open it and look," I suggested. He was happy to let me look, and I wheeled Paul back into the warm hallway to wait hoping he wouldn't try to get up. I unlocked the car and found no keys inside so I drove the car back to the valet station. "What do we do now?" I asked. "All my other house keys are on that key chain."

"We'll have to fill out a lost key form and buy you another key," he said. Just then the first attendant arrived and found my keys immediately! "I don't know why he couldn't find them. They were right there," he said, obviously annoyed. I thanked him, went back to get Paul, and we left the hospital thirty-five minutes later than we should have. The good news was the test results were all normal! But this still didn't explain the reason for Paul's crazy blood pressure fluctuations.

So we could rule out the adrenal functions as an explanation for the low blood pressure but we still couldn't seem to get it regulated. Finally, we learned that Parkinson's disease plays havoc with the autonomic nervous system which regulates blood pressure, a fact that no one had ever mentioned before. How many other symptoms were going to pop up down the road? I had thought we'd reached the end of the list, but apparently there would always be one more thing to worry about. The cardiologist played around with the dosage of the drug to elevate his blood pressure. One week his pressure responded well to the five milligrams three times a day. The next week it would plummet again and he'd be faint. So we increased the medication to ten milligrams three times a day. All would be well for a while and then - boom! The blood pressure spiked to 146/80, and his face was flushed red. By this time I was getting pretty adept at just looking at the color of his face to guess if his pressure was low, high or just right! We readjusted the medication to ten milligrams once a day and five milligrams later in the day. But that didn't work either. I called the cardiologist on a Friday morning when his pressure started out at 126/68 and plummeted two hours later to 51/37. I know the doctor thought I was ill equipped to use the monitor. It couldn't be that low and still have a walking, talking husband! He said to keep him hydrated, and he would see me on Monday! I'm not sure if I was relieved or disappointed when the doctor took his pressure and couldn't get it up over 66/44. The look on his face said it all; shock, concern, disbelief and the realization that maybe I hadn't been misreading the home monitor! "Let me take it in the other arm," he said. "That's the arm from which they took the artery for his bypass surgery. We never use that arm," I told him.

"Well," he answered, "He still has another artery we can use." I nearly laughed out loud when the numbers fell to 57/44 with that arm. After that visit, he increased the medication to ten milligrams twice a day and added another drug to boost it along. I thought why not add another pill to his daily regimen? It just seemed like my husband's poor, tired body was functioning solely because of the different drugs that kept all his parts working. Except for his adrenals; they were still just fine!

CHAPTER 17

Over the course of the eight months since his femur break, his three months of rehab and his five months of home therapy, I had noticed many cognitive changes which unnerved me almost more than the mobility problems. The occasional hallucination like the one when he had a tête-a-tète with my dead mother had not reoccurred. But the confusion and disorientation were definitely getting worse. Hardly a day would go by when he didn't exhibit some kind of confusion or inappropriate question. For example, one morning as we were waiting in the pharmacy drive-through line he asked, "Where did mom go this morning?"

I asked him, "Whose mom?"

"My mom," he said.

"Well, I'm pretty sure she went right up to Heaven about eight years ago." Then he'd get a blank expression on his face until it registered that he had said something wrong. There were countless times in our house when he would become disoriented and think he was going to go upstairs to bed when we were already on the second floor. Sometimes I would ask him where he thought we lived. Invariably, his answer would start out correctly, and he would give me our address. "What city do we live in?" and then he would get confused and answer Columbus instead of where we lived. "No," I answered every time. "We left Columbus 40 years ago. And the same blank stare would be there until he got it right in his head. Most of these moments of confusion occurred when he was either waking or tired at night. There were many mornings when he would be getting up before it was light, and when I'd ask him why he was getting up he would say that he had to take an exam or teach a class. I had to remind him he was retired and had no class to teach or exam to take and he would say, "Okay" and go back to sleep immediately. I, on the other hand, would lie there wide awake waiting for him to try to get up again. He rarely knew what day it was, and many times thought it was time to get ready to go to Church if it wasn't even close to Sunday. More and more frequently he had difficulty remembering relationships. When talking to our granddaughter on the phone, he'd say, "This is Uncle Paul." Or once he told his sister on the phone he was giving the phone back to "mom" when he meant me. I just figured I seemed like mom to him since I took care of him all the time. But the most concerning moment was the night he asked me to give him a tour of our house because there were so many changes! "That wall wasn't there before," he'd say, or "That room is different." It broke my heart to watch his cognition becoming so compromised. Of course, I took him around the next morning when it was light, and we went room to room. I'd ask him if this room looked different. If so, what was different? We have a large house so this took quite a bit of time, but I thought he was satisfied that he knew where he was when we finished. I chalked it up to the fact that when he was in the hospital and rehab for three months, I had made some changes in the décor when I thought we were going to put the house on the market. At least, I wanted to think that was the reason for his confusion. But a few weeks later, the house confusion returned as well as other disturbing mental changes.

One night as we were preparing for bed, he asked me who was sleeping in our bed that night. I was so taken back all I could say was, "Who in the world do you think was sleeping in our bed?" "You are?" he asked blankly. My heart sank as I realized we were entering into a new area of confusion. So many instances that involved his thinking other people lived in our house began to be commonplace. After ordering a pizza one night, he asked me if it was just the two of us eating it. "Well," I answered, "nobody else is here and the dog doesn't eat it, so yes, it's all for you and me." One day after his nap, we were enjoying some time sitting on the patio swing, always a favorite place to hang out before dinner. "Have you met the neighbors next door?" he asked. "Yes, I met them when they moved in eight years ago!" Then I thought maybe he didn't realize who I was, and that was why he asked me. I asked him if he knew who I was, and it did take him way too long to answer correctly.

He spent hours at a time on the commode, usually with his eyes closed. I'm convinced he fell asleep many times because when I'd go in to check on him, he would say some bizarre things. One night, after a particularly alarming bout of constipation, as it was approaching bedtime, he asked seriously, "Are you staying the night?" When these things came out of his mouth, I was so unnerved momentarily because I was not sure if he knew who I was, or if he knew where he was. It was possible at times that he thought he was still at the rehab center because he often asked me if I could stay the night with him there. But I began keeping track of the correlation between mental confusion and bouts of constipation. It seemed the more days he went without a good bowel movement, the more confusion he exhibited. At first I didn't mention this observation to anyone in the medical community for fear they would think my professional diagnosis of "poop brain" was ridiculous. But then one day I did mention it to the visiting nurse, and she thought it made perfect sense. As she said, "The sicker your intestines are, the more your entire body becomes bogged down, so why shouldn't the brain?"

I tried to find jobs for him to do around the house that didn't jeopardize his safety. At one point I had a container of loose change to put into a baby bottle to donate to the local pregnancy center. I asked him to count the coins and tell me a total to put on the slip of paper that came with the bottle. I figured it was probably going to be somewhere between $8 and $10. He had a terrible time doing it, kept dropping pennies on the floor and stacking the individual piles of nickels, dimes and quarters. But when he finished he proudly told me he thought there was close to $240.00. When he went for his nap, I recounted it and came up with the sum of $10.42.

By far one of the most difficult changes to witness in this highly educated, professional man was the loss of knowing how to make things work. He lost his ability to organize email, how to type and send an email or even remember how to open his email account. He would attempt to use the remote control for the TV and completely mess it up although I suspected that his vision was also partly to blame, and he couldn't really make out what each button was used for. This former professor in the medical school, who had published scientific papers, who lectured all over the United States as well as internationally, who taught Pathology in the medical school and directed an entire laboratory of other professionals, now couldn't even write a letter to his brother. His ability to form sentences much less paragraphs was disheartening. It is also a well-known fact that the penmanship of Parkinson's patients becomes tight, tiny and pinched, and this was true for Paul. Not only was it impossible to read, he couldn't keep it in a straight line at all. Not able to hand write a letter, not able to type an email, and with a voice that faded in and out, he was at a loss to communicate on so many levels.

After five months of having him home from rehabilitation at the care center, I had done everything I could to ensure his safety and well-being. But what was the most difficult challenge for me personally was being able to go about my activities both at home and away from home in a timely manner. Everything I had to do, from making our bed to taking out the garbage to checking my email and doing the online banking, everything had to be choreographed around his needs. If I had to prepare a meal, he had to be in my direct field of vision because I couldn't trust him to always remember to use the walker when he rose to a standing position. When I needed to use my desktop computer, it had to wait until he was ready to go downstairs to putter in his office across the hall. I even put bells on the walker so I would hear him when he stood up if I couldn't see him. The laundry had to wait until he was downstairs with me because I wasn't comfortable having us on two different floors. Making the bed had to happen when he was in the adjoining bathroom so I could be close by. Taking a shower depended on his being at the bathroom sink brushing his teeth and washing his face so I could see him through the glass shower door. And as ridiculous as it sounds, I looked forward to the long periods of time he sat on the commode trying to bring his constipation to an end. I could get all kinds of work done while I knew he was seated, and sometimes that was a minimum of thirty minutes! You would be surprised at how much I could get done while he tried to get his bowels to move! I became quite good at organizing everything I had to do around everything he was doing at that time. And yet, even that could get frustrating and downright irritating when he would decide to change his activity after only a short time, and I was still in the middle of my job, like paying the bills which I didn't want to stop doing. It was a constant juggling act on my part to keep him occupied, safe and happy and still accomplish all that I needed to do. I devoted a good part of each day doing things for him like reading books out loud since he could no longer do this long ago, favorite activity. I made sure he exercised every day and monitored how long he worked at it, encouraging him to add a minute or two more each time. I fed him three times a day, medicated him four times a day. I took him to the park with the wheelchair and pushed all thirty pounds of chair and 195 pounds of him around the walking trail until my shoulders, arthritic hands and thighs were on fire. I made sure his IPAD was charged and ready for him to use at some point every day since he liked listening to the TED talks. I took over communicating with his four siblings via email more frequently so they always knew how he was doing and what he was doing, and I read their return messages to him. They no longer sent mail to his computer but rather to mine to read to him. I did all this not always willingly and not always selflessly, believe me. Hardly a day went by that I didn't lose my temper with him for something he had done to imperil his safety. Sometimes it was just annoyance and other times downright rage. I learned quite a bit about myself during these times, and that when I am terrified, my response is angry screaming and bad language. Before this time in my life, I never realized how closely anger and fear are intertwined. But in my more rational moments, I had made peace with the fact that for whatever the reason, this was God's plan for us at this time in our life. I had learned some valuable lessons over the course of Paul's illness which had led me to this conclusion.

For example, in 2009 when Paul underwent the deep brain surgery and suffered the consequences of the surgeon's mishap, it was the first time in our marriage that I lived alone for that long. Early in Paul's career he had many business trips, the longest being only two weeks, and though I hated them, I learned that I could handle any family emergency alone. And there were several. On one occasion, our beloved eleven year old German Shepherd had to be euthanized the same day Paul left for a business trip. I had to deal with the gut wrenching experience of cradling his head in my lap until he took his last breath, my enormous grief, as well as the emotions of our three children without his moral support. On another business trip, our son fell off his bike and landed face down in gravel, losing one tooth and really doing a number on his braces. That resulted in a trip to the emergency dental clinic at Children's Hospital. Why emergencies always happened when Paul was out of town still remains a mystery, but maybe that was even a part of God's plan for me. But his hospitalization after the brain surgery was ten weeks long, and I found it very difficult. The one blessing was that I was so tired at the end of each day that I literally fell into bed, mostly from emotional exhaustion. The days before his procedure, he had tried to show me how to pay the bills which I hadn't done in decades. I discovered that he really had no easy system; some were auto pays, some were snail mail checks to write, some were paid on line. I had been the bill payer when we first got married, but that was way before online banking which was a whole new ballgame for me. But I didn't panic since he was supposed to be home twenty-four hours after the surgery, and we both anticipated that he'd be doing the bills again upon his return. Not only the monthly bills but also our tax return was due shortly, and I had never dealt with figuring out that enjoyable job. It was his to do every year. But then he didn't come home in twenty-four hours but rather ten weeks later. When I realized what lay ahead, then I did panic! Our son showed me how to file for an extension on the taxes, but to make matters worse, I kept finding unpaid bills on his desk from months past and underneath all kinds of junk mail. It was obvious that he had lost his ability to organize our finances, and we were in a terrible mess. He had countless credit cards paying the minimums on all of them each month, and they were eating us alive. To make matters even more difficult, that was the year of the great recession, and we lost nearly $2000.00 every month from our retirement income! Now I was not only in a panic over the health of my husband but the health of our financial situation as well. "For better or worse, for richer or poorer, in sickness and in health, until death do us part" were definitely taking a turn for the worse, and I felt like a disastrous collision of all four was in the making! Finally, a few weeks after I tried to begin this new fiscal responsibility, I called our son-in-law, who is a banker, to help me with some financial strategies to get us out from under. It was a very humbling experience not only to ask for this kind of help, but to share our financial problems with our daughter's husband. I don't know what I would have done without him. I gathered up all the bills that I could find and in tears dropped them on his dining room table and said, "Help me, please."

And he did with calm understanding. He drew up a spread sheet for me to use every month so I could see the big picture more easily, a picture that wasn't very pretty for many months, and he advised me which credit cards to pay off and cancel immediately. When I left his house, I could feel my stomach knots relax, and I could finally get a full breath again. This wouldn't be easy, but it was doable. I wouldn't accomplish it overnight or even over one month, but eventually, it got better. One day at the hospital, Paul asked me if we were going to be okay financially. I will never forget that moment of conflict; part of me was so angry that he had left me with such an irresponsible mess, and part of me felt so sorry for what he was going through physically. How could I tell him in his present state that we were going to be $24,000 poorer in the upcoming year? So I just lied and told him everything was going to be alright when in my heart, I really didn't know how long it would take to be alright. Needless to say, after months of working through this, when Paul returned home in May of 2009, I relieved him of the bill paying permanently! He didn't seem to mind.

Those ten weeks prepared me to be alone, to keep the house running smoothly and pay the bills, all of which I have had to do again while he was hospitalized for three months with a femur break in 2014. I learned that thanks to wonderful neighbors, I could always ask for help if I was afraid of something. I remember when the furnace was making a terrible noise, and I was terrified since I knew nothing about furnaces. I called my neighbor to come over and give me his opinion regarding the cause of this disturbing noise. He felt it wasn't terribly serious, and the house was not going to explode as I was picturing it in my head. And he gave me the name of his furnace repair man who came the next day. On another occasion, someone vandalized our mailbox, and I found it lying on the ground. Two other neighbors went to the store, bought me a new box and installed it! And it was during those thirteen weeks of Paul's rehab in 2014 that I found a house I thought we were going to buy, prepared our house to sell and still spent hours with him every day at the rehab center. It seemed like every experience and difficulty life sent to me only prepared me to take on a more difficult responsibility later. But I'm not sure any of that prepared me to be a caregiver twenty-four hours a day seven days a week. However, if this is what God expected of me at this time, well, there must have been a good reason for His plan. I didn't have to like it, but I did have to accept it with faith, keeping in mind that everything happens for a reason, and maybe someday I'd look back and understand the greater picture.

One of the toughest decisions I had to make was whether or not to continue my volunteer teaching in the OLLI program at my local university. I had been going to the Osher Lifelong Learning Institute ever since I retired in 2003. It was a great way to keep up with my French language skills and meet like-minded retirees who wanted to improve their language skills. I met wonderful people with interesting pasts who had lots to share. The first year I attended, I was just a participant in the class which was moderated by a man named Lester. He had learned French while working in France for General Electric. His pronunciation was pretty bad, and he really had never learned the grammar, but for him, the class was just a ninety minute opportunity to socialize with friends who wanted to use the French language. There was really no learning going on. This drove me crazy, but I did enjoy the people, and I came to like Lester a lot. He asked me to co-moderate with him the following year and I readily agreed. We made a good team; I could convey the academic side of the language, and he had the experience of having lived in the country which I had not.

By the end of that second year, Lester told me he was moving to Pennsylvania to be closer to his son and family. He had just been recently diagnosed with Parkinson's disease! He was obviously scared, and I shared with him that Paul also had the disease. I think I cried all the way home that day. Lester and I kept in touch during the holidays until one day eight years later I received a note from his wife that he had died. After only eight years! Paul had been diagnosed six years before this, and I had no idea if that meant that his life was going to end sooner than I had thought. Was eight years the norm? I shuddered at the thought.

I continued to moderate the class without Lester, and I missed him dearly. There were always a variety of language skill levels, but we all spent ninety minutes trying to speak and understand each other using this beautiful language and having a good time while doing so. I put my heart and soul into preparing lesson plans to make the classes as fun and stress free as possible. Several years I spent an entire morning teaching two ninety minute classes back to back. One was French History and the other Conversational French. For a while after Paul retired in 2006, he created a course called Understanding Disease which was very well received. It was fun going with him on Thursday mornings, each of us still enjoying our fields of expertise and sharing them with other retirees.

During spring quarter of 2014, I missed more classes than I attended mostly due to problems with Paul. Then in the fall quarter he was in the rehab center after his femur break, and I was doing all the crazy house business, and I had no available energy to give to OLLI. My friend, Gloria, an octogenarian fluent in the language, always took over for me when I couldn't teach. I don't know what I would have done without her. Gloria took my place as moderator every winter quarter since I had made the decision in 2003 when I retired that I was never going to commit myself to anything that required driving in snow and ice, and I stuck to that decision. So when spring quarter 2015 rolled around, I had to make the decision to go back to OLLI and entrust Paul's care to someone else for three hours in the morning or to give up the OLLI program entirely. If the class had met in the afternoon, the decision would have been much easier since there is much less to do for his care during those hours. But anyone who cares for a Parkinson's disease patient knows that the mornings are the most labor intensive since mornings are the most challenging for the patient, too. Mornings bring the longest time period without having taken medication, and the going is very slow. Most days caring for Paul to take his meds, eat his breakfast, use the commode, get dressed and complete his teeth, hair and shaving needs would take a minimum of three hours. My regular care assistant, who was well schooled in working with Parkinson's disease and also who was an R.N., was not available on Thursday mornings so I had to start from scratch finding someone I trusted before I could make the decision to go back to the program at OLLI. This was an agonizing time for me because I missed the interaction with the other French language speakers, but I wasn't sure the stress of finding someone for Paul's care and actually trusting her with him was worth it. My usual stress symptoms flared up with a vengeance, loss of sleep and intense stomach pain that required medication and sometimes resulted in vomiting. I called the agency I had used before and asked for help on Thursday mornings for three hours with someone experienced in caring for patients with Paul's condition. Meanwhile while they were searching, I signed on for the eight week teaching assignment trying to think positively and then wrote out two detailed pages of notes for any caregiver who might be assigned.

April, 2015: When they found someone who could give me those three hours every week, I arranged a walk through session from eight o'clock to eleven o'clock the week before the spring quarter began to see how it would go. The girl who arrived was only twenty years old, a single mom of a two year old and not a registered nurse. She was licensed as a nurse aide and had very little experience with Parkinson's. I was heart sick and not at all comfortable with leaving Paul with her. But if I wanted to go back to the French class, I had no choice. Paul and I discussed it and decided to give her one week on her own and then make a decision. Our Care Connection home visit nurse thoughtfully offered to stop in that first morning and check on Paul as well as the care worker. It was most reassuring to know there would at least be another set of eyes and ears on the scene during part of my time away. She would report back to me what her impressions were of the young care giver.

I was clearly anxious leaving him that morning, and when I called home at the end of the class, I was relieved that all had gone well. Paul seemed to be satisfied with her care and the nurse felt the same way. Each week of that spring quarter, all seemed to go well with Paul and his most recent care giver, and I felt more and more comfortable leaving him with her.

In May, 2015, our neurologist suggested that she write a script for outpatient physical therapy for twelve visits since he was no longer qualified for in-home therapy. The downside of this change was that our in-home weekly nurse visits would also have to end since Medicare could not provide a service if he got therapies outside the home in any way. It was a very emotional visit the day she came for the last time. She had been with us every week for six months, and she was just as sad as we were to say goodbye. I personally felt a tremendous loss just because she was another pair of eyes and ears and someone with whom I could share my fears and concerns each week. She was always so willing to go the extra mile to reassure me as she had done that first day with the new care giver. The upside was that Paul was going to get much needed exercise several days a week. It would provide a chance for him to get out of the house and have time to work with another person and which would give me a bit of a break as well. So a new chapter was about to begin.

CHAPTER 18

Spring, 2015: Finally, the longest winter of my life was over. The days were getting warmer, Paul and I could be outside on the patio sometime nearly every day, and we were enjoying our "happy hours" sitting on the brown wicker swing we had bought the previous year. I remembered on that first warm day of 2015, the spring in 2009 when he was in the hospital after his brain surgery. All I had prayed for then was that he would survive so we could relax on the patio swing and thank God for his recovery. That thought came back to me nearly six years later to the day when we sat in the sun, listening to the water rippling in the little fountain and enjoying the various bird songs in the trees all around us. Lunches were eaten at the umbrella table more days than not, and even though he wasn't taking in all the beauty around him since his eyes were closed for most of the meal, he could at least hear the wonders of nature and feel the warmth of the sun. It wasn't the same as it had been, but at least he was there with me.

Having his eyes closed during meals was something I could never get used to; I really hated seeing him hunt for the food on his plate like a blind man. There were even times I was so unnerved by this behavior, I would go and eat somewhere else so I didn't have to look at him. I am not proud of this response on my part, but it seemed better than constantly asking him to open his eyes. And it made me angry since I was still convinced that closing his eyes during meals was just a bad habit. I realized that as a Parkinson's patient, after his eyes were closed, it was often difficult to get them open again. So my angry response was always, "Just don't close them in the first place!" It upset me to see him holding his glass of milk and not getting the liquid even close to his mouth. He could sit like that for minutes on end, glass off center, while he just held it up without trying to tilt the beverage into his mouth. At least he didn't pour it into his lap! When he would hold a fork up to his mouth with nothing on it since he hadn't looked at the food in front of him, I constantly yelled, "Nothing's on the fork, Paul!" I began to hate meal times. Quite often, because he ate with his eyes closed, more food landed in his lap or on the floor. After a while, I just had to pick my battles and wash the floor under his place when he had finished.

The eye closing became such a habit, not just at meals, but when we sat on the porch swing, whenever I would read to him and every night in front of the TV. We would turn on his absolute favorite program, and he would miss most of it. In my frustration I would say, "Why don't you just listen to the radio?" He would answer that he **was** watching the program to which I would answer with sarcasm, "Well, you are truly amazing if you can see through closed eyelids!" Sometimes while I was reading a book to him, his eyes would close, and when I stopped reading, he wouldn't look up to see why. I knew then that he had fallen asleep, and I had no idea how much of the book he had actually heard. A year or so earlier, the neurologist suggested he receive Botox injections to help him with the eye closing, but after undergoing this not-very-pleasant procedure with nothing to show for it but bags of fluid that drained like big pouches under his eyes, we temporarily stopped having it done.

One of the consequences of being a spouse of a Parkinson's patient that I never saw coming early on was the overwhelming feeling of loneliness in the marriage. By this time, there was really very little that we enjoyed doing together. Meals were difficult and stressful, not just because of the eye closing but also because of my fear of the esophagus trapping food and necessitating a trip to the hospital. Evenings in front of the TV were no longer enjoyable since Paul rarely saw a program through from start to end. We didn't go out to dinner any longer mainly because of my fear of the esophagus issue making a scene in public. We didn't have meaningful conversations any longer because the disease was robbing him of finding words or forming complete thoughts. It was a rare occurrence for him to ever initiate a conversation, at least one that made sense. When we would drive anywhere, there would be total silence in the car from the time we left home until we reached our destination. His eyes would usually close and unless I started a conversation, there was none. And the most painful thing to give up was travel. We had talked about our "bucket list", all the places yet to visit and when we would plan to take those trips, but now there was no way we would ever travel again, and it broke my heart. We did, however, continue to go to the ballet by changing our season seating to the handicapped area of the theater. I absolutely refused to forego that time out together. At least it was something.

I could see when he was in the rehab facility that there were going to be other changes that I was not looking forward to. The incontinence he displayed there took me by surprise, and I was hoping it would be temporary and a non-issue when he came home. But that was not the case. I had new carpeting laid in our bedroom while he had been gone for those three months since, between him and the dogs in our lives, there had been many an accident that had discolored the rug. So after I saw him losing bowel and bladder control in the rehab facility, I was terrified that he would ruin the new carpeting! I remedied the potential problem by going to an office supply store and purchasing a heavy, plastic mat like you put under a desk chair to help it role more easily. I laid it next to his side of the bed under the commode. It was the smartest move I could have made since the carpeting would have been ruined only days after his return home! Even though he wore Depends underwear day and night with an additional thick pad added to the inside, I also had to put protective matting on the bed, and there were still occasional nights when he would soak through his clothing, the matting and the sheets all the way through to the mattress cover. There was never a night when he didn't get up to urinate sometime in the wee hours and I always felt the need to get up with him, to hand him the urinal and make sure the urine went where it was supposed to go because of course, his eyes were always closed! There were the nights that he got up to urinate, and I would spring out of bed to get to him in time only to find that he had already soaked the bedding instead and didn't really need the urinal at all.

The bowel incontinence was not as big an issue, but there were a few times when it did present a disastrous clean up event. As accustomed as I had become to cleaning up the bladder problems, I could never handle the bowel problems with anything but panic and disgust. Fortunately, most of the time his constipation was the bigger problem for him physically but a whole lot easier on me. That's not to say that emptying his commode after the resolution of a four day bout of constipation was pleasant! I found myself doing jobs involving his hygiene that I never would have thought I would or could do. For better or worse, in sickness and in health!

I have always said I could do anything if I got enough sleep, but even this was becoming more and more difficult. In addition to the need to help him during the night with the urinal, often he would be getting up in the middle of the night thinking he had to go somewhere, more than likely due to a dream he was having. Invariably, it would be related to his former profession at the hospital. One morning, he was trying to get up at four A.M. to get ready to go to a class. Another day, he was getting up because he had to give a lecture. Or he would have to take an exam. When I asked him what exam he thought he had to take, he said, "Organic chemistry." "Well," I answered, "you really are having a nightmare! Go back to sleep" And he did.

What was very unsettling to me was the continued confusion over who I was. One Sunday, as he was getting ready to go to church, he asked me, "Are you going to Mass with us?" If I would ask him who he thought I was, he would think for a minute and answer "Dee".

"Then who else are you thinking would be going to Mass with us?"

"The other lady," he would answer.

"What other lady?" We would go round and round until I could convince him there was no one else here but me. Then he said, "There are three Dee's!"

"Really?" I exclaimed. "Who are they?" I thought this would really be an interesting conversation.

"Well, there are you and the older lady who went with you to get your hair done yesterday and the one whose voice is different." I wasn't sure where to go with this conversation, but I finally convinced him that there was me, there was the older lady who came to stay with him when I got my hair done and the me whose voice is different when I am really angry with him. That seemed to satisfy him for the time being. When I mentioned this unsettling conversation to my care giver, she said I shouldn't try to set him straight but to just go along with it. I vehemently disagreed.

"No, I don't want him to get away with thinking like this; I feel like I have to tell him what is and what isn't," I cried.

"You're still looking at him as the man he was, your husband of 48 years, but that isn't who he is any longer. His brain is not the same brain. You should just go along with him."

"I don't know if I am ready to do that yet," I said trying not to cry in front of her. She just gave me a big hug. And I continued to correct him.

Shortly after this conversation, we had a follow-up appointment with the neurologist. We had to discuss openly the cognitive changes he was manifesting, something I had never wanted to do in front of him. But the time of tippy-toeing around the issue was over, and it had to be dealt with. I was relieved to know that there was a syndrome associated with Parkinson's called that explained the delusion of thinking there was more than one of me in the house. The script that the doctor had written months before, which I had never given him, when I called our children in a panic for a family meeting after his conversation with my deceased mother, was now going to help alleviate this condition. And it was also time to reduce the dosage of one of his medications that can aggravate dementia issues. Hopefully, combining these new strategies, the dementia would be less of an issue or at the very least, keep it from progressing any faster. On a lighter note, on our drive home from the appointment, I asked him how he felt about the time spent with the doctor. Usually my perceptions of how it went weren't the same as how he thought it went. But I had to laugh out loud when he answered, "I am so relieved to know that there was only one of you in bed with me last night!"

CHAPTER 19

June, 2015: Paul's seventy-fifth birthday and our forty-eighth wedding anniversary were fast approaching. I was determined to make it a special birthday for him since there were so many times I was afraid he wouldn't make it to age fifty-eight much less seventy-five! At one point earlier in the year he had mentioned that he really missed his siblings, all who lived in the west. His sister and youngest brother lived in California; another brother lived in Colorado and another in Washington. My wish was to have all of them arrange a trip to Cincinnati to celebrate their oldest brother since I couldn't think of anything that would make him happier. Unfortunately, that was not to be, and only his brother in Colorado, his wife and son made the effort to come. I was terribly disappointed since all his siblings had been so concerned during his last hospitalization and rehabilitation. I invited the very few friends who still kept in touch with us and of course our immediate family. I did request that even those who could not come, to write something, share a memory, or send a photo that was significant of their time with Paul so that I could compile it all into a surprise scrapbook for him. The siblings who did not come mailed photos, memories and personal messages to him. As I read them all and looked at the old photos, worn and discolored with age, I couldn't help but feel nostalgic for better times. Some of the photo memories had pictures of the two of us together when we were young, thin and agile. Those times seemed so very long ago! The photos that surprised me the most were those taken just five years earlier when we traveled to Colorado for a family reunion for Paul's seventieth birthday. Only five years and the physical differences were shocking. But as I read the inspired words and personal reflections sent by his family members, they helped me to remember the guy

I had met, and why I fell in love with him fifty-three years earlier. These messages created such a conflict of emotion in me reminding me of how proud of him I had been for all he had accomplished professionally, how his intelligence had impressed everyone and what a good and caring man he had been...and still was! The sweet and loving messages from the grandchildren meant the world to me as I read them. I couldn't help but remember his words that fateful day in October, 2000 as we heard the diagnosis of Parkinson's in the doctor's office: "Will my grandchildren be afraid of me?" Not only were they unafraid of him, they thought he was fun, and they loved him dearly. It is still so eye opening to me how different personal perception is. The times I thought he was behaving in front of the grandchildren in a way that was a bit embarrassing to me, they perceived him as just a funny Papa who made them laugh. We really have so much to learn from children!

But these messages and photos from family and friends also reinforced how far he had declined physically. The good and caring man was still in there, but his body and his mind were ever so slowly becoming shells of what they had been. I couldn't help but ask myself if a sudden, unexpected death like Paul's father had had with the massive heart attack, or like the sudden rupture of my father's aortic aneurism that allowed him to bleed out in only four hours, would have been more difficult for those left behind than watching the slow, steady decline of someone we love. After having lived through the former and experiencing the latter, I was convinced that the sudden loss of a loved one, though tough at the time, was definitely easier on a family in the long run.

I approached the upcoming birthday bash with trepidation. It had been a very long time since Paul had been subjected to this much stimulation in any one weekend. I worried that it would all be too much for him, or that he would have one of his choking, esophagus crises in front of everyone, or that he would soil himself noticeably in front of family and friends, or that he would talk, and no one would be able to hear his fading voice or worse, or that he would just sit with his eyes closed all night and not be the social guy he used to be! Since any of those was entirely possible, it seemed like I could never just enjoy the thought of entertaining any longer. There was too much mental garbage weighing me down. Add to this the threat of a stormy forecast negating the possibility of entertaining thirty-five guests outdoors on our wonderful patio and I was an emotional mess.

Paul's brother, sister-in-law and their son arrived at our house Thursday night for an outdoor casual supper, and it was a wonderful reunion and a perfect start to the weekend. This brother was Paul's "Irish twin" who was eleven months younger. They had always been close, and I adored his wife. Whenever we had to leave each other, we always cried, "I wish we lived so much closer!" We had not seen them in five years, and Paul thoroughly enjoyed the evening with no mishaps of any kind to ruin the fun.

Friday morning, they had plans with a former college friend of hers, and our oldest daughter entertained their son while Paul had a physical therapy appointment. After a good nap, we all went together to our other daughter's house for dinner. Aside from Paul's brother spilling his drink on my new phone, the evening was without problems. After dinner, our two grand- daughters played piano, and our nephew, who has four black belts, taught some martial arts moves to our grandson for some moments of real hilarity. This was followed by relating stories about their growing up years in Indiana, and even though, by this time, Paul's eyes remained closed, he was enjoying the stories which brought back many memories and laughing along with everyone. But the next day would be the real test of his stamina and ability to cope with all the stimulation!

We awoke to a cloudy, drizzly morning, and my heart sank as I thought about all the work done to make the yard and patio look beautiful for the party, the cheerful, green chair cushions I would not be able to put outside on our new wicker furniture and the panic that I would have to go to plan B which entailed entertaining thirty-five people for a sit down meal inside the house. Paul was not having a very good morning either, slowed down by lingering fatigue and the ever present enemy, constipation. We had arranged to pick up Paul's brother and his wife and bring them home for a quick lunch and some quiet time for the brothers to bond before the onslaught of people later on. Meanwhile our son and his cousin went kayaking for the morning.

It was obvious during lunch that Paul was still very tired so we made sure to return his brother to the motel so that we could squeeze in a good nap before all the festivities began. I had so many misgivings during this down time thinking once again about all the things that could go wrong. I was honestly afraid I had made a huge mistake planning such a large gathering and subjecting him to even more stimulation. I found myself praying out loud. "Dear God, please help him get through just one more event this weekend. Don't let him choke; don't let him embarrass himself with a bathroom mishap; please make this an enjoyable day for him that he will always remember. And PLEASE don't let it rain on his party!" An hour before the guests were to arrive, the sun began trying to peek through the clouds. I put the cushions out on the chairs and flowers on the tables and hoped for the best. My respite care helper came early to ready Paul after his nap so that I could continue the party preparations. Our daughter picked up all the food from the caterer and delivered it to our door, and I was ready for anything. Paul wore his favorite green shirt that brought out his hazel eyes, and he looked rested, handsome and wonderful.

If an evening could be called "graced", this one was. Our children called it a charmed night. Everyone showed up in a festive mood, and Paul was right in the thick of all the fun, sitting in his wheelchair on the patio. I hadn't actually seen him look this happy in a very long time. The photos showed a handsome man who was surrounded by friends and family who all adored him. Our two granddaughters played Happy Birthday on their violins as we all sang along. I tried to give him a toast without becoming too emotional, but that was not to be. I had to choke back my tears as I said, "Long ago I read a quote by one of my favorite French authors, St. Exupery, who said 'true love does not consist of gazing at each other but of looking out in the same direction together.' That was a great definition, but now it seems like it is meant for the young, and we are not young any longer. Then I found another definition that, for me, is even better, especially since Paul personifies all of it. It says that 'true love is the total acceptance of everything that is right now, total acceptance of all things past and total acceptance of what will be, but also of what will not be.' Here is to Paul and to true love." I noticed several others with tears in their eyes. Paul had never complained about his present condition; it seemed he just accepted quietly all that God sent his way. He had moved beyond any problems in his past, and he seemed to accept whatever was still to come but even more, all the things that he knew would never come because of his illness. He was much better at this than I was, and I had much to learn from him..

After the toast, I presented him with the book of memories, photos and good wishes so many people sent to me, and he was truly pleased. The rain held off, and though it was terribly hot and humid, it really was a perfect evening. Later I found out that it had poured down in the next neighborhood to the west of us and also in the neighborhood just to the east of us! God must have heard my frantic prayer!

Paul slept like a baby that night, but I cannot say the same for me. My feet and legs kept cramping because of all the going up and down the stairs all day, standing for five hours during the party and cleaning up after. I was beyond exhausted, but my body would not let me relax, and it took me several days to feel good again. But in the end, the memories created over that weekend made everything worthwhile.

I wondered what Paul's recuperation time would be since he had not had that much social interaction or physical and mental stimulation in years. As I feared, the following day he had a tough time with his mobility, thinking and swallowing. He fell in the bedroom hitting his head on the air conditioner vent because he walked away from his walker and lost his balance. Then at lunch some of his food stuck in his esophagus again but he was able to clear it on his own with no need for a run to the hospital. For the next few days, he was slower than usual and foggy brained and even a couple of weeks later, didn't really seem to improve that much. I began to wonder if it had been a big mistake to celebrate in such grand style!

It seemed every morning when I got up, my first thought was '*I wonder what this day will bring*' followed with a short prayer for the ability to handle whatever came. Two weeks after the big party, I became so concerned about his inability to walk well, converse, or keep his eyes open, I thought surely one or both of his DBS batteries wasn't turned on. But when I checked them, both were operating well. It wasn't low blood pressure, and it wasn't due to the DBS batteries which could only mean that he was having a really bad day for reasons that are never clear. I tried everything to engage him in conversation, I began reading a new book to him, made sure he got a good nap, but nothing helped. He continued to sit like a lump, chin on his chest, eyes closed and totally closed off. Days like this are particularly hard for me, and I feel helpless and alone. They sap my energy, my resolve and positive attitude, and that is never a good combination. Unfortunately, when I am like this I am also filled with fear, and it manifests itself in harsh words and anger. Of course, that helps even less, and it becomes a vicious cycle.

Over the course of the months since he came home from the nursing home, so many well-meaning family and friends had praised me for being such a good care giver. Since the birthday party, his siblings especially thanked me profusely for taking such good care of their brother. As much as I appreciated all that, and even needed to hear it occasionally, it made me feel like a complete hypocrite after a day of anger and frustration. Traveling this Parkinson's disease highway continued to present any number of conflicting emotions almost daily, and I struggled to balance them all.

Three weeks after the big party, Paul had another day of non-communication, eye closing and general apathy. Finally, that evening, I turned off the television at nine o'clock because he had not seen even one minute of the two programs he had said he wanted to "watch", and I had another moment of anger and frustration.

"What would you like to do right now?" I asked him in the most sarcastic voice I could muster. "Go to bed," was an answer I had not anticipated.

"No, it is only nine o'clock on a Friday night, you got up from a ninety minute nap at five o'clock and you are NOT going to bed this early," I screamed. "What would you like to talk about?" I asked almost jokingly since he never talked to me at all. After about twenty minutes of trying to get a complete thought out of him, a most enlightening but frightening conversation ensued. Everything he started to say in his usual whisper made no sense. He'd begin a thought and then drift off before the sentence was complete leaving me hanging for information. Eventually, what came out of his mouth reeked of paranoia and confusion. We talked about the day months before when I had taken him around the house for "the tour" to get reoriented after his long rehabilitation at the nursing home. He told me he considered that time a "subterfuge" and still did! I was incredulous at hearing him use this word. "What are you talking about? What subterfuge?" I went to get the dictionary and read the definition of the word to him and asked him to tell me how that related to us. He never really did explain what he meant but continued to somehow link that activity with "papers signed" at the nursing home. The only papers he signed were the contract when we thought we were buying a different house and later voided when the inspection failed and the re-financing of our present home which our son-in-law organized to save us nearly $700.00 a month. But he thought he had signed something underhanded which I guess he didn't trust. I told him I would show him those papers the following day so he could see exactly what he had signed. And as I had anticipated, he forgot all about them the next day.

He was still convinced there was a second woman living the house, and then he added that he thought we had two dogs instead of one. There was nothing I could say to convince him there was one of me and one dog so I just had to let that go since the neurologist had warned me of the symptom to explain it. He finally added that he saw himself as a very confused person, and I had to agree with him. But I added that I was trying very hard to help him get rid of the confusion, and I made him promise to ban the word subterfuge from our vocabulary, and he agreed.

These kinds of encounters unnerved me more than anything. I was aware that hallucinations and delusions could be a part of this disease, and that paranoia had always been a problem for him whenever he was hospitalized, but he had been home for seven months in the house we bought twenty-eight years before, and this paranoia really upset me. I tried to imagine how all this confusion must have made him feel, to be afraid, to not trust in his own home, and it broke my heart. But it also worried me because I didn't know how to combat it

CHAPTER 20

July, 2015: Two weeks after the party, we were both still basking in the success of the celebration, or at least I still was. I had fun buying a scrapbook/photo album to compile all the photos taken from various cameras and all the cards Paul had received from far and near. Keeping these kinds of visual records of family events is something I have loved doing ever since our first family vacation when the children were little. Consequently, after forty-eight years, I have amassed far more scrapbooks and photo albums than I have space to store them. Just the year before, I divided nine family vacation photo albums among our three children making sure they each got their favorite trip included in their trio of books. It was time for someone else to store them! At least I eliminated nine albums from my storage area to make room for more!

Paul continued to exhibit some confusion that weekend, and his constipation was also an ongoing problem, further convincing me that a backed-up bowel contributes to mental confusion. We had sat down for breakfast before which he took all his morning medications. The Sunday newspaper was all over the table in various piles and as it usually is, Paul closed his eyes and sat quietly. This behavior still annoyed me, but I could no more eliminate it than I could stand on my head. Besides, as long as he was sitting quietly and comfortably, withdrawn into his world, I could enjoy a second cup of coffee and work on the Sunday crossword puzzle.

Then his breathing changed, became audible and weird enough to make me look up from the paper. There were four long, audible exhales and then nothing. For a moment, I thought he had fallen asleep at the table, and I was afraid he might fall off the chair. So I went over to him and put my hand on his shoulder and said, "Hey,

Hurtubise, are you sleeping over here?" There was no answer. I repeated it and could tell he was unconscious. What was going on? He hadn't stood up and fainted from low blood pressure as he had done on other occasions. I couldn't rouse him, he didn't answer me, and I immediately called 911. The operator asked me if he was breathing, and then I realized I couldn't tell. His chest was not moving at all. I couldn't feel a carotid pulse, and at that moment I was sure in my heart that the exhalations I had heard were his last breaths before dying. 'Till death do us part' immediately came to mind. Was this it? Was this the easy, painless death we all pray for? Was my job of full time care giver over? But then I looked down at the dog at his feet, and occasionally Paul patted her head! What was going on? I stayed with him until the ambulance arrived, now a familiar sight in our driveway. The dog was carrying on, and I had to put her in her cage so she would not run out the front door. Four men came into my small kitchen with all their paraphernalia as I explained what had happened. When they could not rouse him either, they put him on oxygen. One of the first things they asked me was if he might have overdosed on something. What drugs did he take? When did he take them? Was he on any opiates? They worked on him for a long time not getting any response either. By this time I was sure he had died. I called the three kids in a panic, and thankfully they were all at home and answered right away. "Come quick, something happened to dad. He is unresponsive!" They all arrived within ten minutes. By the time they were there I heard the EMT's say that his pupils were constricted and his blood pressure was very low. Was I sure he had not overdosed on something? I continued to panic wondering if I had made a mistake in his medication box. But I had just filled it the previous day and besides he doesn't even have an opiate in his regimen! They couldn't get a good EKG because of the chest batteries from his brain surgery so that indicated nothing new. I don't know how many minutes had gone by between the time of his strange breathing and the time they decided to spray Narcan into his nose. It must have been at least fifteen or twenty minutes of his being unresponsive. And then he opened his eyes! They continued to question me about what drugs he was on since the Narcan is a spray that blocks the effects of an opiode. I showed them a list of all the medications he took that morning, and the success of the nasal spray to bring him around made no sense to me at all.

They eventually got him into the ambulance, and he was responding to questions. Thankfully, the kids did not lose their dad, and I did not lose my husband that morning. But we were all pretty shaken up, and I felt terribly guilty for having upset them so badly. But everything I had said to them on the phone was true at the time. Something had definitely happened to him, and he was unresponsive, and we all drew the same conclusion. He was dying. They wanted to drive me to the hospital, but I insisted on going alone. It gave me something to think about. I arrived at the emergency entrance shortly before the ambulance as did our son, and our two daughters arrived by the time Paul was in a room. The EMT told me upon their arrival that Paul said in the ambulance that he heard everything that had gone on in the kitchen. He heard me call his name, make the 911 call; he knew I was upset. He heard the EMT's arrive and knew they were working on him. Then he told them, "I just didn't feel like talking! I was upset about an article in the paper about Pete Rose." WHAT? The EMT then asked me, "Does he suffer from dementia or could he have faked the whole thing?" I was incredulous. "Yes, he is experiencing some dementia but NO, he would never just fake something like this. Besides, he never even read the article about Pete Rose. We had mentioned the headline at breakfast but that was it." How ridiculous! He wasn't even looking at the paper at the time he zoned out. Later in the hospital room, I asked him about this conversation, and he said he didn't remember any of that. Knowing my husband as well as I did, I was sure he just made up a story to downplay the gravity of the moment and told them something he thought they wanted to hear. He was quite good at that!

The ER staff was efficient and professional doing everything to get an answer as quickly as possible. They did a urine scan to check for infection; they did a CT scan of his brain to check for any bleeding, and all was fine. All the lab work came back with nothing unusual. There was no explanation for what had happened. After hydrating him and re-checking his blood pressure, they discharged him two hours later. I was glad once again they didn't take my blood pressure! At that moment, I think he was healthier than I was. We went home, ate a late lunch, and he took a nap. I collapsed in a chair and began informing his siblings, reliving the terror of the morning over and over. I admit that the two glasses of Scotch I drank later on helped enormously!

The following day, I called the neurologist and the cardiologist to get some answers. The neurologist could give me no answers. She knew he had an appointment with her at the end of July, and since the CAT scan had been good, there was no reason for her so see him before then. However, she did say that perhaps he experienced a bradycardia that slowed his heart rate way down, and that would have been why I could see no chest movement. The cardiologist said he should do an echo cardiogram to check on the heart structure and function. Paul had had one of these many years earlier that showed a narrowing of a valve so he wanted to see a more recent picture. We couldn't get an appointment for three weeks but he didn't seem to think it was more urgently needed. As I began trying to put all the puzzle pieces together based on things each physician had told me, I became convinced that Paul did not just pass out from low blood pressure but rather experienced some kind of cardiac event. He had not had a heart attack; his heart enzymes had indicated nothing at the hospital to be alarmed about. I began to fear that seventeen years after successful cardiac bypass surgery, perhaps his heart was just wearing out. Were we facing another, different chapter in his health journey?

After his siblings received the news, our sister-in-law wrote back that the previous year she had been diagnosed with bradycardia and had also had the echo cardiogram and a pacemaker implanted. What she added really got my attention. "I heard everything that was going on around me, but I just didn't feel like talking." At this point, I was convinced that Paul and she shared the same diagnosis, and I was anxious to move his echo cardiogram up instead of waiting eighteen days! But there were no openings with any of the doctors in the same practice before our scheduled date, and there was nothing else to do but pray that nothing more would happen before then.

Three days after the big scare, I was not feeling well. I thought it was just the occasional stomach spasms that I self-diagnosed as irritable bowel disease for as long as I could remember. It was, in fact, my usual stress symptom followed by muscle spasms. Unfortunately, it was the fourth of July holiday weekend, and by the time I realized it was not IBS but what I determined to be a flare up of diverticulitis, my doctor's office was closed. When I got up that Friday morning, the official holiday, I realized I had better get some medical attention. I also awoke to a refrigerator and freezer whose temperatures were on the rise and most of what was in the freezer was now mush. So not only did I have to do the usual care of my husband who doesn't do well first thing in the morning, I had to find an appliance repairman who would come on a holiday. Once that was accomplished, I began making multiple trips carrying a large plastic bag with what groceries I could salvage downstairs to our mini fridge in the bar area and the extra freezer, all the while holding my side which was screaming at me with stabbing pain.

Thankfully, the repairman came earlier than later and did what he could, relaying the good news that "They just don't make appliances like they used to. I'll probably get another call from you tomorrow. Be prepared to spend $800.00 for a new compressor." He told me he reset the temperatures for both refrigerator and freezer for thirty-two and zero degrees but not to open the doors for twenty-four hours. I thanked him and went immediately to the Little Clinic to see the nurse practitioner at the grocery store. I signed in at noon and was told I was on a list and to come back in two hours. The day was not getting any better, and I limped home, my gut pain feeling awful, and ate lunch, watched a bit of Wimbledon tennis on the TV until two o'clock. Upon my return, with Paul waiting for me in the parking lot, I explained my symptoms and received a script for two very potent antibiotics that I had to take for ten days. One of them had a side effect of stomach discomfort and to make matters worse, I couldn't even soothe my discouraged self with a glass of wine!

The following morning, I approached the refrigerator with dread and said a little prayer before opening the door. To my amazement, the temperatures read thirty-eight and zero degrees, and I almost cried with relief. Now all I had to do was make the multiple trips bringing salvaged food back up to the kitchen and hope that the temperatures would stay where they were. After all that had been saved was returned to its frosty home, it was disheartening to discover that what had filled every inch of my mini fridge could fit on one shelf in the kitchen refrigerator!

The antibiotics were slow to make a difference other than the stomach upset forewarned in the packaging. After five days of feeling worse than when I went to the clinic and a terrible taste in my mouth necessitating the purchase of a package of gum and a huge bag of mints, I dreaded taking the offending antibiotic three times a day. I felt so bad that I could no longer determine if my discomfort was from the infection in my gut or from the medication. I tried disguising the taste of the disgusting pill by eating ice cream, yogurt, milk and cookies, anything to change the side effect. After all, I was supposed to take it with food, I rationalized. But absolutely nothing made any difference. By the ninth day on this horrible antibiotic, a Saturday night, my body rejected it and I couldn't even swallow the pill. On Sunday I went to the emergency clinic, and I was sure there was something terribly wrong with me. I had never felt so bad. Thoughts raced through my head. What would happen to Paul if something happened to me? Where would he go? Who would be able to take care of him? What would happen to my little dog? I had myself in such a state I couldn't stop crying. The doctor there told me the diverticulitis was gone and what I was feeling was due to the antibiotics. What he told me next floored me. "When I have to prescribe this particular antibiotic I always tell patients that it is not going to be fun, but to please try to get through seven days!" I had been on it for nine out of the 10 it had been prescribed. "Throw the rest away," he added, and if I had felt better I would have hugged him!

I had my scheduled follow up appointment with my doctor two days later, and by then I was feeling nearly 100% again....until the phone rang that morning. It was a different doctor from the clinic telling me the urine sample I had given showed bacteria which was very difficult to treat! I had to go back on an antibiotic! I literally screamed into the phone, "NO, No, No. I feel fine. There can't be another UTI." He repeated that there was and he had called in a prescription. I was in tears at my doctor appointment, and I gave them another urine sample which showed no infection at all! Even forty eight hours later, there was no evidence of an infection. That doctor must have read someone else's results when he called me. My physician told me not to take any more medications. No need to worry about that, I thought!

To make matters more difficult, Paul had a twenty-four hour period while I had been so sick, during which his urine output was alarming, soaking through layers of protective bed coverings multiple times a night and requiring endless changes of underwear and padding during the day. I did countless loads of laundry on practically no sleep since he needed my help to change clothes and bedding during the night. I was alarmed that with all that urine output he might get dehydrated again, and when that happened, his blood pressure would plummet. It just seemed like a domino effect with one problem after another popping up. One system was constipated and another couldn't be controlled. Once again it was a weekend with no way to phone the urologist. I talked to my respite care helper who works with many Parkinson's patients, and she said not to worry. It seems to go with Parkinson's and stops as mysteriously as it begins. And she was right.

The three weeks leading up to the echo cardiogram passed with no further incident, and we finally got in to the doctor. The technician who scanned Paul's heart asked him, "Have you ever had work done on your heart?"

"Yes, I had bypass surgery in the late 90's," he answered.

"Did you have any work done on a valve?" he continued. I watched his face as he peered more closely at the screen.

"No, I didn't." I was convinced at that moment that something had changed, and we were in for more trouble. My mind raced to the horrible possibility that he would have to undergo more gruesome open heart surgery to repair or replace a valve, and I doubted he would be able to survive that kind of invasive surgery now. An hour later, we finally had the conference with the cardiologist.

"Well," he began, "the cardiogram doesn't really look bad. There is a little bit more calcium deposit around the main valve but not enough to warrant any action at this time. We'll continue to monitor it though." I asked him if when the time came for surgery, how it was done.

"Oh, we don't even do an open heart procedure for this any longer," he quickly answered, probably noting the fear in my eyes. "We go into the groin artery just like an angioplasty now."

Then I proceeded to ask him about the possibility of a bradycardia explanation for the terrifying events of June. He didn't think that was even a possibility given the pulse rate he sees each time we are there so that eliminated the need for a pace maker at this time. Okay, so far so good, I thought. No immediate surgical procedures to face. But I still needed answers!

"What do you think caused his non-responsiveness for such a long time then? I need to know how to prevent this from happening again."

"Well," he proceeded slowly, "We know he was not getting enough blood flow to the brain to give him the energy to respond in any way. He was in a semi-conscious state and too weak to be responsive, but he could hear everything going on around him."

"What could have caused this interruption in the blood flow to his brain?" I still wasn't getting any helpful information, and I was getting more and more frustrated.

He suggested hooking Paul up to a fourteen day cardiac monitor to record all his heart activity and then meeting again after the results had been read. It was a complicated wireless device that I would have to check multiple times a day, routinely change electrodes on his torso every three days and charge the device twice a day. I was not looking forward to this responsibility at all, but it had to be done if I wanted answers. They hooked him up in the office and gave me a phone number to call in a few hours after they had sent the order to the medical device company. His device would be activated over the phone. But after two unsuccessful attempts to get a good reading the technician on the phone asked me, "Does your husband have any kind of mechanics in his chest?"

"Yes, he has two deep brain stimulator batteries there."

"Well then, I am sorry, but he cannot use this device. We cannot get a good enough reading due to so much interference from his batteries. You'll have to mail the device back to us." Great! I thought. Back to square one and still no answers!

Just two days later, again on a Sunday morning, he was sitting on the commode while I was in the next room drying my hair. I thought I heard his walker move (thanks to the bells I have attached to it) and when I went to check on him, he had fallen back in another faint with his eyes wide open. He came right out of it when I yelled his name and was obviously a bit dazed for a moment. I asked him how he felt and what had happened. Apparently he had tried to stand up and again he felt dizzy. I brought him bottles of water and took his blood pressure. As I had expected it was 79/47! Why did this continue to happen even with his medication? After three bottles of hydration, I finally got two consistent readings of 95/69 with a good pulse rate. So it was time to get on with the day as though nothing had happened. It reminded me of morning sickness; throw up after breakfast and then get on with the day! This still stressed me out each time I saw that wide-eyed fainting posture. I had no idea what we could do to change this unpredictable pattern and having no ready answers wasn't an option.

Several days after returning the cardiac device to the manufacturer, the cardiologist called back to say he was ordering a forty-eight hour electronic monitor, and I would have to hook him up to it myself. Once again, I was on the phone with a manufacturer and being talked through the directions. Once Paul was hooked up and the device activated, we walked back to the bedroom about fifteen minutes later where he fainted again. I called the phone number on the device after he checked back in with me and asked them if anything had just been picked up on the device. I was shocked to know nothing unusual had shown up. Then they informed me that only electrical activity of the heart would show up, not the results of low blood pressure. I was sure that forty-eight hours later, we would have nothing new to learn. After I mailed the device back, the cardiologist called and said just what I had anticipated, no problems, and of course, still no answers. There was still no explanation for why Paul had been semi-conscious for twenty minutes one month earlier. The only suggestion the cardiologist could make was to increase the dosage of Paul's medication. I thought, "Why not just add one more pill?" I was becoming more than just a little frustrated. There had to be a better way, but I had no idea what it would be and apparently the medical community didn't either!

CHAPTER 21

The morning Paul completed his final physical therapy appointment paid for by Medicare, I began feeling like another urinary tract infection was starting. This could not possibly be, I thought. If it were true, it would be the fourth one in eight months, and that just wasn't normal for me. I called immediately and got an appointment at my doctor's office with the nurse practitioner since my doctor had no openings for seven weeks! He said, "I see here that you were just here two weeks ago. What is going on?" So I informed him about the reason I had seen the doctor two weeks before, also about the weird phone call I had received that same morning telling me I had a serious UTI, and that my doctor had checked my urine sample and said there was no problem. But he would send it out to be cultured to be safe. The nurse practitioner looked at my chart and said that the doctor had called me two days later telling me that there was indeed a serious UTI, and that my chart said I had taken the call and indicated that I understood! What was going on? I had received no such phone call! "Well," he added, "your sample today shows that you do have that very same infection, and you need to be on the only antibiotic known to attack it." I was devastated as I knew that this particular bug was very resistant to drugs and could be tricky to cure. Had I had this particular infection all the other three times I had been medicated for a UTI earlier in the year but with the improper antibiotic? Is that why it kept coming back every two months? Had I done myself a huge disservice therefore making it harder to cure this time even with the correct drug? As the questions kept popping into my head I was becoming more and more alarmed especially since, once again, I had no answers. Only this time the questions were about my health instead of Paul's. For better or worse, in sickness and in health….what would be next?

I picked up the antibiotic and began taking it immediately. I was really feeling awful and afraid that this was the serious infection the emergency clinic had told me I had earlier. By the second day on the drug I was feeling much better and encouraged that I could beat this superbug. Then the phone rang, and the message from the doctor's office was that the urine culture had come back and it appeared that there was hardly any infection worth noting and nothing to confirm the superbug. Discontinue the antibiotic; there was no need to continue medicating! What? One day I am infected, and the next day I am not; then I am infected, and then I am not! This was bordering on the ridiculous, and I really didn't know what to do. Fortunately, part of the decision was made for me because I had an appointment to get my teeth cleaned on the fourth day of the medication, and ever since 2011 when I had a total hip replacement, I was required to take an antibiotic before any dental procedure. So I really didn't have to make a decision to continue or stop the medication until the fifth day. There were moments when I was sure the infection was still present so I opted to finish the drug to be safe. It turned out to be a wise decision.

A few days later the doctor's office called again to tell me they thought in light of all the UTI's I should probably see a urologist. But I told them I was not going that route, but I had made an appointment with my gynecologist. Again, it was a good decision as all was well, and there was no reason for any further treatment! But not without further drama!

The morning of my appointment with the gynecologist, Paul didn't look good at the breakfast table again. He had urinated copious amounts during the night and early morning and was probably dehydrated before he ever came to the kitchen. I was in the midst of taking his blood pressure and giving him a bottle of water, but he couldn't even hold it much less swallow it. He began to fall out of the chair in a faint again, and I had to hold him up as I dialed 911. This time the EMT's told me his BP was very low, but his sugar numbers were sky high. The combination wiped him out, and off we went again to the hospital. They were convinced he was diabetic. I got myself together and then remembered my own appointment later and called to cancel it.

Like déjà vu, Paul was hydrated with an IV drip and blood taken to run every test in the book. I looked at the clock and it was ten thirty. He was looking better so I made a most impulsive decision to try to get to my appointment, and I left him hooked up to the fluids. I called and they told me I could still come right way. Of course, when they took my blood pressure it was higher than it had ever been! Why is it, I thought, that nothing was ever easy anymore?

One hour later I was back in the ER with Paul who looked better, was more alert and ready to be discharged, again with no good explanation for what had happened. Even his sugar numbers had come back to an acceptable level. With no answers or even suggestions from the medical community, I decided it was up to me to find the solution to prevent these terrifying events from reoccurring, but how I didn't have a clue.

So, after having a good cry when my sister stopped by to check on us later that afternoon, I ended my personal pity party with new resolve to be pro-active in solving this enigma. What did I know so far? What facts was I sure of? And there were only two, really. The two culprits that Parkinson's disease was affecting fifteen years after diagnosis were blood pressure and sugar levels. A dangerous low in the first and an even more dangerous high in the second had created a disastrous combination. Once I could think clearly again with all emotion set aside, I realized that while this disease would continue to be challenging and unpredictable, there were certain things I could control.

Was there a possibility that my husband was beginning late life onset of diabetes? It seemed to me that the poor guy had inherited every bad health gene from both his parents: his heart disease, which was the only one I feared on our wedding day forty-eight years earlier, he had acquired from his father; his gall bladder, which had been removed decades earlier, from his mother; Parkinson's disease from his mother's family tree was our ongoing life now, and I became aware that diabetes did exist on both sides of his family. We had tackled the cardiac issue in the late ninety's, the gall bladder even before that, Parkinson's had reared its ugly head in 2000, and now I was not about to allow diabetes into this man's body! Who knew when I repeated the words 'in sickness and in health' that this one vow would become so cumbersome? Something had to change.

August, 2015: His physical therapy at the gym had ended thanks to limits of Medicare spending so we decided to go back to the Fitness Studio he had been using before his fall a year before. He went twice a week with one on one training to reestablish core strength and to try to strengthen the muscles in the leg he had broken. He was supposed to use the recumbent bike at home on the other five days of the week. At least this was a start in improving his life.

I knew that Paul had a sweet tooth ever since we met, and ice cream was a serious weakness. He insisted I buy a large container of his favorite dessert every week, and before I had taken on the responsibility of serving him, he would empty an entire container in just a few days. Even after I became his server, the helping was way too large, but at least the container lasted a full week! He drank more sugary colas than water, and the cookie jar had become his partner in crime. Now I had some place to start!

I thought back to that morning in late June when I thought he had died, but I couldn't remember what he had eaten. But this latest episode rang a giant bell in my head. His breakfast had consisted of a big bowl of Raisin Bran, which I discovered upon reading the label, contained eighteen grams of sugar in one cup. His serving had been larger than one cup by far. He had sweet prune juice for his constipation, and he finished the meal with a very decadent piece of coffee cake that probably had enough sugar to hype up an entire village. And right after that, his sugar had spiked. No wonder! Add to that the fact that the night before he had soaked the bed not just once but twice, which happened sporadically thanks to Parkinson's ability to toy with the kidneys and bladder whenever it chose to do so, and therefore Paul was probably dehydrated before he ever got out of bed. This was something else I could try to control. I knew I couldn't control the loss of these enormous amounts of fluid during the night, but I could surely control replenishing the fluid before he set foot out of his bed. A plan began to emerge in my head.

Our pattern before all this had been for Paul to take his constipation and two blood pressure meds as soon as he awoke. He wasn't allowed to eat for thirty minutes after taking them, and normally he would just go back to sleep until I got him up for breakfast. My new plan called for him to stay awake, sit up in bed and drink an entire bottle of Smart Water which included electrolytes with the hope that his hydration levels would return to normal whether he had soaked the bed or not. I took his blood pressure before he put one foot on the floor to establish a starting point and invariably it was high, around 145 or 150/80.

Then he came out for breakfast which still consisted of cereal (a smaller portion) but with the addition of a cut up banana for the potassium. There was no more sugary coffee cake, which I have to admit I missed terribly, and I always had another bottle of Smart Water handy just in case. Although after his meal, usually his blood pressure continued to drop, it did not drop to the point of being alarming. For the first week of this new plan, his coloring never looked ashen, he seemed more alert, and he never complained of any light headedness. And even better news was that the bananas were helping somehow with his constipation! I was ecstatic and knew we were on to something productive. By the second week, although he still wanted his ice cream at night, I had found a sugar-free Cherry Cordial that tasted exactly like the real thing, and he never knew the difference. The one difference was that I cut his portion down to half of how much I had served him before.

Then out of the blue, he had a bad morning again, displaying the pale complexion and listlessness that had always been a sign of low blood pressure and sure enough, he said he was a little dizzy. The monitor read 69/47! What? How could this be after all the good things we had accomplished? I made him consume more Smart Water and checked his blood pressure every ten minutes until it reached 95/69. His color returned and he seemed fine. I had to accept the fact that this disease would continue to present unexpected challenges no matter what we did, and that there really was no such thing as being totally in control. This last fact really upset me, but I still felt that we were on to something positive. Diet and exercise were essential in maintaining any quality of life with this disease, and we could only do whatever we could to stave off the occasional complications. Parkinson's had toyed with his blood pressure once again, but this last time we managed to put it in its place!

Several weeks went by with no major scares until one morning after a bad night of bed soaking his blood pressure plummeted again after breakfast. This time it was just as low as the previous time, 69/47. I repeated the Smart Water routine but to no avail. It wasn't doing the trick this time. I was so nervous I called my daughter to come over and be with me for moral support. She was noticeably scared and it takes a lot for her to show it. She was so worried she broke down and cried, something she never did in front of him. It was really the first time any of the family saw what I had to deal with so often. Eventually after three bottles of water, his blood pressure went up to 85/60, high enough that I felt he could safely stand and go back to the bedroom.

I decided to call the cardiologist and make an appointment that day with anyone who would see him. His doctor was on vacation but the nurse practitioner got him in. She made the decision to increase the dosage of his medication and change the timing of when he received it. We were to go back in two weeks for a follow-up with his doctor. When I got home, I phoned his urologist who was also on vacation and again spoke to his nurse practitioner. He decided to take Paul off the Flomax for a while to slow down the urine output. It had occurred to me earlier that both these doctors were in the same health system with the ability to confer on a mutual patient. I suggested that maybe they could do that, but I got absolutely nowhere with that request with either of them! For the following two weeks, this combination of changes seemed to be helping. The bed wetting decreased and there were no further blood pressure issues. I couldn't wait till the appointment with the doctor.

After checking Paul in the office, the cardiologist seemed pleased with the changes, but I was incredulous when he said, "Oh thank goodness he is off the Flomax!" I asked him why, and his answer floored me. "Flomax lowers the blood pressure." He had seen that drug in his medication list for several years and certainly during the nine months we had been dealing with the blood pressure problem, he had to be aware Paul was taking it. Why, I wondered, would he allow him to take a medication to lower the pressure and then prescribe another to raise it? This made no sense to me whatsoever. Once again I suggested that perhaps it would be a good idea for the two doctors to confer about Paul especially where medications were concerned. It seemed like an intelligent suggestion but once again I got nowhere!

CHAPTER 22

In the fall of 2015, as the holiday season approached and my life began getting busier than at any other time of the year, Paul seemed to be getting worse. It wasn't a blood pressure thing this time but rather a decrease in his mobility, his inability to keep his eyes open and a general apathy about life. As infrequent as our daily conversations had become, now they were non-existent, and I have to admit it was an extremely lonely time for me. Fortunately, I have never been bored, and I had new outlets to keep me sane. My fourth children's book had just been published, and I knew I had lots of work to do in marketing it; my fall quarter course at The Osher Life Long Learning Institute at the university was getting under way one day a week for eight weeks. Thank goodness for respite care workers. But as much as I enjoyed these activities, it was heartbreaking to see my once active husband have absolutely no reason to get up in the morning. In fact I became so concerned about his inability to function I checked his chest batteries frequently to see if they had somehow stopped working, but everything was always working fine. Fortunately, we had an appointment with the neurology department already scheduled, and I was anxious to have him checked out. As usual, he had a fairly good visit with no real explanation for his behavior at home. We were fast approaching the first anniversary of the day he came home from the thirteen week rehab experience. I thought I had never lived through a more difficult year in my life!

To make life even more interesting, in October, as I was racing down the carpeted hallway and wearing new shoes, my right foot rammed into the carpet and my body went flying forward, and I literally landed flat on my face. I suppose it was a blessing that it was on carpet instead of the hardwood upstairs, but I had the wind knocked out of me. My nose felt like it was broken, and my right arm hurt so badly I was afraid I had dislocated something. My right knee was skinned with rug burn, and I actually lay there moaning for a few minutes. I can't remember when the last time was that I fell; it had to be decades before. I got up slowly, and my knee really hurt. Just as I got up, there stood Paul holding on to the door jamb of his office and checking on me, but without his walker. I screamed at him to stay where he was as I hobbled to get his walker and keep him from falling, too. What a pair we were. After getting him back into a chair, I went into the bathroom and looked in the mirror as a beautiful black eye was starting, and the right side of my nose was bruising. And then I cried. No bones broken, only my pride, but I knew something was wrong with my knee. After seeing the orthopedic doctor and having an x-ray, he told me nothing major looked wrong and to try ice and rest. Ice I could do, rest not so much. If it didn't feel better by the end of the year, I was to call him. Well, it didn't feel better, and he ordered an MRI in January which indicated that I had torn the meniscus! I could try physical therapy or have surgery. So physical therapy it was.

Meanwhile I decided that Paul had to have a project to work on so I ordered an expensive machine that would transfer all our VCR tapes to DVD's. I figured it would take him all winter to get this task done as we had amassed a huge number of tapes over the years. He was actually looking forward to doing this, and I was overjoyed to see him anxious to get started, but when the box arrived, my heart sank. There was an entire book of complicated directions to set up the machine correctly to the TV with a very specific kind of disk that the machine could take, and we didn't have any of those. After many phone calls I found one store that carried them, and we started with a box of fifty disks.

It was evident after many attempts that this was going to be a more difficult task to figure out than I had thought. Who knew that there were so many different kinds of disks, or that just because you successfully transferred one tape to a disk it might not be accepted into all DVD players? We realized that he was going to need help from someone more tech savvy than he or I. After several weeks, we still had not accomplished anything. Then finally with some help from our very young respite care helper, who was more comfortable with technology, he got one VCR tape copied to a disk. But when I went to insert it into a different DVD player, the words WRONG TYPE DISK appeared on the screen. I wanted to scream. Several more weeks went by with no further attempts made to figure it all out.

Thanksgiving was fast approaching, and we were at our daughter's house one afternoon to see her newly finished four season room. As usual, his eyes were closed as we sat in this new space, and I was exclaiming over every beautiful detail of the room and its decor. Suddenly, he stood up as though he wanted to go somewhere else, and we asked him what he was doing. He attempted to say something in his usual near whisper so it was not unusual to ask him to repeat, but when he did, the words were unintelligible. Julie looked at me with alarm, and we both had the same thought I am sure. Something bad is going on in his brain again. My first thought was another brain bleed since this language anomaly had not happened since his neurosurgery six years earlier. He was mobile; there was no drooping on one side, no indications of a stroke, just the bizarre speaking in tongues. I decided we should leave, and I would make an assessment on the way home whether we should make a side trip to the hospital. We sat in her driveway for almost ten minutes since I was honestly afraid to leave until I could get some idea if he was okay or not. I kept asking him how he had felt in that new room. Now he was forming words correctly, but he couldn't seem to complete a sentence. Eventually the words "weak", "weird" and "confused" came out. We left for the ride home and got caught in a big traffic jam, giving me more time to assess the situation. I asked him his birthday, my birthday, our address, how many children and grandchildren we had. He got most of it right so I knew there was fairly good cognition going on. I made the decision to go straight home. He was able to tell me later that he had just felt very confused.

I gave him a snack, a bottle of water, and then I took his blood pressure. It had been nearly thirty minutes since "the event" had occurred and his pressure was 127/72. That is considered high for him so I had to wonder if it had been higher thirty minutes before. Did he have a mini stroke, a TIA? We would never know for sure. After his nap, he was back to normal. I was not. The thought of adding a new worry to the ever growing list of potential health issues was almost too much to think about at that moment. What would this mean if indeed it had been a mini stroke? Would there be another and another until perhaps a major stroke would be the end result? What if Parkinson's disease would not be the major health issue in the total picture of things? Was I going to need to learn about new symptoms of new problems and what to do when they occurred? The very thought of that possibility was overwhelming to me, and I felt like there was just no more that I could handle. But whenever I stared to succumb to these feelings, I had to wonder how much more frustrating and frightening it must be for Paul to go through all these physical crises? I shared this latest medical news with his siblings and discovered that Paul's mother had had many mini strokes leaving her very confused each time, confused... the same word he had used in describing how he had felt

Eventually, I phoned both his neurologist and his cardiologist to keep them in the loop on this latest scare. Both agreed a trip to the hospital would have been unnecessary since even a CAT scan would not have shown a TIA, but the cardiologist thought it sounded like it could have been a TIA and ordered an ultrasound of the carotid arteries to check on blood flow to the brain. It was nearly four weeks until we could get an appointment! However, two weeks before that scheduled appointment, I had to call 911 again when he was fainting and becoming unresponsive after eating breakfast. As terrifying as these moments are, and sometimes it can take thirty to forty-five minutes for him to rebound, I know that they are caused by a combination of dehydration and too much sugar in his meal. The pattern continued that morning and though the EMT's wanted to take him to the hospital, I said it wasn't necessary. They asked me if I had power of attorney, and I had to admit that I hadn't gotten around to doing that yet, but Paul was back to normal enough by that time to respond for himself, and he agreed with me. I realized that morning that I could not put this task off any longer.

CHAPTER 23

The Christmas holidays were fast approaching and like most busy wives, mothers and grandmothers, the list of "to-do's" was endless. With all the unpredictability of Paul's condition day to day, I had learned that it is not enough to be organized, but rather I had to be organized beyond anything considered normal! Even if the Christmas dinner wasn't for two weeks, the dining room table was set just in case I had an emergency to deal with and wouldn't have the time if I waited. It became almost an obsession to get things done no matter how early it seemed. I felt like I was always waiting for the other shoe to drop, and who knew when it would happen. So "get it done now just because I can" became my mantra.

The holidays were crisis free, thank goodness, and Paul did well throughout the craziness. There was Christmas Eve Mass, the onslaught of eight excited and very noisy grandchildren and their parents on Christmas afternoon, followed by dinner and a song fest. The December 26 was my sister's seventy-fifth birthday party and another day of festivity and socializing. Then we hosted another dinner party on December 27 to celebrate our son's birthday. On none of these days was it possible for Paul to get his usual afternoon nap, and I was concerned about that. Fatigue is not a friend of Parkinson's disease. But he surprised me and got through it with no immediate problems.

On New Year's Eve day, we finally made it to the cardiologist for the ultrasound test on his carotid arteries. What a way to end a very difficult year, and we both prayed that nothing serious would show up. And like just about every other test that had been done on him over the course of the year, there was nothing to indicate a problem or a cause for the possible TIA he had experienced earlier. Good news but once again, no answers, no explanations. No satisfaction.

I welcomed in 2016 with renewed hope that this would be a better year but on the second of January, with no explanation, he zoned out on me after breakfast again. I couldn't bring him around and was forced to call 911, and our daughter to come for moral support. The EMT's arrived within minutes and found him unresponsive as they had in times past with a very low blood pressure once again and a slightly elevated sugar. It took three men to get him off the kitchen stool to lay him on the floor. His blood pressure began coming up immediately, and after a while, I could tell he was back and "with it" again. It didn't help that our dog also got sick that morning and was vomiting. What else could go wrong to welcome in the New Year? This time, the EMT's insisted on taking him to the hospital, and we complied, and our daughter stayed to take care of the dog. Two hours later, after a normal chest x-ray, lots of blood work that showed nothing other than a mild elevation in sugar and a mild dehydration, he was discharged. This was becoming all too familiar and a frightening nuisance!

I was completely frustrated after this episode since none of the usual precursors to his other fainting spells had been present. He hadn't had a soaking bed night; he hadn't had a sugary breakfast, and I was sure I had been doing everything right to keep this from happening. I cannot remember a time when I felt more defeated. For better or worse, in sickness and in health were definitely taking a turn for the worse for him physically and me mentally.

Meanwhile our daughter went searching on-line for any studies correlating Parkinson's and diabetes. She found a research article published only four months earlier showing a new connection between the disease and a problem in the communication system of the pituitary gland, the hypothalamus and the production of insulin. It wasn't a condition unknown by the medical establishment before. It had just never been associated with Parkinson's before! It was called Diabetes Insipidus. I told the cardiologist about this study, but all he did was change the time of the day I gave Paul his blood pressure medication!

Five days later it happened again. This was unusual to have two episodes in less than a week. But fortunately, my respite care helper was there with him. I had a premonition that I shouldn't leave the house that morning because he had a mega bed soaking that previous night. It was an unbelievable amount of urine that he had put out, enough to soak through five layers of protective bedding followed by filling the urinal upon waking! I knew from the previous episode, that getting him onto the floor to lie flat was the answer, and together, she and I managed to accomplish this without throwing out my back! Sure enough, within minutes, he was coming around, his blood pressure coming back up. His pulse was irregular but eventually, evened out. We sat him up against the kitchen counter and kept monitoring his pressure in these different positions. When we felt he was all right, we managed to get him standing, and his pressure remained at a healthy level. I was relieved to have managed without calling 911, but I did call the cardiologist and the neurologist to keep them in the loop. Of course, the cardiologist was out of town. I was so grateful to have had my respite care helper there with me because I knew I couldn't have handled him alone. I needed to have a new breakfast plan in case this happened when I was alone! I was tired of the 911 calls and the runs to the hospital only to be discharged after IV fluids.

I made the decision that from that day on, Paul was going to have his breakfast in the family room, sitting on the couch and watching TV. If he zoned out, all I would need to do was put him flat on the couch and there would be no lifting required. I could even elevate his legs with the throw pillows that were there if necessary.

The doctor called me back the following day after he had received the message about Paul. I couldn't believe it when he said, "I have been giving Paul's situation a lot of thought since there seems to be a pattern of this happening after breakfast." He suggested Paul see an endocrinologist "to check on a hormone in the brain regulated by the pituitary gland which keeps fluid retention and output in check. It is called Diabetes Insipidus." This from the same doctor who just earlier told me he didn't think there was sugar problem and to "Let him eat whatever he wants!" I knew he was referring to the very article I had told him our daughter found, but he seemed to think this new idea just came to him! He gave me the name of a doctor to call for the screening for this hormone.

I called our neurologist's physician assistant and shared this information to get her take on it before I made an appointment.

She was familiar with the condition but had never seen it linked with Parkinson's. She looked it up online while I was on the phone with her and said she would share this information with the Neurologist and get back to me later. I was surprised that they both felt I should hold off on a screening for this deficiency since if indeed he had the problem, it would manifest itself all the time, not just every once in a while. Somehow, it was getting more and more difficult to know what to do, whom to believe or if anyone really understood all the idiosyncrasies of Parkinson's disease. My gut told me that nobody had this disease figured out at all!

My other respite care worker was a retired social worker who discovered a franchise of Hospice that offered 100% free palliative respite care for the duration of life if the patient had a disease that would continue to get worse. I needed a script from the Neurologist and a medical power of attorney in order to qualify. The term Hospice conjures up so many awful images as it is usually associated with "end of life" issues, but this particular franchise extended its services for the duration of life, and it was almost too good to be true. They provided a nurse aid three mornings a week for two hours to be my moral support during the scary breakfast hours and give me a break from that stressor; they paid for all medications related to Parkinson's disease! That in itself was a miracle since just the weekend before I paid $200.00 for just two refills of his meds; they provide an RN visit once a week to monitor his vital signs, and they would provide any supplies or equipment we might need down the road. So I set up a meet-and-greet with the nurse in charge, Tracy, to see if all this really was too good to be true.

Miraculously, it was all true, and when she left, I asked Paul what he thought. His response said it all. "Wow!" was all he said. So we signed on, and the following day their Social Worker came out to finalize the paperwork and meet us. And small world that it is, she was a former student at the high school where I had taught. She was not one of my students, but we recognized each other immediately. A few days later, she returned, but this time she brought the chaplain to meet Paul, and they enjoyed a very nice visit. The only person yet to meet was the nurse aide who would be coming three mornings a week.

Mary was a petite woman in her early fifty's, laughed easily but was all business with Paul. I liked her right away, but Paul wasn't sure. His comments amused me. "She's kind of like you. Let's get it done!" Yes, I liked her even more. I could feel the weight lifting off my shoulders little by little as soon as she arrived in the mornings. It wasn't a lot of time, but the two hours she was there I knew I could "clock out" and relax a little.

Paul was continuing to eat his breakfast in the family room on the couch in case he had a fainting spell; he could just be lain down instead of trying to get him on the floor as I had had to do the previous time he fainted. But as the days wore on, my shoulders were becoming knots of tension as I tried to get him up, from the couch, from the commode, from his desk chair. It was getting more and more difficult. Less than twenty-four hours after mentioning this to Mary, a lift/reclining chair was delivered at the door, free of charge! The following week, a hospital table came to make his meal times ever so much easier for him and for me. This organization was living up to all the hype, and I continued to be amazed at their generosity and compassion.

CHAPTER 24

February, 2016: The first month under the umbrella of Hospice care was going smoothly. My helper who had told me about their services continued to come on Monday afternoons for three hours, Mary, the nurse aide from Hospice, came for two hours on Tuesday, Wednesday and Friday mornings and Carol from another home care service came on Thursday mornings for three hours. I had twelve hours a week of not being the only one responsible, and my tired body could feel the difference. It didn't take very long for me to begin to feel emotionally dependent on their presence in my home. I had wondered if I was going to dislike all these people coming and going in and out of my house, but just the opposite was happening. I have always been fairly independent and used to handling everything I needed to get accomplished, both physically and mentally, but suddenly my emotional vulnerability was pushing through my barriers of perceived strength. All who knew me always said how strong I was; if they only knew how untrue that felt to me now.

On a sunny day in late February, Carol was taking care of Paul, and I needed to pick up a prescription at the pharmacy. I decided to go for a walk at the park before going home since the sun had broken out, and it was warmer than usual for a February day. I drove to the park, took my phone with me and began the mile walk. I was about as far away from my car as I could have been when Carol called and said, "Paul did it again," meaning he fainted. He had wet the bed pretty much that morning but not the usual "soaker nights" I associated with his fainting episodes. I told her to lay his new recliner back as far as it would go, take his blood pressure and get him more bottled water, and I would come right home. I tried running back to the car, but the torn meniscus in my knee made that a laughable sight so I just hobbled as fast as I could, drove through a red light and broke the speed limit getting home. By the time I flew in the door he was conscious, eyes open and talking again. So we put the new chair to good use by taking his blood pressure every five minutes and gradually raising the chair until he was completely upright. When we got three consistently good readings in each position, we raised him a little more until he was finally able to stand up. I thought it was odd that when Carol took his pressure the first time, it was high, for him. This time it didn't seem like it was a plummeting blood pressure that caused him to pass out. That seemed strange to me creating more questions than relief. After two more good readings in the standing position, I asked him if he could walk back to the bedroom. And then it happened. Everything he tried to say was gobbledygook. Just like at our daughter's house in November, he could not speak correctly. It had been three months since that episode, and I remembered that the speech corrected itself after about forty-five minutes, and I was hoping that would be the case again. Carol and I got him back in the recliner and checked his blood pressure again. It was high, but the alarming thing was that his pulse was weak and irregular. I immediately phoned the hospice nurse, Tracy, who told me she would come if I needed her, to keep observing, and if it seemed that he wasn't getting any better, to keep her informed. She was at least forty-five minutes away. Then I called Paul's neurologist and asked her what I should do, call the life squad or not. She said her concern was the combination of the speech problems with the irregular, slow pulse. She thought he should be checked out. I called 911 again, and I knew what they were going to say. They wanted to take him to the hospital, and Paul didn't want to go, not at all! By this time, Carol had left and our daughter, Julie, came to be with me. It was she who talked her dad into going to the ER, but later he didn't even remember that she was there with him. Something was definitely happening in his brain. Of course, by the time the ambulance got to the hospital, Paul was fine, his eyes were open and he was speaking intelligibly. I thought, here we go again. A day lost in the ER and they will find nothing. The doctor ordered a CAT scan of his brain to see if there was a bleed, and it showed nothing. There was a very slight elevation in a heart enzyme reading that didn't indicate a heart attack, but it indicated that something was different from their previous readings on file. She wanted to admit him for twenty-four hours for observation, but after being there four hours already, he refused, and that was fine with me. The doctor was very understanding, realizing we had been there so many times, and she knew I was "all over it" and knew what to recognize if another problem arose. So we came home to a dog that was very happy to see her daddy.

In late February I had to go to the funeral of one of our neighbors who had died of cancer. His wife and I had talked several times during the two year course of his disease. She said she thought of me every time she drove by our house and wondered how, after seven years of care giving, I could continue to do it all. She talked about the constant worry, her fatigue and her inability at times to know what to do for her husband, all with which I could readily identify. Her husband was still hanging on and living at home until the last three months of his life when his bones began shattering one by one. At one point in January, he had five surgeries in four weeks to insert rods into his arms and legs. Finally, after two days in Hospice, he died peacefully.

For me, this funeral was terribly difficult. The church was one of the more beautiful I had ever been in, with lots of wood and glass and sun pouring into the space. The music choices were many of the same I had chosen for my eventual funeral mass and the pastor's eulogy one of the most upbeat and inspiring I had ever heard. Despite all that, I couldn't help but project myself into her place, picturing myself as the grieving widow, flanked by our three inconsolable children and eight grandchildren. Till death do us part. My neighbor was experiencing that final vow. My mind wandered as I imagined how Paul's eulogy would be? Who would give it? More than likely our pastor would be the presider as he had visited Paul in the hospital several times when I had feared for his life, and he was well acquainted with our situation.

When the casket and the family arrived at the church, I went outside to hug my neighbor who clung to me as she cried, "We never thought we'd be doing this so soon." It was all I could do to stay until the end of the Mass. I drove home as fast as possible on a Saturday morning only to find Paul in one of the worse states I had seen him in yet. My helper had come so I could go to the funeral, and she had never witnessed this situation before. She clearly didn't know what to do. She told me he had been pretty non-responsive most of the morning, grunting more than talking. I called Hospice to come as soon as they could, and the nurse on call was someone we had not met who knew nothing about Paul. She was as good as nothing. His blood pressure wasn't bad, but he just couldn't respond for over an hour, didn't know me and later had no memory of the entire event. She called the Hospice doctor who said, without ever having seen Paul, that he probably had had a seizure! I called the Neurologist who disagreed with this diagnosis and still felt that it was just a malfunctioning autonomic nervous system due to Parkinson's. Never have I been able to get the neurologist, cardiologist or ER doctors to agree on anything. Eventually, after about two hours, he came around to his normal self and was able to walk around and function again. But the collective symptoms of this latest episode had not matched any of the previous episodes. Just when I thought I knew the rules of the game, the game kept changing.

When the nurse left, she asked me if I had considered "placement". For a moment I didn't understand what she was saying, but then I realized she was talking about putting him in a nursing facility. I was so angry with her at that moment; I wanted to throw her down the stairs. She had been with him for only one hour and already thought he should be somewhere else.

The next day, after I had calmed down, I thought that maybe I should just dig out Paul's long term health care policy, acquaint myself with it before I actually needed it and see just what benefits he had. I called the 800 number and spoke with an agent who would tell me nothing without Paul's permission. I told her I had power of attorney over finances and health issues but she said I would have to fax a copy to her before she would tell me anything, or if Paul could give her permission over the phone, she would be happy to talk with me. At that moment, given Paul's tendency to paranoia, I didn't want him to know I was even looking at this issue for fear of worrying him. I hung up the phone and searched for the power of attorney papers. I located the health POA since it had been completed just recently, but I couldn't find the financial papers anywhere. After another half hour of panic, I found them, all seventeen pages of them.

When he woke up from his nap I decided to tell him I had called the agent because I wanted to know what his policy covered for "in home nursing" in the event we would eventually have to go that route. I told him I wanted to be able to keep him home at all costs, and that was the reason I had called, but they needed his permission. He seemed fine with that rationale, and I felt better than if I had had to go behind his back.

Before I could find the time to revisit the insurance issue, Paul had another mild episode only five days after the last frightening one. My Thursday helper was there, and I had already decided I wasn't going anywhere just in case something happened, and my instincts were right again. He didn't have nearly as bad a time and rallied quickly for a change. But the Hospice nurse decided to come anyway to double check and to share information she had learned about the possible diabetes insipidus we had discussed earlier. This was not going to be an easy solve as I had hoped. The test for this brain deficiency was an eight hour rigorous test done at the hospital and required constant monitoring. That alone could be very difficult on him. If it was found that he had the disease, the blood tests would determine dosage of a drug that could help but have potential side effects. At least she found that the drug wouldn't interact with any of his other medications. It was another moment of being overwhelmed, in over my head with additional responsibility and feelings of defeat. Paul and I discussed it and we thought it would be smart to have a family meeting with our kids since five heads would be better than two in making this very important decision.

A few days later I returned to the insurance issue and found what they would pay for in-home care (180 days), but what they would pay for nursing care in a facility barely covered what it would actually cost. All of a sudden, the mega amounts of money we paid monthly for Medicare, AARP and long term health care weren't going to be enough if we needed this kind of help down the road. Even with the inflation clause built into the policy, either it didn't keep up with actual inflation or it couldn't keep up with the soaring costs of medical care. I decided to check out one very nice facility five minutes from home and discovered, to my utter dismay, that even with insurance, we'd have to pay $6100.00 every month out of pocket. How in the world do people accomplish this? I had heard of people going bankrupt because of medical care, but I had been so sure we had covered all our bases, this never even seemed real for us. There was not even enough in our savings account, (which was healthier than many people) to cover one year! I was in tears the rest of the day.

I decided right then to use the money Hospice was paying for Paul's pharmacy expenses and put it to more in home help. There had to be a better solution. "For richer or poorer" kept popping into my head now as well as "better or worse, in sickness and in health".

March, 2016: The following Monday I called the Endocrinologist who was recommended and was told I couldn't even get an appointment for a consult for close to eight weeks! There was no way I could allow that to happen so I called another one and got an appointment in four days! Julie went with us so there would be an extra set of ears to help gather information as well as an extra body for moral support. For over an hour, she and I were getting more and more frustrated with this doctor's curt style, shutting me up when I tried to ask a question while she sat glued to her computer screen. Granted she knew nothing about Paul and was trying to learn facts posted after the most recent ER visit, but her manner was rude and condescending. She asked me for the exact number of ounces of fluid Paul takes in daily; how could I answer that definitively? She asked how many ounces of urine he secreted daily and during the night. Obviously, I wasn't wringing out diapers and bed clothing to have that answer. She said she couldn't even order the eight hour blood test without knowing those figures. I had to have him catheterized for twenty-four hours and also monitor every ounce of fluid he took in and excreted within that period.

Throughout the visit, Paul sat in the wheelchair, unresponsive, chin on his chest as usual with eyes closed most of the time. At that moment she surprised me with the question, "Has he ever had his thyroid checked?" I honestly didn't know, but my guess was NO. She checked in her computer for the blood work done during the many hospital visits, and there had never been a test for thyroid. She ordered one immediately.

The next day we got the results of the thyroid test which showed that it had been non-functioning for well over a year at least, and he needed another pill for that! I wondered if anything in his body was working right at this point. I felt like all his systems were being affected by Parkinson's, and his body was just wearing out, and this terrified me. I Googled Thyroid Disease and Parkinson's and discovered it was the one area of the Endocrine system most frequently associated with Parkinson's. Why, I had to ask again, didn't the Neurologist suggest doing this test months ago or even years ago?

The biggest surprise occurred when I finally spoke again with the endocrinologist and found out exactly how bad his results were. The normal number for a thyroid blood test should be four or less. His was 174! He should have been comatose or dead! No wonder he couldn't keep his eyes open! No wonder he looked like a big lump of nothing all the time! What was keeping him alive? How many times since his heart surgery had I asked myself this question? Our daughter's friend, who also had a thyroid problem, told her that when she was diagnosed her number had been eighty-six, and they told her to go to a hospital immediately! She couldn't believe Paul's results. There had been at least four times in the last fifteen years that he could have easily died. A weaker man probably would have. I was at the point of believing that my husband was indestructible.

The endocrinologist was out of the office for four days and couldn't write the prescription until her return, and that was totally unacceptable to me. Now that I knew how very sick he was with this newest problem, I couldn't wait to begin treating it. Instead the Hospice doctor wrote the script the same day I got the results. It wasn't filled until the following day and I had to wait another day to give him his first dose since it had to be taken as soon as he woke up. The problem with thyroid medication is that it has to build gradually in the body. Too much too soon could cause heart issues. So he had to start with the smallest dose for two weeks, then add a little more for two weeks and then the full dose for two weeks and the doctor would check him again.

I finally talked to the endocrinologist on the phone when she got back to the office, and she was like a different person. She allowed me to ask questions, was more compassionate and made me feel like everything was going to get better. But the thought of having to wait another six weeks to see results left me feeling depressed. Fortunately, after only four days, I could see a minimal change for the better. Before, I had had to pull 200 pounds of dead weight out of bed with a therapy belt every morning. Now, I no longer needed the belt. I still had to give him a boost but he was doing more of the work himself. I was so elated I almost cried. After a week, he told me that he was feeling better although he couldn't really explain how. But his walking was easier, still not great, but easier, and after the first two weeks were over, I could hardly wait to see what the next dosage would do for him.

I kept careful track of his day to day progress for six weeks and though it was more difficult for me to notice changes, the Hospice nurse who saw him only once a week, could readily see improvements. The follow-up appointment couldn't come fast enough for me. I will never forget the look on the doctor's face when she saw him. She couldn't stop smiling! "Look at him," she exclaimed. "He is sitting up strait, eyes open, even talking to me!" She gushed on and on, and it was a moment I will always remember. I felt like maybe things were going to continue to get easier for both Paul and me. The blood test this time showed that his magic number had dropped almost 100 points from 174 to 77. He still had a way to go to reach the goal of number four, but she increased his dosage again and said she wanted to see him in two months. Then I asked her what would have happened to Paul if we had not found this problem when we did. Her answer sent chills through my body. "He would have slipped into a coma and that would have been that." I cannot describe the mixture of emotions I felt at that moment. If we had not found this doctor, "till death do us part' would not have been that far away. It was evident to me at that moment, that he had been slowing slipping away from me for the last fifteen months, the deterioration accelerating in the last three months. I also knew that if we had waited the eight weeks to see the first doctor I called, he probably would not have lived that long. Everyone would have thought he died from advanced Parkinson's disease when in fact his death would have been caused by a Parkinson's complication, an illness that could have been treated, hypothyroid! Relief and gratitude were two of the emotions I felt but also anger and disbelief that no one had never checked for this. I wondered just how many other patients they had who would benefit from this simple blood test? And so I called them. It was difficult for me to keep my emotions in check when I spoke to them. I asked why they had never asked for this test and their answer astonished me. "We have never seen this correlation before." "How would you know if you never checked it?" I practically screamed into the phone. "I know you have other patients who faint frequently. Maybe they need to be checked, too." Then they told me this is the kind of test a Primary Care Physician would request, and Paul's primary doctor should have requested it. This made me even angrier since it was like passing the buck. "He doesn't have a primary care doctor because he has so many specialists who see him. He has a neurologist, a pulmonologist, a urologist, a cardiologist, a gastroenterologist, a psychiatrist and now an endocrinologist," I shot back. "But since the thyroid is the one gland that Parkinson's can affect, it should be in your domain to recognize the symptoms!" The response, patronizing as it was, at least indicated something. "We will see this as a teaching moment."

On one of the weekly visits from the Hospice nurse, she showed me the title of an article she found: *Constipation, the Thyroid Symptom No One Talks About!* I couldn't believe it. Was this serious problem he had suffered with for so long also going to be improved with thyroid medication? In 2013 he had been hospitalized with the serious bowel impaction and became septic. He could have died then, too, but didn't. Was it possible that his thyroid had been malfunctioning even longer than we thought? The neurologists had always attributed the constipation to Parkinson's, just like every other symptom he had. Watching his progress on thyroid medication was definitely going to be interesting!

I began keeping track of the number of days since Paul's last fainting episode. He had not had a loss of consciousness since the first day of thyroid medication. For fifteen months, we had been dealing with these episodes in the mornings, sending waves of terror into me every day anticipating another crisis. We treated it with blood pressure meds and still he fainted; we treated it as a dehydration problem, but the twenty-four hour catheter test showed that he was not dehydrated and still he fainted. Now we knew that all the drama and all the medical crises requiring frightening trips to the hospital were due to one thing only, a malfunctioning thyroid! God had taken care of us once again.

CHAPTER 25

May, 2016: After eight weeks on the thyroid medication, the changes for the better were becoming more evident to me as well as to the respite care workers. He obviously had more energy, but the eye closing was still a most annoying problem. But these changes for the better came with a down side as well. His mobility was improving, his walking getting better especially in the morning. But I did notice that when he had been sitting for long periods of time, the first dozen steps he took upon getting up were very difficult. Because he favored the right leg due to the femur surgery in 2014, and because the left leg was the one most affected by Parkinson's, he had a difficult time getting the left foot to function well when he got up. As my arthritic grandmother used to say, "It takes a few minutes to get my motor running." His motor was definitely hard to get running. If I weren't holding him by the back of his belt, his knees buckling would have sent him down to the floor. But although his energy level was up, cognitively, he didn't make the same progress. There were several times when he was in his chair in the family room, and I was working in the kitchen and could see him (thank God) that he got up to walk to the kitchen without his walker in front of him. If I had not been there to witness this, he would have fallen on his face on the hardwood floor. I was noticing more and more that his energy was improving but at the same time his brain was not telling him his limitations. It was a disastrous combination that had to be monitored carefully. For me personally, it felt like a step backwards because I didn't feel free to leave him unattended or at least out of my range of vision for even a minute.

One morning after the Hospice nurse left and he had done a better job of walking, he asked me when I perceived his being able to get rid of the walker altogether. We had had this conversation several times before, and I had never sugar coated it. So I was not happy that he was asking this same question again.

"You will never be able to walk again without your walker."

"Why have you come to this conclusion?" he asked almost incredulously.

"Why have you not come to this conclusion?" I shot back. "Do you really think you can walk from here to there with no support?"

"Yes, I do," he stubbornly continued.

"Then you are in total denial of your limitations. No amount of thyroid medication will eliminate the fact that you still have Parkinson's disease, and you will never walk without support again." I felt mean talking like this, but I refused to be dishonest or patronize him. "When you are at the point of giving up the walker, it will be because you will be in a wheelchair! End of discussion!"

One of the things we used to enjoy doing together was playing the board game, Sequence. It was a game I took to the hospital after his brain surgery to help me gauge his cognitive progress since there is a good amount of planning, eye hand coordination etc. The last time we tried to play it after the broken femur surgery, he just couldn't do it, and I was heart sick. Something had happened cognitively that kept him from being able to go through the simple steps necessary to play the game. So I put it away for over a year. After the ninth week of thyroid meds, I decided to ask him if he thought he could remember how to play the game. And he said he wanted to try. I was truly nervous about doing this, but I thought it would be worth it to see. He had just recently had more Botox shots in his eyelids and was able to keep his eyes open more so maybe he would be able to play again. I was elated that after the first few moves, he played very well, very slowly but well, and was only one move away from winning the game before I drew a winning card. We decided then that we were going to get back to playing every day.

Later that same night, he kept his eyes open during our TV watching, and I was really happy that we had enjoyed a more "normal day" together when suddenly the mood changed. He began asking me questions like, "Where are the girls?"

"What girls?" I answered.

"The two girls who live here," he said.

"There are no girls who live here. How many people do you think live here?"

"There are four of us, Dee, me and the two girls," he insisted.

"Do you see other girls living here?"

"Yes, sometimes," he said. I thought, oh great, here we go again with the crazy talk. Then he said, "Jan is your sister, right?"

"Yes, she is."

"And she has two sisters, right?"

"No, she has only one sister, me. Who do you think is her other sister?"

"Suzie," he said.

"No, Jan has two daughters, Suzie and my godchild, Deanna."

"Oh, you may be right," he finally agreed. Conversations like that really unnerved me especially after a day when I thought he was thinking so much more clearly. We went to bed shortly after this, and I left him sitting on the side of the bed changing his clothes while I went to lock doors and turn off lights like I do every night. When I walked back toward the bedroom, there he was away from the bed without his walker, just as he fell on the floor. I could see that he hadn't hurt himself falling on the soft carpet, and my anger and fatigue got the best of me. "What were you doing?" I screamed. He said he had wanted to walk to the bathroom. He actually had to maneuver to get around the walker to leave the bedside commode to walk unsupported. I was beyond furious with him. "Now do you realize you cannot walk without support? Now do you believe me? What good does it do for me to take care of you all day long if you make one stupid decision like this and ruin everything? If this had been on the hardwood, you could have broken another bone, and then we'd be going to the hospital again. I have had it with you!" I was screaming out of control, my fear and rage totally taking over the moment. And because he was tired at the end of the day, he was having trouble figuring out how to get up on all fours to try and stand up. He was so heavy, close to 200 pounds, that there was no way I could lift him. It's at moments like this that I want to hit him and sadly, I did shove him a few times on the back. I know if I were to watch someone else do this to an elderly, disabled man who had just fallen, I would be horrified and ready to call it "senior abuse". Sometimes I scared myself by the intensity of my emotions merging together. Then the guilt takes over. He did eventually get himself up, and I got him to bed. It was at this moment that I realized that I cannot allow myself to get too encouraged by anything because everything can change in an instant.

The next day, I was curious to see how he would be after the ugly way we had ended the previous night. All seemed fine, and we were ready to begin anew. I had decided to move on and not mention the incident again. We played another game of Sequence, but he didn't play as well as the previous game which had gotten me so excited. When we finished, I asked him if he would put the game pieces away while I started to make lunch. This involved putting the various colored chips into their plastic bags, putting the deck of cards loosely into the box and folding up the game board and putting it into the box. I figured this would be an easy task and would probably take him longer than it would me, but that would give me time to get the lunch made. I finished the lunch preparations only to find him totally confused by the task. There were colored chips still all over the table, he was putting cards into the plastic bags instead of chips and nothing was done right much less finished. My heart sank as I said nothing, gave him his lunch and finished the job for him.

Later that afternoon, it was time for his nap, and I usually go into the adjacent bedroom to work on various tasks and stay close enough that I can hear him when he wakes up. I was on the phone talking to our daughter when suddenly I heard the bells on the walker, and I ran in to find him once again on the floor with the walker next to him. Normally, he can't even get out of bed by himself, but that day he did, walked out to the front end of the bed and was going to back up to the hope chest to sit and put on his slacks. He is never supposed to back up with the walker, but he did and fell again. I guess the upside was that he did use his walker this time. He had tough time getting himself up, but I refused to help him. He eventually made it without my help.

June, 2016: June10 was our wedding anniversary, and this year we hit forty-nine years. He would not have remembered, just like last year, if I had not reminded him the night before. And like last year, I got out the wedding album, and we went through page by page remembering whatever came to mind from each photo. These are very poignant moments for me but necessary opportunities to remember the guy I had married and how I had felt on that day. I remember when each photo was taken and the emotion I felt at the time. Was that really only forty-nine years ago? It seemed like so much longer. I looked at him, the young, thin redhead with the devilish grin, and tried to rekindle those same feelings. Of course, neither of us was the same young, thin person we were those many years ago, but so much of that twenty-seven year old groom was just gone now. I remembered my parents' fiftieth anniversary and not long ago my sister and brother-in-law's fiftieth. I had to wonder if we would even realize ours. What made this even more difficult was that my parents were still young and vibrant on their anniversary and danced the night away at their party. The same was true for my sister's big night. I knew our celebration, if he made it till then, wouldn't be anything like theirs. What would the next 365 days bring?

On a particularly "down" day I was telling my helper about some of my feelings of late, and she told me, "Dee, you're grieving. The man you married isn't there anymore. He has been slipping away gradually for the last sixteen years. If he had just died suddenly at age fifty-eight with the anticipated heart attack, your grief would have been overwhelming and sudden. But your grief has been building over sixteen years, little by little, as more and more of the life you had together has gone by the wayside."

I knew she was right. So many things had already died that I was sorely missing and about which I was angry and sad: our unfinished bucket list of travels, our ability to boat, (the boat that's still unsold), to road trip in our RV as planned. (The RV we had to sell after using it only once) Our entire list of retirement plans had proven impossible to accomplish. They weren't just put on hold; they were dead. Friends had dropped out of sight; freedom to go out whenever and wherever I wanted without paying someone to stay with Paul was impossible; going out to a restaurant was difficult and stressful for me as I worried about every bite he swallowed getting trapped in his esophagus. I was doing the best I could to weigh the negatives with the positives, but there were just some days when the positives felt very tough to find. And what scared me the most, was that even with the newfound help I was getting from Hospice, Visiting Angels and my helper, Bonnie, I never felt like I should have felt. I thought I should be rejuvenated and ready to dig into my life when I got home, but instead I dreaded pulling the car into the garage and taking hold of the reins again. And every night when I finally tucked him into bed, I said to myself, "Thank you, God, for another day done."

We celebrated our birthdays, his seventy-sixth and my seventy-second with our three kids and our eight grandkids, and it was a wonderful evening. It seemed like the only time I was really happy any more was when I was with my family. Not just because I could relax a little because there were more hands to help me with Paul, but because those were just about the only times I found myself laughing now. The children invigorated me; I never wanted to leave them when we were all together. But invariably, any time we had a day or a night out, the following day was terribly difficult. It seemed like it took him another twenty-four hours to recuperate from any kind of socializing. The day after our birthday party, we were scheduled to go to a cousins' reunion at my sister's house. He was so out of it that day, I knew it would be a disaster so I made the decision to pay my helper and go by myself. I felt guilty doing it, but I just needed to enjoy myself even though it cost me a bundle for the number of hours I was away. When I mentioned this to our daughter the following day, she surprised me saying, "Good for you, mom. You should do that more often!" I couldn't believe how much better I felt hearing her say that. Maybe I wasn't such a mean, selfish wife after all!

Every other Wednesday, we babysat for a few hours for our son's two daughters. I used to do this alone before Paul became my full time care giving job. But ever since his broken leg eighteen months before, he had to go with me. The last "Mémé Wednesday", as the kids called it, found him unable to function again, and Bonnie said she would come over so I could go alone. It had been such a long time since it was just the kids and me. They asked where he was, and I told them he wasn't feeling well. Then I asked, "What should we play?" They both smiled, their faces lighted up and they shouted, "Hide and Seek", something we always used to do but hadn't been able to do with Papa along in the wheelchair. We found ourselves having so much fun again, and it was just another indication of how much even that child care experience had changed for me. I felt so conflicted because I felt guilty for enjoying myself more alone than with him.

By the end of June, the day arrived to return to the endocrinologist for the new thyroid numbers. She was elated to tell us that the new number was down to thirty-one from the seventy-seven it had been three months ago. She increased his dosage again and scheduled a thyroid ultrasound and check back in two months. Maybe after six months of treatment, his thyroid would be back to normal. I could only hope.

CHAPTER 26

July, August 2016: These two months went by in a hurry; Paul and I spent some time every day on the patio, sometimes having lunch, sometimes just reading together, sometimes just enjoying the sun, the music of the fountain and the ever present birdsong. He would doze off in the wheelchair, and I would lie down on the swing and savor all the sensory input!

In July, it was also necessary for Paul to see the neurologist again after I did a quick check of his chest batteries and found that the right side was registering a problem. It seemed that since that side had to work harder to supply the amount of voltage to match the left side, the shelf life of that right battery was wearing out. It had been three and a half years since both had been replaced four years after the initial brain surgery so it became evident that the time in between replacements was getting shorter. I guessed this was to be expected since the disease had had three and a half years to worsen. The physician assistant checked him out at the office and said that he should be scheduled for surgery sooner rather than later. I knew he had been through this once already, but I couldn't keep my "worry gene" from overworking. They scheduled his procedure for July 28 at two thirty in the afternoon. Of course, now he had to have a pre-op physical, blood work drawn and an EKG. Fortunately, the hospice doctor, who is now considered his primary care doctor, came to the house to do the physical. Scheduling the EKG at the cardiologist office was easy enough to accomplish as well. But getting the blood work done was not so simple. Because his new primary care doctor was not in the system where he had blood work done before, we couldn't make an appointment there. So we had to go to a facility close to home that was first come, first serve. It was a Friday. My heart sank when we arrived, and I saw the waiting room completely full with a few more patients waiting outside the office. We signed in, and I had to count the number of names ahead of us…twelve! It took an hour before we were called back only to be told that he was not pre-registered in their system, and we would have to make a phone call to get that done before they would draw his blood. Twenty minutes later, I gave the technician the written orders for a Metabolic Panel and a CBC and she drew his blood. I was so relieved to know that I had covered all bases, and he only had to show up for the surgery a week later. The following Monday I got a phone call from the surgeon's office telling me that we had to go back because the results of the CBC were not there. She also told me that she needed them immediately and to tell the technician to mark it STAT. So off we went again, but first I called them to let them know what they hadn't done on Friday, and I told them there was no time to wait for an hour. Could we move to the head of the line when we arrived? They said YES! Hurray! Something was going right. The technician was abundantly sorry for not reading the entire order the first time.

The problem facing us now was that Paul couldn't have anything to eat after midnight on the twenty-seventh, and his procedure was supposed to begin at two thirty in the afternoon the next day. He had to get most of his medications in that morning with as little water as possible, but normally he takes his three Parkinson's meds with food. Oh well, there was nothing we could do about that. This surgeon, the very same one who had botched the brain surgery in 2009, is notorious for running late, and this day was no exception. He didn't even begin the procedure until three thirty, and I was furious. The surgery was uneventful, and after an hour in surgery and another hour in recovery, we closed the facility at five thirty. The hospice nurse said she would meet me at home to help me get him in and settled while I prepared something for the poor starved guy to eat! I was so very grateful to have another pair of hands to help, and after I prepared his dinner, she fed it to him, and I was able to take a glass of wine out on the patio and decompress! We both got a good night sleep that night.

The following day, I had to watch him carefully, put ice on his two incisions fifteen minutes out of every hour for the first twenty-four hours and monitor his walking even more closely than I already did due to the after effects of anesthesia. I knew he would probably sleep off and on most of the day, and he did. After five days, I was concerned that his exhaustion was not getting better so I called the neurology office to get some reassurance that this was normal. They told me that the last time he had the procedure, the disease was not as advanced, he was still walking with a cane and hadn't yet fallen and broken his thigh. After considering all that, plus all he had been through due to the additional complication of thyroid malfunction for at least eighteen months, it was no wonder that this seventy-six year old was going to recover very slowly, and it was OK.

Three days after his surgery, his brother and sister-in-law were in town, and they arranged to visit him before they went back to the airport. I wasn't sure about this since he has to work so much harder to be sociable on a good day, but this was post-surgery. However, it was his brother whom we see maybe once a year and Paul wanted them to come. However, there was a set end time since they had to get to the airport at a certain time. But I was so sad and upset by the time they left because it felt to me that their conversation with him was condescending and patronizing. But when I asked him later how he felt about the visit, he said he enjoyed it. That was really all that was important, I know, but somehow the fact that he didn't feel patronized or feel the conversation condescending made me even sadder. Had he really slipped that far? And I knew the answer was yes. But then, maybe I was just being defensive and overprotective.

August, 2016: Paul was scheduled to see the ever late surgeon two weeks after the surgery. The appointment was the same day as his Botox shots, and there was an hour of down time between the appointments. I asked if there was any way we could either make the Botox appointment later or get him in to the surgeon earlier since their two offices were across the hall from each other. All he was going to do was look at the healing incisions and say, "You're good to go. See you later!" But no one could seem to make this simple task happen. After the Botox appointment finished I asked again if he could squeeze Paul in for the five minutes it would take the surgeon to see him. Again, they refused, and after waiting forty-five minutes, they told me it could be another ninety minutes. That's when I refused and told them to reschedule Paul for the following week. We eventually kept this appointment and only had to wait another ninety minutes!

By the end of August, Paul was once again doing and saying things that bothered me. One night, as I was getting his bedtime meds together, I turned around to take them to him and found him walking out to the kitchen pushing the wobbly hospital table instead of his walker. For six months, our routine had been for him to wait in his recliner for me to bring him his meds, but for some reason he decided that I wanted him to come out in the kitchen! Again, I lost it. In fact I lost it so badly, I scared myself. I said some hateful things which I regretted as soon as they came out of my mouth, but I was unable to control my anger at that moment. We cleared the air before we went to sleep but I felt terrible, guilty, sad and scared again.

Another night he was talking to his brother in California who had called late. I didn't want to take the call since Paul should have been preparing to go to bed, but he insisted on talking to him. After fifteen or twenty minutes I returned to the room to hear Paul say, "You know, Jerry, for the last year I have been living in Deanna's house." I took the phone from him only to hear his brother say to me, "How nice of you to let Paul live in your house." He was laughing and taking Paul's confusion in stride, but I was not laughing.

On another evening, as I was finishing my wine, he asked me, "What is that you're drinking?"

"It's wine," I answered. "Why?"

"I was just curious. It just seems like you and Deanna both like it a lot." Oh, not this again! I could have just let it go but for some reason I felt compelled to disallow this kind of thinking. So I said, "Who do you think I am?" When he answered that I was some fictitious lady, I said it was time to go to bed!

CHAPTER 27

September, 2016: As summer was winding down, I couldn't shake an overwhelming melancholy that ordinarily wasn't at all like me. Not that I haven't had my pity party days along the way, but this was something different. Even now, it's hard to put into words. The latest visit to the endocrinologist had been very good with a light clearly at the end of the tunnel. The check-up at the cardiologist had been good as well. His recovery from the battery replacement surgery was complete. Yet, I was at a loss to make Paul's days meaningful for him as his apathy continued and his ability to do even the smallest things seemed to be deteriorating. As one of my caregiver helpers said, it was harder on me to watch the mental decline of a former Ph.D. professor than it was for him to be going through it. I hoped she was right. One of the most challenging things for me mentally was continuing my own life, my own activities without feeling guilty for doing so when he had nothing to wake up for in the morning. I knew intellectually that this was stupid, and that I had to continue my book writing for children and my French class at UC for my own sanity. These activities were therapeutic for me. But then I would remember that Paul and I used to go to the university together and teach our respective classes and go out to lunch afterwards to talk about them, and the sadness of leaving him behind would take over. I tried to include him in my book writing by reading things to him for his critique. But other than that, there wasn't much else I could do. Emotionally, I was having a tough time getting past this.

I was paying a lot of money every month for respite care so I could go out and get a massage, or go to a Yoga class or have lunch with a friend. But instead of being grateful for this, I began to resent the fact that I had to pay someone every time I wanted to go anywhere or do anything. I was always aware that the clock was ticking, and I had a deadline to get back. Gone were the days of driving twenty minutes to my favorite shopping area and spending the day browsing in all my favorite shops and driving twenty minutes home. If I wanted to go anywhere, it had to be five to ten minutes away so I didn't spend all my precious free time in the car. And to make matters worse, I never wanted to come home to resume my duties. I began to resent having to do urine soaked laundry every day; I grew impatient when it took us ten minutes to walk from the bedroom to the family room. I was irritated at having to repeat the same cues over and over: big steps, Paul; Head up, Paul; Keep your eyes ahead of you and not on the floor, Paul. It never changed; it never got easier for him to do these simple things without having to be reminded of every move to make. I looked forward to putting him to bed for a nap and resented when he woke up too soon. It was becoming increasingly difficult to find any joy in anything, and this scared me to death. I felt like even a visit from three rabbits couldn't help me through this!

Spring and summer have always been my favorite times of the year, but even this was depressing. If the air quality was poor, or it was too hot, we didn't spend much time outside because of his asthma. And there was no way I could sit outside alone and leave him inside since I couldn't trust him to stay seated and avoid falling. Before I was a full time caregiver, I would spend hours at the pool, worshipping the sun and reading a new book. Now I'd have to pay someone to be able to do that, and that certainly wasn't going to happen. Forget traveling in the summer as we had done our entire married life. Now I'd have to pack two suitcases just to hold all the diapers, protective pads and bedding necessary to keep him from ruining a hotel bed. And even then, there was no guarantee he wouldn't still ruin someone else's mattress. On days when the morning hours were cooler and the air quality was acceptable, I would take him out on the patio and read to him, or take the wheelchair to the park and take him for a walk. He enjoyed this change of scenery, but it was hard on my back and arthritic hands and feet to push 230 pounds for very long. Where was the joy in my life now? It seemed the only time I experienced joy was when I was around our grandchildren, but even that beautiful time together was more limited since they were all getting older.

Dreams have always been a subject I loved to explore. Now I was having more and more disturbing dreams that left me uneasy when I awoke. Sometimes they would be about Paul as a young guy, walking unaided and enjoying life with me. I would wake up feeling so sad. Sometimes they would be about Paul as he is now but walking unaided and falling. But the most disturbing were the ones in which I would be angry with him, hitting him, screaming at him and crying. All my inner rage would come out in my sleep, and that scared me even more. I considered going to a psychologist to get help but resented the fact that I'd have to pay a caregiver as well as a hefty fee to a professional to tell me things I probably already knew. So I put that idea aside. When anyone would ask me how I was doing, I was starting to find it difficult to answer with an upbeat response. I felt pretty sure that no one honestly wanted to know how bad I really felt, but I found myself not being able to fake it anymore. I knew I didn't want to live my life like this, and I knew enough psychology to realize that anger suppressed over time will manifest itself as depression. I knew in my heart that this was happening and that something had to change. And since Paul wasn't going to change, at least not for the better, something had to change in me.

The first step, I thought, was to identify precisely all the things that I was angry about. Then look at each one squarely and decide if there was something I could do about it and if not, let it go. If there was anything I could do, I had to be proactive and get it done. And so I began to make my "angry at" list.

1. This miserable disease called Parkinson's: Yes, I was angry that it had taken our golden retirement years and turned them upside down. Could I do anything about it? NO. It was the hand we were dealt, and we had to believe it was part of a bigger plan. Let it go!

2. Fair weather friends: We used to see people frequently to go to movies, out to dinner, to each other's homes for dinner, etc. Where did they all go? When Paul had his DBS surgery in 2009 and landed in the hospital for ten weeks, so many friends were there to support him and me. It was the first time, really, that I realized how much I needed people. I valued the company, the conversation, the sharing of tough

times and the moral support. Now, seven years later, we saw hardly anyone as couples. Our best friends for twenty years vanished; his wife, who had hung on for a few years, rarely called. We had two couples we still saw from time to time, one with whom we had gone to the ballet series for decades and another former colleague of Paul's and his wife, who were out of town more than they were here. A few of my girlfriends still contacted me regularly and emailed to see how I was doing. I valued them so much. Was there anything I could do about this? NO! Paul had really never worked at "guy friends" before he had Parkinson's. So we weren't going to be getting together with many men. The only thing I could do was to continue to cultivate my girlfriends for fun and moral support and say "Forget the rest of them!"

3. Loss of planned retirement hobbies: As I mentioned earlier, travel was supposed to continue forever, and now that was gone. Could I change it? NO! But I made it a point to look back at our travel photo albums from time to time and to share that with Paul, too, to stimulate his memories. Boating had been a huge part of our life for years and giving that up was probably the most difficult thing for both of us. Could I do anything about it? NO! Let it go. We had bought an RV when we gave up boating but had to give that up, too. Let it go!

4. Freedom to leave him alone: This was probably the biggest adjustment I had to make, and I hated it. Could I change it? NO! But I had to be willing to pay whatever was necessary to have time to myself, and instead of resenting the expense, be grateful I had the money to do that.

5. Shared fun with grandkids: I really felt bad for the eight grandkids that they didn't have a "fun grandfather" to hang out with. And as I had written previously, my time with them was hampered when he was with me. Could I change it? NO! But I could still work to spend time with them alone when possible. As they were getting older, I loved texting them and hearing about their days.

6. Jealousy: I mentioned this before, and I didn't know how to handle this one since it has never been my nature to be jealous of anyone. But when our two granddaughters' other

grandparents lived within walking distance of them, and they owned a condo in Tennessee and had a boat there to enjoy with them, I was beyond green with jealousy. The kids were supposed to be spending time with us on our boat, weren't they? Could I change it? NO! Had to let it go.

7. Loss of my soulmate, best friend and conversation partner: As Paul's ability to converse declined, my life at home felt lonelier and lonelier. I still tried to engage him in conversation, but it was such an effort for him to complete thoughts, find the word he was searching for and frankly, to make any sense at all sometimes, that it was hardly worth the effort. Could I change it? NO but I could continue to try.

8. Having to do difficult care giving tasks: Looking back, I knew I had successfully gotten used to doing a few "yucky" things I never dreamed would be necessary when I said "I do" back in 1967! I had learned to deal with urinary incontinence; it no longer phased me. Thank God for Depends and thick pads to put in them. I had gotten used to inserting a suppository up Paul's behind when the constipation was a problem; got out those latex gloves and got the job done! Gave him an enema when the suppositories didn't work; that was a tough one, but I did it. But dealing with bowel incontinence was a job I had not yet been able to handle with compassion. That was a work in progress. If anything could make me lose my composure that was it!

After I completed my list, I realized that I had quite a lot to be angry about. Admitting all these things was a bit overwhelming. Then I saw an article on the internet written by another wife of a Parkinson's patient. The title of the article was "It's OK to be Angry!" Really? It is? Well, maybe I'm not such a bad person after all. Maybe just being allowed to acknowledge that fact could be a start, and realizing that it was pretty normal to feel that way just might make it easier.

CHAPTER 28

October, 2016: We returned for the next thyroid blood testing only to find that, though the magic number was better, it was still a few points away from normal. It had come down from thirty-one to five so she increased the dosage one more time. Finally in late October, after eight months of therapy, he reached the goal of 1.99! I should have been elated, but the day we were supposed to go to the doctor's office for the results, he had a terrible morning. He was so bad, I had to cancel our appointment and ask them to phone me with the results. He told me later that he thought he was dying. He said he hurt all over, and his asthma seemed worse. He could hardly talk above a whisper or hold up his head. I was so alarmed, I called the Hospice nurse to come right away and check him out. She had not seen him like this for over seven months and was just as bewildered as I was since all his vital signs were perfect. He had no fever, and after a couple of Tylenol and some puffs on his inhaler, he was able to get up and go out to breakfast. She sat with him, and I told her I needed some quiet time alone. It is difficult even now to describe what I was feeling. I was in tears because I knew that his thyroid had been continually improving, and we hadn't had any scares like this since before he had begun thyroid meds. So what was it this time? Were we starting yet another crisis period that I wouldn't know how to handle? I had honestly forgotten how it had felt to be so terrified every morning before we found the answer at the endocrinologist office. The thought of facing that kind of fear again with no explanation for it overwhelmed me. Then it occurred to me that the cardiologist had taken Paul off one of the two blood pressure drugs after his thyroid had improved. Maybe that had been a mistake. I called him, and he agreed that Paul be put back on both of the drugs. The following day, the doctor office called me with the thyroid results indicating that it was normal. He had weathered another storm that obviously could have killed him. I couldn't help but wonder just how many lives this husband of mine had. This thyroid crisis, if left undiscovered, would have taken his life, the doctor had told us. He had survived open heart surgery when the surgeon couldn't give me a reason why he was still alive; he had survived a brain bleed when the surgeon doing the DBS surgery caused a seepage in his brain; he had survived his kidneys nearly shutting down after that brain crisis; he had survived a near fatal bowel impaction, sepsis, multiple serious falls and now a malfunctioning thyroid. I am convinced that a lesser man would have died long ago. God must really have had a need for him to still be here!

November, 2016: The month of November is officially the start of our family's holidays with our daughter, Jennie's birthday on the fourth. The occasions when we can manage to have the entire family here at the same time get more and more difficult as their lives get busier and busier. So having three kids with November and December birthdays helps get us all together more frequently along with Thanksgiving and Christmas thrown in there. November came and went with no medical drama to speak of. Paul wasn't moving very well, but that wasn't anything new or alarming. But it did seem that his asthma was making itself known with his breathing becoming more labored from time to time, plus he had been having a productive cough that no one could explain for what seemed like a year. Cold weather as well as exercise had always induced the wheezing, and the weather was definitely getting colder. Paul was asking for his rescue inhaler more frequently especially at night after having walked from the family room to the bedroom. I made a mental note to call the pulmonologist if this didn't improve.

December, 2016: We had the whole family together in early December for our daughter, Julie's, birthday. It was just a Happy Hour get together with drinks and gift exchange, family fun and great conversation. Paul seemed fine other than the occasional cough and wheezing. This is such a busy time for me with all the Christmas shopping, wrapping, cookie baking and the hundreds of details that go along with the wonderful season I love so much. Paul and I decorated the travel tree in the family room, each ornament producing a memory from the vacation where it was purchased.

The grandchildren had already decorated their tree downstairs over Thanksgiving weekend, and later Paul and I enjoyed decorating the big family tree in the living room. The house was completely decorated for Christmas by the time we celebrated Julie's birthday.

By the second week of December, Paul was asking for the inhaler more and more, and the Hospice nurse suggested we get a nebulizer to give him breathing treatments to help him through these episodes. His feet, ankles and legs were more swollen than usual making it almost impossible to even get his slippers on some days. On Thursday, December 14, the nurse and I talked about this. I asked her if she thought there was any congestive heart failure going on. She reassured me that she had actually considered this and listened to his lungs even more closely than usual and heard nothing to suggest that. I breathed a sigh of relief chalking up my concerns to asthma and lack of physical exercise.

By December 17, we were supposed to go to hear our granddaughter play viola in the Northern Kentucky Youth Sinphonia concert. We had never been able to get to one of these concerts, and I really wanted to go. But that Saturday, Paul seemed particularly bad, had very little energy, bad wheezing, and I made the judgement call to get my helper, Bonnie, to stay with him so I could go alone. I knew he would have enjoyed it, but I really didn't want to be responsible for him while enjoying this incredible group of young musicians. And since I had never been to this facility before, I didn't know what the handicap facilities were. That evening, he asked me to use the nebulizer before he went to bed as the wheezing seemed worse. I thought it calmed things down afterwards, but I made the mental note to call the pulmonologist the following Monday.

During the night, I awoke to the sound of his breathing as he slept, faster and shallower than I had ever heard it before. I actually tried to mirror his breathing, and it was ridiculous how hard his lungs were working. As the early morning hour to get up approached on December eighteenth, I awoke again to see him holding his left arm up in the air. When I asked him why he was doing that, he said it hurt. This set off alarm bells in my weary head, but he said it had gotten stuck between the mattress and the bed rail. It seemed he always had a safe, plausible explanation for everything so I did nothing, a fact that would come back to haunt me. All day Sunday, his breathing sounded labored and his mobility terrible. But if I had to walk with those swollen, puffy feet, I guess I would have trouble, too. And I didn't have Parkinson's disease. Then at nine thirty Monday evening, December nineteenth as we were watching TV, he asked again for the nebulizer, but the treatment did nothing to help him. We went back to the bedroom to get him ready for bed, and he asked for the inhaler again! One last puff and he was in for the night, or so I thought.

At eleven forty-five he woke me up asking for the inhaler again. I asked him if he wanted me to call 911, but he said no. He went back to sleep until two in the morning Tuesday when it was obvious he was in terrible distress. This time I did call 911 and told them I thought my husband was having a severe asthma attack. They came within five minutes, and it didn't take them long to realize this might not be asthma at all. I, however, was still under that assumption. They had to cut his pajama top off, administer oxygen, and from the way they were talking, although I didn't understand the medical lingo, I could tell this was serious. Then they told me he had to go to the hospital. I find it difficult even now to describe how I felt at that moment; I was on auto pilot, in a sleepy yet adrenaline charged state, calm on the outside, churning on the inside. "Get dressed! Take care of panicked, unhappy dog! Take Hospice binder to the hospital! Call Hospice about the turn of events." My brain was just a continuous checklist, devoid of real emotion. As they were taking my sweet husband down the stairs, he was wearing a big breathing apparatus over his mouth and nose, and all I could see were his eyes, staring at me with a look of complete fear. There must have been a hundred thoughts going through his head. He didn't have to say a word; his eyes said it all, and I will never forget the terror I saw there. *Is this goodbye? What is happening to me? I am scared!* My heart was breaking for him. All I could say was, "It's going to be alright. You're going to be okay" but I really wasn't sure. One of the EMT's asked me then if he had a DNR. He does because Hospice requires the do not resuscitate. He said he had to see it. All I could say was "Is he dying?" He paused a little too long before answering. Then he said, "Well, at some point, his heart is going to get tired of helping him breathe like this." And then he walked out of the house leaving me standing there in disbelief.

We have been to the hospital so many times, and I know the drill perfectly, but this was like no other ER experience. As they hurried him inside, there was a room already waiting with five doctors and nurses already waiting to attend to him. The EMT's must have called ahead and told them they had a very serious situation. I'm glad I really don't know what they said. I sat off to the side helplessly watching as they worked on him, answering questions as fast as they asked them. It became clear that they knew they were not treating asthma. I look back on those first few moments and realize now how out of touch I really was, what huge blinders I had on. They took a chest X-ray, drew blood and performed all the many tasks they perform in a true emergency. The results came quickly; this was not asthma but congestive heart failure, and the night his arm was raised in bed, he was having a heart attack! Bloodwork showed his heart enzymes were very elevated. His survival at that point was uncertain.

It was now three thirty in the morning, and I was still processing the fact that I had allowed forty-eight hours to pass without acting on my gut instinct that the pain in the left arm meant trouble! Paul has always had a way to explain away symptoms as something much less serious than they really are. We'd been married nearly fifty years; when was I going to learn to trust my gut instead of his safe, convenient explanations?

It was evident that he was going to be admitted so I had to call Hospice to come to the ER to sign off on their services until he returned home…if he ever returned home! I sat there waiting for the Hospice nurse to arrive, watching my poor husband still wearing the breathing contraption helping him to survive. When she arrived I felt I had to apologize to her for making her come in the middle of the night, and she was very sweet and most supportive. She stayed with me until she felt I was going to be alright. Finally they put Paul in a room in the new tower recently completed. The thought occurred to me at that moment that we hadn't gone to the Open House for the public to see this newly built part of the hospital. Now we were seeing it in all its technological glory for real.

At six in the morning I left him to come home to my poor, scared dog and care for her needs. I tried to lie down, but sleep would not come as horrible thoughts raced through my head. It was December twentieth, and I wasn't sure he would make it to Christmas. More inane thoughts popped into my head. What if the dining room table was set for an after-funeral meal with family instead of a joyous

Christmas meal? What if we would never decorate the three Christmas trees together again? They were ridiculous mental ramblings, but I couldn't turn them off. I have always loved Christmas, the decorating, baking, shopping, wrapping. If he died now, would I ever be able to enjoy this time of year again? Would our family ever be able to enjoy it again without sadness getting in the way?

I returned to the hospital around nine thirty not entirely sure what I was going to find. The heavy breathing apparatus was removed, and oxygen tubes in his nose replaced it. He was resting comfortably. They had given him an IV diuretic to drain the fluid from his lungs, and he was breathing more easily. Now it was just a waiting game to talk to the hospitalist and the cardiologist. They finally spoke with me about how serious this was. Our son, Jamie, arrived shortly before my talk with the hospitalist, and he heard everything she had said. When the consult was over, Jamie said, "You know, Mom, I always knew it would be his heart that would take him." I couldn't believe it. His heart health had never crossed my mind, not in the eighteen years since his bypass surgery. Even the nurse had ruled out congestive heart failure.

The cardiologist wanted to do an echo cardiogram that day to see just how extensive the damage was to his heart and what might have to be done. We waited all day, and after much questioning the nursing staff, we were finally told that the lab was swamped for echo cardiograms, and they were taking them in order of gravity. I guessed that was kind of a good news/bad news moment. They must have thought his case was less serious than others! But now we wouldn't have any real answers until the following day.

I didn't want to get to the hospital too early because our little dog was acting even more scared and confused. She wouldn't eat, and it was obvious that she needed attention, too. I called in the troops and asked our kids to help out, stop in to see her, give her some love and maybe take her for a short walk. When I arrived at the hospital, the echo cardiogram had already been done, and another waiting game to find out the results began. Meanwhile the diuretic Paul was taking was doing a great job of clearing all the fluid from his lungs, and he no longer needed the oxygen tubes. After what seemed an eternity, the doctor came in. The test showed that there was decreased pumping ability in his heart, and the only way to really know what to do was to perform an angiogram, going through his groin with the tiny camera to view the heart vessels up close and personal. Of course, we agreed it should be done immediately. He then reminded us of the DNR status and wanted to know if we wanted to rescind it for the procedure. He said if for any reason something happened and they needed to resuscitate him, the current DNR wouldn't allow him to do that. So Paul signed off the DNR, and the doctor told us he would talk to me before doing anything more extensive than the angiogram. And off they went.

Two hours later, the doctor called me and told me what he had found. The news was good and bad. The good news was that there was no valve involvement; if there had been, major surgery would have been involved and way too risky to perform. The bad news was that of the original five bypasses Paul had done eighteen years earlier, only two looked good as new, two were totally blocked again, and the fifth one he couldn't see well enough to evaluate. The choices were to try and open them again which would have been very risky with no guarantee that the outcome wouldn't be worse. He didn't say what those risks were exactly, but I felt my heart beat harder and the familiar sense of dread set in. Before I answered him, my mind took me back to that day in March, 1998, when I watched the cardiology surgeon take Paul into the OR for his bypass surgery. I still remember well the feeling of dread that that could easily have been the last time I would see my husband alive. That wait had been excruciating, and the thought of having to wait like that again was terrifying. So I asked him what his decision would be if the patient were his father. He answered without missing a beat, "I would err on the side of caution and do nothing more." That's all I needed to hear.

To say I was relieved isn't totally accurate; of course I was glad I would see Paul alive again. But I also knew they had solved nothing, and the future was going to be a day to day uncertainty. We would continue to treat him conservatively at home, adding the diuretic to his daily regime to keep fluid off his lungs and hope he didn't have another crisis. He had lost twelve pounds of fluid in three days. There was nothing else to do. And when he was discharged two days later, December 23, the surgeon warned me to bring him back to the hospital immediately if any of his symptoms showed up again. Suddenly, the onus of responsibility to get it right felt like a ton of weight on my already exhausted shoulders. But we made it home for Christmas, and we wouldn't think about anything else for now!

Meanwhile, back at home, our little dog still was not acting right, wouldn't eat and was obviously missing her daddy. I was hoping she would perk up after I brought him home. We were having a hospital bed delivered the day after discharge, and I needed to call in the kids to help me move furniture out of the bedroom to make room for it. Out son-in-law, all three of their children and our daughter beat us home. I had described what needed to be removed and placed elsewhere in the house, and our daughter was going to supervise the project. Along with them, the hospice nurse wanted to be there when we got home to sign him back into the program. When we finally arrived at six forty-five PM after everyone else, it was like grand central station, lots of chaos, noise and excitement to have Paul home. The dog was very happy to see him, and after everyone left and quiet was restored, I thought maybe everything was going to be okay. But that was not to be.

After forty-nine and a half years of marriage, my husband and I spent our last night in the same bed together, and he slept like a log; I, on the other hand, was awake most of the night listening to his breathing. It proved to be a long and exhausting night, but fortunately, an uneventful one. I realized I was going to have to get over the fear of not listening for a problem, or I would never get any sleep.

The hospital bed arrived the following day, and although it didn't add anything decorative to our bedroom, it fit in the allotted space, and Paul found it to be very comfortable. That was all that mattered. I wondered if I would sleep better with him farther away from me, or if that would make it harder for me to hear if all was okay. My body's needs took over, and I slept soundly for the first night in more than I could even count.

It was Christmas Eve, and we had originally planned to go to the seven o'clock Candlelight Mass. But he was too fragile, I thought, to go to church, be in a crowd and exposed to any number of germs, and I couldn't justify taking him. There was no way I would miss Christmas Mass, however, so our son-in-law agreed to hang out with him so I could go. Our son picked me up, and we met our daughter and her three children there. Ordinarily, I would have been happy to be with all of them, but it was overwhelming to me that someone was missing. This was the first Christmas Mass that Paul and I had not attended together in over fifty years and the void was gut wrenching. I did fairly well until the choir sang *Silent Night* after Communion, and try as I did, I could not stop my tears as they sang "all is calm; all is bright". Our granddaughter noticed my tears even though I tried to hide them, and she just held my hand.

Christmas came and went, and to my amazement, Paul rallied enough to handle all the joyous grandchildren noise, gift giving, happy hour, dinner and song fest that followed. I knew he would be exhausted, and we would probably pay the price the next day, but the one thing he had insisted on in the hospital was that he had to be home for Christmas. And he made it!

Because he had been diagnosed with anemia, he was sent home from the hospital with a prescription for iron tablets which he had never taken before. After a couple of days, he became very sick with iron toxicity and began vomiting. I flew out of bed to see this disgusting, dark junk bubbling out of his mouth, and I admit that I panicked. In the dark, I didn't know what I was seeing. Was it blood? Was he dying…again? I turned on the light and could see that it was the color of the iron tablets. I called the hospice nurse who called the doctor, and together they decided he had to stop the iron pills. He vomited several times, the same black stuff and had several very bad black bowel movements. The hospice doctor said he really felt that his anemia was due to his body fighting chronic diseases, and that iron wouldn't help him anyway. That bottle of pills hit the garbage can immediately!

After twenty-four hours, he was doing better, but our little dog who missed nothing and picked up on every bit of tension and anxiety in the house, was not so fortunate. That night, she began vomiting, and by three thirty she was vomiting blood! I felt like I was caught in the middle of a terrifying nightmare. I knew I had to get her to the twenty-four hour emergency vet clinic, but I couldn't leave Paul alone in the house. Once again, I called our daughter and told her it wasn't a dad emergency this time but a dog crisis. I needed her husband to come over and be in the house so I could take the dog to the clinic. I put a blanket on the front seat since it was a very cold night, and off we went. This really was my worst nightmare; driving in the dark, it was snowing, I wasn't sure of the directions to get there, and I had a very sick dog. I prayed out loud the entire way, did make one wrong turn and figured out how to remedy the error and thanked God that there was absolutely no traffic at four in the morning since I made several illegal maneuvers. The clinic took her right away and suggested I leave her there, and they would call me before eleven o'clock with a diagnosis and treatment plan. They originally quoted me a fee of $1400. And I had to pay fifty percent before I left. Knowing I would receive 700 rewards points on my bank card, I whipped it out and paid.

I arrived home at six in the morning exhausted, worried that now I might lose our precious puppy and tried to lie down. I had not slept in two nights, but I had to prepare Paul for a cardiology follow-up appointment at nine thirty. The hospice nurse came to help me get him bathed, dressed and breakfasted while I tried to get myself together. It wasn't a pretty picture.

The visit to the doctor was uneventful for the most part. He agreed that the decision to not try to open the blocked vessels was the right one. If he had tried, the old grafts would probably have ruptured, causing a stroke and probable death! Was it any wonder the surgeon at the hospital didn't explain what could happen? I asked him what the odds were that Paul would have another heart attack, and he said that it was more than likely he would at some time, but then what he said next did me in. "You can't live like that. You have to stop worrying!" I burst into tears and cried, "I can't!" Really, I thought? Stop worrying? Did he really believe that was even remotely possible? He didn't remain in the room long after that and told Paul he'd see him again in three months. He was a wonderful cardiologist, but he had no clue how to deal with a crying woman!

We hurried home so as not to miss the call from the vet. They needed to conduct more blood tests, and she needed to stay another night. Now the bill was up to $2000.00. I told them that given her history of stress related illness, I felt this was all her reaction to the stress of the previous month. Their response was that most pet owners say that, but it's usually something else. Of course I told them to do whatever they needed to do. The final result was what I had said all along. There was nothing physically wrong with her. She was just a very nervous little dog who empathized with her mom and dad. She would recover when we both settled down, too. It seemed like 2016 not only started out badly with Paul's malfunctioning thyroid, but it also ended badly with an ailing heart. I was never so happy to say goodbye to a roller-coaster year.

CHAPTER 29

January, 2017: We rang in the New Year a few hours earlier than midnight since neither Paul nor I could stay up to watch the ball go down in New York. Mental and physical exhaustion has a way of changing perception of what's really important. Besides, it was already 2017 somewhere in the world! The first 2017 visit from our wonderful Hospice nurse, Tracy, occurred on January 2. I thought she looked more serious than usual. Tracy has a fabulous smile and hearty laugh that can fill an entire room, but she seemed more subdued this time. Eventually, she told me she wanted to talk to me about "where to go from here." I wasn't sure what she meant by this, but she tiptoed around her words to finally get to the point.

It seemed that Medicare was cracking down on coverage for Hospice services in cases like Paul's. Bottom line, she explained, was that if he were to have another heart attack, get treated in the hospital and return home like he did this time, Hospice could no longer bill Medicare for their services. Then she stumbled through the next part of her explanation. He has the dreaded DNR, the do not resuscitate code, and if he were to have a second heart attack, our choices would be to do nothing to help him survive, basically to let him die or, in the case of his surviving on his own, sign off on Hospice services and relinquish their support altogether. "This is the hardest part of my job," she said through tears.

There were a million thoughts racing through my head, and I wasn't sure I completely understood this. It seemed so crazy, so insane. My first thought was, how would I ever manage without the help of these wonderful people at Hospice? So I tried to put it in perspective. "In other words, what we have to hope for is that a second heart attack would kill him outright so we don't have to make the choice to save him or not?" Her response was thoughtful and sympathetic.

"Every time something like this happens, and it's not a question of if but rather when, it takes a big chunk out of you, a big chunk out of your family including the dog, and more importantly, a big chunk out of Paul, who is already physically fragile. A second heart attack on top of continued worsening of Parkinson's would be a lot for him to sustain and have any real quality to his life." Paul was listening to this conversation, and I knew he and I would have to talk about this after Tracy left. She did say that this was not an imminent threat, but that we should really talk about all this as a family, and she would be glad to sit in on that meeting to facilitate things. It was important that we all be on the same page if and when the time came to deal with it.

After she left, Paul and I did discuss it. I reminded him that in the hospital that first day he had said to me, "I don't think kickin' the bucket would be such a bad thing." I remember I looked at him in shock. "What did you say?" I replied almost incredulously. He just smiled and said he was only kidding. But I wasn't sure he was. Now, he swore he didn't remember saying that, but I told him that if he didn't remember that moment, more than likely, he had meant it when he said it. Then I asked him, "If in your heart, you think kickin' the bucket wouldn't be so bad, why am I trying so hard to care for you to keep you around?" At that moment I completely forgot that I had made a New Year's resolution to not give in to anger any longer! He didn't answer, but he agreed he would give serious thought to what Tracy had said.

After a few days, I mentioned this new Hospice information to our daughters. Julie tried hard to process it, and her voice cracked when she finally said, "Mom, do you think his body is just getting too tired to go on?" I had to agree that it was probably true. As I have said so often, a weaker man would have been dead long ago. But how long can his body keep up the good fight? Our daughter, Jennie, said she had thought about this a lot and wondered if it was just selfish on our parts to want to keep him going. How could it be our decision what kind of life or death he chose? Why should we dictate how his life should be despite the lack of quality it has? These were all answers that took me by surprise and which I felt were truly difficult but mature and heartfelt on their parts. I had yet to have this conversation with our son, and I was curious how he would respond. In most situations he is logical and a natural problem solver. He is decisive and quick to find solutions and tries hard to keep emotions out of the equation.

About the middle of the month, I was having a very tough time getting Paul up in the morning. By now, he was 186 pounds of dead weight, and even with the hospital bed which allowed me to sit him up, I still had to bring his legs over the side of the bed. He had absolutely no core strength to keep himself sitting upright. I had to try to get him to scoot himself forward enough so that his feet touched the floor and then hold on to the handles of the walker. A wet wash cloth in the face helped him wake up enough to open his eyes for a few seconds to get oriented to his surroundings. All this was difficult, but the hardest part on me physically was yet to begin! At this point I had to try to get him on his feet without falling backwards on the bed, swivel him around and then back him up to the bedside commode. If all went well to this point, then I had to keep him up with one arm and take down his briefs, which were usually heavily soaked with urine, with the other arm. Then he had to ease down to the commode seat. By the time all this was accomplished, my arms, shoulders and low back were screaming with pain. The massage therapist would try to work out the knots in my body, but then I would come right back home and undo all the good she had accomplished. Something had to change.

One Monday morning, I lamented about this to the Hospice nurse and even asked her to come back to the bedroom so I could pretend to be Paul, and she could pretend to be me and show me a better way to get this morning chore done less painfully. She agreed that, even with the hospital bed, it was too difficult, and that I had been doing everything I could do, but that something definitely needed to change to spare my sore body parts! That afternoon a huge piece of medical equipment was delivered to the house. It took both the deliveryman and me to get it up the steps. It was called a sit/lift, and my heart sank when I saw it. For one thing, it was ugly, plus it was heavy and cumbersome, and moreover, it took up so much room in the bedroom I didn't know where to put it. He gave me a quick ten minute in-service on how to use it, and I admit I was very intimidated. I still had to get Paul sitting up with his legs over the side of the bed, and then I had to wrap this large, security belt around his waist, latch it closed, attach straps from the belt to the handlebars of the machine, push the "up" button on a remote control which would slowly lift him from a sitting position to a standing one. His feet were on a plate which added his 186 pounds to the weight of the machine, and then I had to maneuver the entire contraption around to back him up to the commode where I would then push the "down" button until his derriere was on the commode. The first day it really was a comedy of errors, and I was truly glad that no one had seen it. I had gotten him successfully seated on the commode but then realized I had forgotten to take down his briefs! I had to raise him back up, remove his underwear and sit him back down. Then I had to remove the heavy security belt, pull the contraption around to the other side of the bed to make room for his walker and return his walker to the front of the commode. By the time I got all this finished that first day, I was sweating profusely and nearly in tears from the effort. Was this really going to make my life easier and less painful? On the second morning, I remembered to remove his briefs but didn't have the urinal close by before he urinated all over the floor just seconds before getting situated on the commode. I was in tears. At that moment, I didn't see this as a solution to anything. By day three, I managed to get a pattern figured out that was more efficient, and although still labor intensive, my shoulders stopped burning! I was really starting the day getting my cardio!

January ended on a bad note. The cardiologist had ordered an ultrasound scan of Paul's carotid arteries, a test he had done once before just one year prior. I didn't even remember what the results of that test had been, or if anyone even told us so they must not have been noteworthy. But now, especially after having had a heart attack, Paul needed it repeated. Paul and I are so different. He went in to the test expecting nothing bad; I had just the opposite fear. Normally, I am not a pessimist, but so much had happened over these last few years, I could only imagine the worst. And as I had feared, the left side showed a seventy percent blockage. When the doctor called with these results, I was heart sick once again. If Paul were stronger and in better health generally, he could have tried a stent to unlock the artery but now, that could cause a stroke or worse. It was the same risk as we had heard in the hospital regarding an angioplasty to reopen the two blocked graphs. All we could do was continue with the blood thinners and hope for the best. I felt like he was a walking time bomb, the "big one" waiting to happen. It was just one more thing to be worried about. Paul was actually surprised to hear these results, and I couldn't help but think that he really was in denial most of the time. But he admitted to me when we went to bed that he was scared. I told him that I was scared, too, but that I would do everything I could to keep him around as long as possible, but that he had to meet me half way. And when he asked me for ice cream every night and I said no, he had to quit pouting!

The following day, I felt a kind of quiet peace, a kind of resignation to God's will. I knew that I had done and was doing everything anyone could do and probably more, and that each day would now be a gift to enjoy together. It was time I would need to relish. I continued to pray that the "till death do us part" scenario would be kept at bay a while longer. I felt my anger melting away, replaced with a better attitude about my all-consuming care giving job. I didn't expect everything to be happy and rosy; I knew there would be days when this quiet, positive attitude would probably fall by the wayside, but at least it was a start. So maybe January ended on a not-so-bad note after all.

CHAPTER 30

February, 2017: Winter has always been my least favorite time of year for so many reasons, not the least of which is that I detest cold weather. If I had the choice, I would never drive in snowy or icy conditions, and I have always avoided that stressor at all times when possible. Lastly, it is typically flu season, not to mention all the other nasty germs that invade our bodies when we are exposed to so many potentially sick people indoors. For that reason, I have always been vigilant about protecting Paul and his fragile immune system from any conditions that would expose him to these winter culprits. For several years, I had made the decision to forego Mass on Sunday from the beginning of flu season to the end just because of the crowded conditions in the church, the need to shake hands with those around us in the pew during the "Sign of Peace" and the taking of the communion host from a distributer's hands. I figured God would understand my logic, and for the first couple of years, Paul remained healthy, from a microbial point of view at least, because of my efforts. I even made it a priority to tell our children to keep any less than healthy grandchildren away from us.

January came and went with no illness, and I felt good about our renewed efforts to keep it that way. But during the first week of February, our good luck ran out. I awoke at three thirty in the morning to an odd sound that sounded like squirting of some kind. I got up to check and discovered Paul projectile vomiting all over the bed. It was everywhere on the bedclothes and on his pajamas. He was barely awake through this nightmare, and I was grateful that the head of his hospital bed was slightly elevated or else he would have choked on the vomit. I was in a momentary panic since I couldn't even move him and his 185 pounds of dead weight, and within seconds I knew I needed help. Fifteen minutes later I called Hospice to ask the nurse on night duty to please come as soon as possible. She didn't arrive till another ninety minutes had gone by, and by that time I had been successful in removing his pajama top and the top sheet and blanket, but He was still lying in all the vomit that had fallen to the bottom sheet. And to add insult to injury, I could feel that his bedding was soaked with urine despite the many layers of protection he wears each night.

When she arrived, she looked for a moment like she didn't know how we were going to get the bedding off underneath him. But together, we rolled him to the side so I could pull the soiled sheet, protective padding and urine soaked paper chucks out from under him. Then we rolled him to the other side and repeated the procedure. We raised the bed up more and he promptly vomited again. After cleaning him up again, she asked, "Where do you want me to put him?" "There's only one place to put him, and that is on the commode," I answered. We had to get him off the bed so I could remake it, and the only way to do that was to use the new "sit/ lift" equipment to raise him up, turn him and lower him onto the commode like I do every morning. Because he was so sick and out of it, it took both of us to get this accomplished. She was on one side of the bed and pulled him over to get his legs over the side and his feet on the floor; I was on the other side of the bed pushing him forward from behind. I still had to get the big belt around him, so with my head pushed into his back, bracing him up, I got the belt fastened. Then she said, "I don't know how you do this by yourself every morning!" But she didn't realize the hardest part was still to come. After he was hoisted up to a standing position, I told her to turn him around and back him on to the commode. She tried to move the contraption with him standing on it, and she couldn't budge it. She looked at me incredulously as I told her to step aside and showed her how it was done!

While he sat on the commode, she gave him a sponge bath while I remade the bed, making sure I added many layers of protection. Then she phoned in a prescription for an anti-nausea medication, and she even drove to the pharmacy and picked it up. I was very, very grateful. She phoned Mary, the Hospice nurse aid who was scheduled to come at 8:30 for the usual shower morning, and told her what had happened. She stayed with me until Mary arrived. I thanked her profusely for her help. Mary came laden with more briefs, wipes, liner pads and protective bedding pads. I told her I couldn't imagine where Paul picked up this intestinal germ since he hadn't been around anyone who had been sick. She told me that she may have carried it when she was here a few days earlier since she had been around sick children right before then. I realized at that moment, there was only so much I could do to keep him and me safe.

He slept until one o'clock in the afternoon and never threw up again, and I was most grateful for the anti-nausea drug. It was a short lived episode, but it was evident that even something like a simple stomach virus was not ever going to be simple for me again. I don't know what I would have done without Hospice help! I was terrified that I would get the germ since I had handled all the soiled clothing, and I was afraid that I wouldn't be able to do all that is necessary on any given day to care for him if I got sick. So I promptly had a serious talk with God. I said, "God, You told me in a dream decades ago that You would always be with me. Please be with me now and don't let me get sick. You know all that I have to do, so if You want me to do it, don't let me down now!" I was so sure my chances of getting sick were high despite my heartfelt prayer, so I barely ate anything for several days to keep my stomach as empty as I could just in case. And God took care of me. After four days of continued good health, I really felt like I had dodged a bullet.

A few evenings later as we were watching TV, he looked over at the couch with a confused look on his face. I asked him what he was looking at. His response made my heart sink. "We're missing a person."

"Who are we missing?" I asked, almost afraid to hear his answer.

"We're missing one of the Deanna's." Oh, I thought, not this again!

"How many Deanna's are there?" I continued.

"Three," he said.

"Really? Who are they?" I asked.

"One is very sure of herself; one is quiet." And he stopped.

"And the third one? Who is the third one?"

"Kind of a combination of the other two."

I looked at him and explained that I was the only Deanna who lived here, and that at times I am all three of those people. But there really is only one of me. Then I put him to bed.

A few days later, I had an appointment to get my hair highlighted again. I returned home a bit more blond than usual after these appointments. When Paul saw me, he didn't say anything, and I thought, "Oh no. I bet he thinks there's a fourth Deanna living here now!"

Valentine's Day, 2017: As I wrote in chapter one, this day has always felt like an anniversary for me personally since it was fifty-four years ago today that I made the mental commitment to choose Paul for my life partner. For most of those years, Paul brought me flowers which I always loved receiving. But for the last few years as his health and independence had declined and made it impossible for him to do this any longer, it was a tradition that, sadly, went by the wayside. This year it felt different since only two months prior, I hadn't been sure he would be alive on Valentine's Day. His heart attack in December really rocked my being and put so many things into perspective. I decided that maybe it was my turn this Valentine's Day to buy him a bouquet of flowers. I found a beautiful red and white bouquet with a glittery red heart pick, a heart-shaped chocolate cake and a funny card, and I presented them to my forever valentine on the thirteenth with an explanation of why I was doing this. I wanted to tell him early because for the previous few years, he had sweetly asked our daughter to buy him a card so he would have something to give me. I needed this year to let him know that I didn't feel the need to get a card "To my wife" that our daughter picked out. Also, I didn't want him to feel bad on the fourteenth when he didn't have a card or flowers for me. He seemed pleased when I explained that now it was my turn. It was a special Valentine's Day.

CHAPTER 31

March, 2017: February came and went with no drama other than the fact that Paul began to have the loose, productive cough that had plagued him off and on for a long time. I, of course, began thinking the worst. Was this the beginning of another congestive heart failure episode? In a panic I asked Tracy to come and check him out. I have no idea what I would do without the attention of these Hospice nurses. She listened to his heart, his lungs, took his temperature, blood pressure and checked his feet and legs for swelling. She neither saw nor heard anything that alarmed her and felt he had a virus that had been lurking in his body off and on for a while. She told him to take a Z-pack for five days and see if it helped, which it did. But more importantly for my mental health, she explained something I really needed to hear. She told me that congestive heart failure doesn't start in the lungs. It starts with swollen feet; then it moves up the legs and up the rest of the body, and finally when it has nowhere else to go, it fills up the lungs. Of course, this made sense to me now. Paul's feet and legs had been swollen for such a long time prior to his heart attack. Coughing was not the alarm sign; swollen feet and legs were. This came as such a welcome relief, I nearly felt too weak to stand up. At least now I had a better understanding of what to look for, when to push the panic button and when not to. My daily gauge for that was how easy or hard it was to get his slippers on in the morning.

March came in like a roaring lion with terrible storms. Being very gun shy of wind storms after living through a tornado in Kettering in 1969, the prediction of what was headed our way prompted me to ready a space in our lower level with supplies in case of a disaster. I took two days to prepare the downstairs bathroom, the innermost safe room in the house, with extra clothing, first aid kit, bottled water and energy bars, extra dog food, and the jewelry that was the most expensive or which had sentimental value. I had a second list of things to grab at the last minute: Paul's meds, dog leash, my purse etc. I was ready for anything. Ready until I realized that if the tornado sirens went off during the night, I wouldn't even be able to wake Paul up. Even if I could, he probably wouldn't be able to walk to the stair lift. What good was the room if we couldn't get to it? I didn't get much sleep that night since the predictions were for three different storm lines to come through during the wee hours. As predicted, the first wave hit at two in the morning with torrential rain, thunder and lightning; the second at four o'clock, but it was the third wave that hit at six o'clock that knocked the power out with high winds that were so loud I could hear them even with my earplugs in. That's when I panicked and naturally, Paul slept through the entire thing. I prayed that the tornado sirens wouldn't go off, and they didn't. I was literally in the fetal position under the covers with the dog curled up next to me and praying. Ninety minutes later the power came back on but the wind was still threatening. What I didn't know then was that a funnel cloud had set down just one block away from our house with much damage to homes and taking down enormous trees for an entire square mile. The sirens had not gone off to warn anyone! God was with us again.

A few weeks later, Paul had invited two of his friends and former colleagues to come for a visit and have lunch. They stopped at a local restaurant and brought lunch with them for a treat. They said that if I wanted to use the time to go out and run any errands, they would be fine. Ordinarily, I would jump at the opportunity to get out for a while, but I was not comfortable with them being responsible for Paul's care especially when food was involved. So I politely declined, said I'd join them for a cup of coffee and then go downstairs to my office if they needed anything. We had just about begun to eat when Paul started making the throat noise that tells me he has food stuck in his esophagus, a sound I had come to detest. The guys looked terrified, and I said, "Now you know why I don't like to leave him during a meal." The thought of this happening when I wasn't there was terrifying. They would not have known what to do for Paul. I tried to help him clear the stuck food for nearly fifteen minutes, but it was evident he needed to go to the hospital and have another endoscopy. I was so upset, first of all for Paul that his reunion with his friends was such a disaster, but also for them to have to witness this very disgusting problem. Talk about losing your appetite! It's not a pretty picture! But I was also angry that Paul wasn't more careful while he was eating. It was a big piece of ham from his sandwich that was stuck. All I could think was *Why didn't you chew it? Why can't you be more careful?*

I kept apologizing to Paul's friends as we made our way to our respective cars. They reassured us they would reschedule. We got to the hospital, and there was only one place to park which was a tight squeeze. There was no room to put a wheelchair by the door so getting him out of the car was a real chore, but somehow we finally did it. By two o'clock he was in a room, hooked up to the IV, blood taken and chest X-ray done. I asked them who the GI doctor on call was, and when they told me, I broke down and cried. As luck would have it, the same doctor who had let him suffer for five hours a year ago until he finished watching the Super Bowl playoffs was on call! The nurse kept telling me to calm down, and when I explained why this was such upsetting news, I said, "Tell that doctor we will not jump through all the hoops he made us jump through the last time. We need the endoscopy immediately. My husband had a heart attack in December, and I will not let him experience that kind of physical distress again." I guess they listened because the doctor arrived thirty minutes later and got the job done. When he walked in the room, I am quite sure he remembered us because his behavior last time resulted in him being written up by the hospital staff as unacceptable. With sarcasm dripping from his mouth he asked, "Well, what did we eat this time?" I told him and left the room as quickly as I could. It was all I could do to hold my tongue. I went home to let the dog out, and when I returned twenty minutes later, the procedure was already finished, and the doctor was nowhere to be found. At least I didn't have to see him or talk to him again.

It seemed like every time Paul had to undergo anesthesia now, it took him longer and longer to rebound. The procedure was done at three o'clock but we didn't get home until six. He slept from eight to nine o'clock in the TV room, and I put him to bed then. The clocks sprung ahead that night so it was really like ten o'clock and he slept through until eight the next morning. I had a terrible time waking him to give him his morning medications, and he was still so out of it, I had to feed him both his breakfast and his lunch. Twenty-four hours after his anesthesia, he finally came back to life and could feed himself his dinner.

I also knew that I needed to follow up with his doctor because he would be scheduling another procedure in the near future to stretch the esophagus again. I had many questions to pose when this happened. Since this swallow problem is not unusual with Parkinson's patients, is this stretching procedure something to do only after an incident like he had just had? Is this something we should do annually as a preventative? How did the esophagus look this time after a year since the last procedure? How dangerous is it to repeat this stretching so many times? Is there a risk now that he is taking two blood thinners? The questions just kept on invading my mind, usually in the middle of the night. Somehow, when that happened, there was no turning off the spinning wheels!

The stretching procedure was scheduled for two weeks following the ER visit. I answered all the questions asked, and then I asked about the two blood thinners he was taking. The secretary said that those two were okay. I was honestly nervous every time Paul ate anything, and my meal preparations during those fourteen days were a real challenge. For example, his ham and cheese sandwiches at lunch were transformed into open-face diced ham covered with ultra-thin Swiss cheese on very thin white bread and broiled till the cheese melted. Then it was cut into small squares. He ate lots of yogurt, pudding, mashed banana, Jello, mashed potatoes, meat cut into tiny pieces smothered in gravy, diced sausage, pancakes and syrup cut into tiny pieces, goetta, spaghetti with the pasta cut into small pieces. I couldn't wait for the two weeks to be over so he could get the procedure done and eat more normally.

We arrived at the medical center at ten o'clock, checked in and waited to be called back for preparation. He hadn't been able to eat or drink anything beforehand, and he was really hungry. I had given him the most important medications with some water, but that was all. We finally went back to the preparation area where he was given the IV which took a second nurse to accomplish. His veins were not cooperating that morning. After an hour, he wheeled into the OR, and I gave him a kiss for good luck. I returned to the waiting room where, five minutes later, a surgical nurse came out and asked when was the last time he had taken the two blood thinners? I said, "The aspirin was yesterday afternoon and the Plavix this morning." She looked at me like I was an idiot and asked, "Didn't anyone tell you not to give him those for a week before the procedure?" "What?" I said. "They told me those were okay to continue." She said she would have to tell the doctor because those were definitely not okay, and he might not be able to have the procedure done. I was furious to say the least. A few moments later the doctor emerged to talk to me. I looked at him and just said, "Really?!" His response was, "Yes, really!" He apologized for the mistake the secretary had made on the phone. "But," I said, "he had the endoscopy in the ER, and he was on the blood thinners then with no problem." He said the problem was that just doing an endoscopy would have been safe enough, but doing the stretching could cause a bleed. Then I further explained that the forms his office had sent me mentioned other drugs that weren't safe, but that the two Paul took were not on the list, further indicating no reason to stop them. Then he said that the secretary must have sent me the wrong procedure form. He indicated he could still do the procedure that day, but there would be risks, and he felt with Paul's fragile health, he had to be more careful. I could not believe this frustrating setback. "How long will it take to get the drugs out of his system so you can do the procedure?" I asked.

"About five days," his said. "But," he continued looking dismayed, "I will be in Florida on vacation then, and someone else from my practice will need to do it." He could tell how disappointed I was, and he assured me he would choose the doctor he felt would take the best care of Paul. I could do nothing but trust him. When he left, I said, "Doctor, have a good time in Florida." He just smiled and walked away.

The stretching procedure was rescheduled for the following week, giving Paul six days to discontinue the blood thinners. The receptionist looked surprised to see us again so soon. She asked, "Weren't you just here last week?" The same reaction came from the prep nurses before the procedure. One did remember the circumstances from the last time and she said, "Well, let's get it done this time!" Paul asked her about the physician who was going to do the deed. She reassured him that he was very good and had done hundreds of these procedures.

All went well. The doctor talked to me afterwards and told me he stretched the esophagus as wide as he could, and all should be okay. He seemed to wake up more quickly this time, and we were home only three hours after we had left. Not too bad. One more fun day at the hospital finished!

CHAPTER 32

April, 2017: My Catholic faith has always been an important part of my life. In fact when Paul and I were dating, it was his attitude regarding his Catholicism that continued to draw me to him. We were on the same wave length when it came to spiritual issues in our lives. We could discuss it openly. Before I had met him, he had spent five years in the seminary at Notre Dame, giving him an entirely different perspective on Catholicism than mine, but nonetheless, we were both committed to our faith. That's not to say that there weren't periods in his life when the fervor waned, and there were periods in my life when I didn't feel as close to God as I had wished, but those times inevitably passed, and our faith always drew us back in.

Lent has always been an important time for me, a time for reflecting on self-improvement, spiritual reading, and extra attendance at Mass during the week. Paul's fragile health had a way of disrupting this aspect of my life, adding just one more way my life had changed. Before the time that Paul couldn't be left alone in the house, I had spent an hour every week in the Adoration Chapel at our church, praying, meditating and writing out my petitions in the presence of the Blessed Sacrament. But I had to give that up when he couldn't be left alone. The last few years, we had stopped attending Mass during the winter flu season because of his compromised immune system; plus he couldn't get the flu shot because of his egg allergy, and I was afraid to expose him to large crowds. We managed to arrange for someone from the parish to bring us Holy Communion every Sunday to at least feel some spiritual nourishment. We tried to always attend the Lenten Taize service at church because very few people took advantage of this very inspiring prayer service, and we could sit far away from everyone in a candle lit church, chanting those wonderful, short, mesmerizing prayers that provided a meditative environment. But as the six weeks of Lent got us closer and closer to Easter, I found the lack of attendance at Mass for such a long time to be upsetting. I just felt such a distance from God, an estrangement from my faith that left me uncomfortable…and it made me angry. I knew in my heart that God understood my absence from parish attendance, and I was quite sure He knew everything that was in my heart. The fact was that I almost felt like my entire life of caregiving had become one, long, continuous Lent, one never ending period of sacrificing everything that we used to be able to do together…and it made me angry. And it scared me, too.

Good Friday was a day I had never missed going to church. As a child, my mother took my sister and me to church for three hours, from noon to three o'clock, the hours that Christ hung on the cross. It was a way of life for us as a family. That practice continued into my adult life although the Church no longer spent three hours for the service. But still Good Friday was an important day. Even that changed on Good Friday, 2017, when Paul had a neurology appointment scheduled for the exact time when we would have been at church…and it made me angry. Even going to Mass on Easter was going to be a problem since there is no Saturday early evening Mass, nor is there a Sunday evening Mass on Easter. Our choices were Sunday morning at nine thirty, too early to get Paul up and moving, and eleven thirty. We couldn't do that either since the only way we could get the family together for Easter was during lunch time. Paul had missed Christmas Mass because he had just gotten home from the hospital after his heart attack, and now we were both going to miss attending Mass on Easter Sunday…and it made me angry.

Easter came and went, family having been all together for the traditional egg hunt and lunch. Having all of them around always recharges my batteries, and for a couple of hours, I found myself laughing and enjoying life again. But Paul wasn't laughing, wasn't talking, and wasn't keeping his eyes open…nothing. In fact the entire weekend he had been like that, and by Sunday night, he began having the familiar wheezing and shallow breathing. It occurred to me that with the temperatures outside so wonderful, I had opened all the windows. But my not having any seasonal allergies, I wasn't aware that the air quality and pollen count were off the charts. By Monday, nothing had changed; in fact, I thought his breathing was worse, and he requested his inhaler several times. I remembered that Tracy reminded me that congestive heart failure starts in the feet and moves up, not in the lungs. I kept checking his feet for swelling, and they were no worse than usual. I decided to close all the windows and see if that helped.

Tracy and I had a heart to heart talk that Monday, and I broke down in tears as I admitted how afraid I was again. I was exhausted from fear. She tried to reassure me that she was there for me no matter what, but then she added, "It is going to get worse. I will bring you some books to read. They're not fun reading. But they will help you manipulate through the final journey of Paul's life." I was stunned to hear her talk like this and she quickly added, "He's not there yet, but you should read these to know how to recognize the signs." I think I cried off and on the rest of the day. By bedtime, just walking slowly from the family room to the bedroom was enough exertion to send Paul into an asthma response. I was alarmed, of course and felt like this was going to be a reenactment of the crisis in December. I gave him his inhaler and put him to bed. It took a while for his breathing to calm down and he went to sleep. I didn't!

All night I listened to his breathing. Was it too fast? Was it too shallow? Then the deep, productive cough started up. I got up and looked at him multiple times and finally by five o'clock I got up and got dressed just in case I would have to call 911 and go to the hospital again. By six o'clock I called the nurse aide who was going to come for Paul's shower later and asked her to bring a nurse with her to check on Paul. I was just too afraid to trust myself and make the wrong decisions again that I had made in December. I kept replaying the final advice the cardiologist at the hospital had given me as we were checking out. "If any of the symptoms come back, get him back here right away. Don't treat him for asthma!" And in the next moments, I remembered what Paul's own cardiologist had said a week later. "You have to stop worrying!" At some point after that doctor visit, I had found some inner peace. I knew I had done everything I could do for him, and there were no medical procedures for his heart that were safe enough to do. Now it was in God's hands, and I just had to go along for the ride. But somewhere between New Year's Day and

Easter Sunday, that inner peace had disappeared, and I was back to living in terror. And I hated it!

By nine o'clock the nurse aide and the RN arrived and checked him out. All his vital signs were good; he just couldn't walk without the wheezing and labored breathing. They decided after giving him some allergy medicine that he needed the breathing treatment of the nebulizer. That seemed to help enormously, and he responded much better. I had planned to spend the day outside gardening with him on the patio, but they quickly squelched that plan and told me to keep him indoors for the day since the air quality was so bad. I even brought the transport wheelchair in the house so he didn't have to walk from the family room to the bedroom. So on this perfectly gorgeous spring day, instead of enjoying the sunshine and the garden, I stayed in, watched him and washed windows! I wondered how I was ever going to get the yard work done if I couldn't bring him outside to keep an eye on him while I dug in the dirt. And I hated it!

He received two more breathing treatments and had a much better night, and so did I. The following morning, dear sweet nurse, Tracy, came back to check on him. I had noticed that his feet were more swollen than they usually are first thing in the morning, and she agreed they were more swollen than when she had seen him two days previously. She took his vital signs and noted that his oxygen saturation was also lower than it had been. She called the doctor to see what he thought we should do. He said it was not necessary to go to the hospital because all they would do was a breathing treatment and an IV of Lasix for the fluid buildup. We could do the same breathing treatment at home, increase his Lasix for a couple of days, and then he prescribed a steroid for five days for the asthma. It seemed like a doable plan, and I felt better. After she gave him the breathing treatment, she listened to his lungs again and said they were so much better. We didn't need the wheelchair to go to the family room, and he walked out without so much as a tiny wheeze. The doctor was scheduled to visit Paul the following day.

The doctor visit was fairly unexciting. We learned nothing new, but he did say he was not concerned that this was a heart issue. If Paul were to go to the hospital the only difference would be that the Lasix would be given IV. He told us that he really didn't hear any fluid crackling in the lungs except for a very tiny amount way at the bottom of his lungs and the asthma wheezing really was very minimal. Of course, Paul was just sitting there and not walking around. He said to continue the plan we had begun, and Tracy would reevaluate him on Monday.

When he left, I had a moment of panic. It was Thursday afternoon at two o'clock, and there would be no further professional assessment until the following Monday. I was going to be on my own again for three and a half days, and I was terrified to be alone for the long weekend. Every time Paul got up to walk somewhere, I prayed that there would be no asthma attack. And I hated it!

I texted Tracy and told her how I felt. Her response was most heartfelt. "Call me if you need me; I think the meds and time will help...you can do this; you are not alone I promise!" She was right; the weekend went without incident, and in fact Paul didn't need a breathing treatment all weekend. He finished his steroid on Sunday, and Tracy was due to come back Monday. I couldn't wait to see what she thought the next step would be.

She did notice that his breathing was better and the lower lung crackling the doctor had heard was gone. I told her he was really putting out the urine. The Doctor suggested he back off the eighty mg of diuretic to sixty and wanted to keep him on that dose forever. He also prescribed a new inhaler to be used daily as a preventative. Of course the big test was still to come; he hadn't been outside for over a week, and the pollen counts were still off the charts. I was praying that the month of April would end better than it had begun.

The first test of the battle between Paul's bronchial tubes and Mother Nature came on April 29 and 30. It was a busy weekend with the last ballet of the season on Saturday, and all went well. Of course he was only outside from the parking garage to the theater. Sunday was another test, not so much for pollen and asthma but for stamina. We managed to return to Mass for the first time since late fall and the beginning of flu season. The church was decorated for the Easter season with flowers everywhere; it was truly beautiful and so good to be back again. We made a quick stop at Arby's next door after Mass to grab a small lunch to eat in the car before going to our granddaughter's high school spring musical where she played violin in the orchestra pit. The play lasted much longer than we had anticipated, and we didn't get home until five o'clock. I was concerned that he wouldn't be able to last this long; six hours in the wheelchair/car was a first. But other than having a sore derriere, he was fine. He went right to bed for a late nap when we got home, but he was still wiped out for the remainder of the evening. I wondered then what the following day would be like since a busy weekend inevitably had repercussions on Monday. But at least we ended the month of May on a good note.

CHAPTER 33

May, 2017: The Monday after our very busy weekend played out as I had anticipated. It would be twenty-four hours before Paul had any energy at all. Monday mornings were when Tracy arrived, and I was always very glad to see her so she can check out my guy! She agreed he seemed tired, but his vital signs were all good except his oxygen saturation was just a wee bit lower at ninety-five percent. This did not cause her to be concerned, however. His feet were very swollen, and the swelling had begun to inch up his ankles, the warning sign I worried about. But she heard nothing in his lungs to indicate a repeat of congestive heart failure and just attributed it to the very long hours he had been sitting the day before. He remained in the recliner quite a bit that day with his feet elevated, and the swelling did go down. I talked with her privately for a while once again stating my concerns about his overall health. I told her I had read the books she had sent about "end of life" issues, and that I found it reassuring that one of the first signs is loss of appetite. No one had a better appetite than my husband. Eating had become the three high points of his day! But I also told her I was well aware that it's not usually Parkinson's that kills the patient. And in Paul's case I felt quite sure that his heart would be what would do him in, and that could be quite sudden. So honestly, the loss of appetite would probably be an irrelevant warning sign. She agreed.

Meanwhile, our fiftieth wedding anniversary was just five weeks away, and our kids were beginning the preparations for a celebration. As Julie worked on the e-invite, I found myself getting more and more excited. She put a color photo of the two of us dancing at our wedding reception in the invitation, and when I saw it, I immediately remembered the exact moment when it was taken. How we had both changed in fifty years! So young, thin, looking at life through rose-colored glasses, I remembered how much in love I was with this red haired, leprechaun-like young guy, and how safe I had felt in his arms, our whole life ahead of us. We both looked so care free, so oblivious to all the high points and low points of our future together. I couldn't stop looking at that photo, lost in memories. I couldn't help but think, *"ignorance truly was bliss"* and that *"all we really heard in the wedding vows were for better, for richer, and in health."* I thought about my parents' fiftieth celebration, both of them so full of life, surrounded by life-long friends and family dancing the night away, and of my sister and brother-in-law's fiftieth just a few years before ours, again at a reception crowded with family, old and new friends, music and dancing. Ours wouldn't be quite like that. I wasn't sure what it would be like.

I finally made the decision to have a simple Open House at our home after the Mass so that his bigger, more comfortable wheel chair and the stair lift would be available, and all his bathroom needs would pose no problem as they would somewhere else. Once I had made that decision, I began to relax about the whole affair! The invitations were emailed out, and within a few days, RSVP's were coming in. Maybe there wouldn't be dancing, but there would be family, there would be friends and nothing else mattered.

Somewhere packed away in a box in the garage was a collection of old audio cassettes. I knew among them was the tape recording of our entire wedding Mass that my dad had arranged to do. After I found it, I was almost afraid to play it for fear that a fifty year old tape might break. But I held my breath and inserted it into the cassette player.

Our Mass had been a con-celebrated High Mass, one of the first to be said in English after Vatican II did away with the Latin Mass. Our celebrants were Paul's Jesuit uncle, Father Mark, and Father Adolph, the Franciscan priest who had married my parents, my sister and brother-in-law, and who had been a surrogate grandfather to my sister and me. Father Adolph did the actual wedding vows, and his voice still sounded deep and strong on the fifty year old tape. The words he spoke to us before the actual vows moved me to tears as I heard them again. He spoke of the importance of what we were about to undertake, about the hopes for the blessings of children, grandchildren and good friends to share our life together. I got goosebumps listening to his message all these years later, realizing that despite the hardships we had been facing over the past decade, we had enjoyed all the blessings of children and grandchildren and the friends he had spoken of, and the ones who still loved us would be there with us to celebrate. I decided at that moment to play that part of the tape at our party and to toast the moment when these words had first been spoken. My excitement was building after speaking on the phone with the priest at the church where we were married. He asked many questions to give him a better understanding of us as a couple. He explained that he would welcome us at the beginning of Mass, include us in the Offertory Petitions and give us a special blessing at the end of Mass. It started to feel very real.

CHAPTER 34

June, 2017: The big day was fast approaching and the closer it got, the more my stress level rose. Our three children had been planning a big party back here at our house after the Mass. I requested it be here instead of at one of their homes since all the bathroom needs, handicap needs for Paul were here, and it would just be easier. But despite the fact that all I had to do was get Paul and me ready, get to the church on time and come back to our party where all the work would be done by our children, my stress kept getting the better of me. For three weeks before the big day, I began to experience the very familiar irritable bowel, stomach pain and diarrhea that have plagued me for as long as I can remember. I couldn't keep food in, couldn't get a good night sleep, and I was losing weight every day. And since losing weight has never been easy for me even when I was trying, I was getting concerned. Needless to say, I was more than concerned, I was scared. For the first time, my fears of whether Paul would make it to June tenth took a back seat to whether or not I would make it! I kept telling myself if things didn't get better after the party, I would go to the doctor.

June 10, was a gorgeous day just as it had been fifty years ago. The nurse aide from Hospice came to help me with Paul's shower and get him ready while I got my hair done. We left in plenty of time to arrive a half hour before Mass started at the church. The priest came out to meet us and to congratulate us. He wanted to make sure he had all the details about us correctly memorized. I gave him a copy of my latest book, <u>Saints Alive, Annie's Very Own Miracle,</u> since much of the story took place in this very church. One by one, our family began to fill in the three pews he had reserved for us. I had told him I didn't think we would need that many, but I was wrong. Soon, our friends who had been invited to the party showed up at the church as well, surprising both of us. I began to relax and feel better physically. I kept remembering so many things about the years I had spent at this church and school when I was growing up; it was memory overload, and I truly felt that I was home.

The priest personalized the Mass for us in a most special way, informed the congregation why we were there, blessed us, and at the end of Mass, before dismissing the congregation, told them a little bit about Paul and me. He even plugged my book and promised to order a few copies for the school! The entire congregation applauded us, and it was very emotional and Paul looked so happy.

We got back to the house after our kids had opened up and were there to greet early guests. It couldn't have been a more perfect celebration. I did play the tape of our vows, and it was another emotional moment when Paul tried to stand up without help to kiss me. His friend, Pete, helped him up, and there were wet eyes in the room when we embraced. He managed the evening well but had to go to bed before the kids had finished the clean-up, and he needed two days to fully recuperate. I knew that would be the case. I, on the other hand, was feeling much better for those two days, my stomach pain disappearing completely.

Unfortunately, it didn't last, and just when I thought I wouldn't need to call the doctor, all the symptoms returned. There was just no rhyme or reason for it that I could pinpoint, and my fears returned. I managed to get an appointment with a physician assistant right away who referred me to a gastroenterologist for further testing.

The doctor who scoped Paul all the time when he gets food stuck in his esophagus walked into the examining room. "Surprise," I said; "It's me this time." Then he asked me the usual opening questions as to what brought me in to see him. I described my last four weeks' worth of symptoms, my family history and anything I could to help him get this over with quickly. Then he said, "I see this with caregivers all the time. All your energy goes into the job, and you don't care for yourself. So I know you must be feeling pretty bad if you actually showed up here!" Wow! He really nailed it, and I had a tough time holding back the tears, another symptom that was getting more and more frequent. He ordered blood work and said he thought I should have both upper and lower GI scoped and get some answers and fix the problem once and for all instead of trying to self-diagnose. Of course, I knew all along this was coming, and I just dreaded it. The blood work came back showing nothing of concern, and the surgical procedures were scheduled. The problem was that since I would be anesthetized, someone had to be with me that day and drive me to and from the hospital. I had always been that person for Paul, but who was going to be able to help me? I also needed for someone to be with Paul while I was gone. Bonnie could only help me on Monday afternoons, and as luck would have it, the doctor scheduled these procedures on Monday afternoons! Okay, God, so far so good. Now I just needed help for me. This was not as easy as I thought it would be. Julie had said all along that she would take care of me, but the date the doctor chose conflicted with family travel for her. Jennie and Jamie would not be able to take off work to do it so I had no choice but to change the date of July twenty-fourth. This was a terribly low moment for me. If ever I missed my mom, it was at that moment. With all my heart I wanted her back to take care of me again. How pathetic was that?

The procedure was all set for July 31, and I had all my bases covered. I really was feeling much better; almost a week went by with no symptoms at all, and I began wondering if all this was much ado about nothing. But then when Tracy came for her weekly visit on June twenty-sixth, I asked her about a few things that concerned me. I had noticed over the weekend that Paul's feet were more swollen and his ankles, too. Oh no! I thought. Is the swelling moving up again? So I mentioned this to her, and she agreed they were more so than the previous week. Then I made the mistake of saying, "This congestive heart failure is going to get worse, isn't it?" She nodded yes. I continued in my masochistic questioning. "Will you tell me what to expect?" I have always believed we don't ask questions to which we already think we have the answers, but I wasn't quite prepared for hers. She said that eventually, the diuretics would not keep the fluid off, and it would continue to get worse. Eventually, he probably wouldn't be able to walk and need the wheelchair all the time and be in bed much of the time. He would eventually need oxygen, and she would have to see him daily instead of weekly. Then there would be around the clock supervision till the end. "Unless he had a massive heart attack or just didn't wake up one morning," I said, which she added would be a blessing. Wow! I knew I asked her for the truth, but all this hit me like a ton of bricks. She said there would be no way I would be able to care for him by myself. Shocked, I then asked if based on her past experiences, what kind of time line was she thinking of regarding Paul's condition? She said that by the fall, I should be looking at either a nursing home or getting much more help here at home, and that I should probably have a meeting with the three kids to get them up to speed on helping me more. She offered to be at the meeting if I wanted her to be. The fall? Really? That was only a few months away! Surely not, I thought. I cried off and on the rest of the day. How could I tell the kids this news? I really had to think about how long I would put it off.

Naturally, the following day, all my stomach problems returned with a vengeance convincing me that whatever it was, emotions set it off. I decided to wait before talking to the kids until after my procedure in July. Let them enjoy the summer without this dreadful news. Besides, Paul had cheated death so many times before; maybe Tracy's predictions were wrong. Paul had a cardiology appointment coming up and I would just not think about it till later.

July began with nothing alarming and then again nothing exciting or fun. I had a tough time with the fourth of July for some stupid reason. I have always loved cookouts, fireworks, the memories flooding back to the fun holidays I had spent growing up. Now nothing was fun; there would be no way I would be able to have a cookout any longer; all our kids and their families were busy with their own functions; by the time any fireworks would begin, Paul would be needing to get ready for bed. I could hear the fireworks somewhere off in the distance, and all I wanted to do after I got him tucked in was go outside and try to see something sparkling in the sky. I admit I had a good cry that night and gave in to a short lived pity party. Tomorrow would be just another day. It was our routinely scheduled day to hang out with our son's daughters for a couple of hours, and even that was no longer fun. I was afraid they couldn't have cared less that we were there. The days of babysitting and making a difference in their lives were clearly a thing of the past, at least that's how it felt. It seemed that nothing brought me joy any longer and that scared me to death.

Meanwhile, all the symptoms that had sent me to the doctor in June had disappeared, and I really questioned if it was really necessary to have the surgical procedure scheduled for July thirty-first. I had also made a discovery that added fuel to the fire, and that was that coffee, which I was hopelessly addicted to, may have caused some of my intestinal problems. So I switched to half decaf, half regular, since I knew going cold turkey would produce headaches I didn't want to experience. Voila! It seemed to work, and I had many days in a row with absolutely no physical problems at all! I was elated and questioning even more if I should go through with the procedure. I admit I was looking for any reason to cancel it!

On a Monday in July when I was on the massage table, and Paul was in Bonnie's care, I got a text from her that said, "He's hallucinating; wants to go home and is very agitated." I texted back for further information; I tried calling and got no response. The masseuse asked me if I wanted to finish the massage, and I said that I had to leave immediately. Not knowing what I was going to find when I got home, I went sixty mph on residential streets until I pulled into my garage. He was just fine by then, and I wasn't happy with her for what I perceived was an overreaction, but what was done was done. I had to remember that she was not a nurse, and all that mattered was that she was not comfortable caring for him.

Paul and I had a few good days after that. We went to Mass and tried to just spend good time together. Thursday of that week, July 20, we had another crisis; we were walking back from the family room to the bedroom, and Paul was having a terrible time walking. It was all I could do to keep him from falling. He claims I pushed him, and that's why he slumped to the floor; I had learned that according to him, everything was always my fault. He didn't lose consciousness, but there was no way he could get up even with my help. I tried everything, and I could see I was in trouble. Jennie was at work, Jamie was on vacation, Julie was the only one to whom I could reach out for help, but she didn't answer. I had no choice but to call 911 and get help. It took two big, strapping guys to get him to his feet, and the walk back to the bedroom was awful. They took his vitals and an EKG. His blood pressure was normal, but his pulse was very slow, only fifty-two beats/minute. The first EKG showed something funky going on with the ventricle. They suggested he go to the hospital, but he refused. I called Tracy who said not to go to the ER since all they would do was IV hydrate him and send him home. If it was a cardiac blip on the radar, they wouldn't be able to do anything anyway due to his overall fragile health. She came an hour later to check him herself, and by then his pulse had returned to sixty-six beats per minute, and he was fine. I knew he had a checkup with the cardiologist coming up in a few weeks, and I would be sure to raise some questions then. To be safe, I brought his wheelchair upstairs to eliminate the stress of walking and possibly falling again.

Adding insult to injury, we were experiencing a serious heat wave with humidity creating a heat index of 104 degrees. People with respiratory issues were told to stay indoors since the air quality was very bad. I don't know if it was the heat or the aftermath of the previous day's stress, but Paul had a terrible time waking up. Just getting from the bed into the wheelchair was a chore for him...and for me. The nurse aide was due to come for his shower, and it took the two of us to get him safely into the bathroom. Usually the shower makes him feel better, but this time he seemed to be having breathing problems. She decided to give him a breathing treatment before he ate breakfast, and even then she had to feed him. It was like he had absolutely no energy to even hold a fork. I called Tracy again and asked her if she had time to do another check some time that day since we were going into another weekend when I would have no help and, as always, she made it happen. She gave him thumbs up and wished us well as we had our granddaughter's eighteenth birthday party and also haircuts the following day, July 22.

I have to admit I really wanted to go to the party, but I was dreading the day. I knew I would have to get Paul up, medicated, dressed, fed and ready to go for the haircuts on time. I would have to carry the wheelchair down to the car again, hoist it in and get him into the car. Once again, he was having a terrible time getting into and out of the car; his feet just wouldn't move. And it was over ninety degrees. I was soaked with sweat already, and it was only noon. Then I had to get the wheelchair out of the car, get him in it, then hoist it back in the car later, get him out of the car at home, carry the wheelchair from the car to the upstairs, get him back in it, all without his being able to move his feet! I was nearly in tears. After a quick lunch of a chilled smoothie, I tried to get him from his recliner in the family room and back into the wheelchair to go to bed for an early nap since we had to go to the party at his usual nap time. And

I couldn't do it. His feet were frozen in one spot, and he could not figure out how to get into the chair. I was in a total state of panic at that point. It took us nearly ten minutes to finally get this done, and I knew after his nap, I would have to repeat the entire procedure to get in the car and go to the party.

Our son-in-law and grandson met us at the driveway, and even he could not get Paul out of the car and into the wheelchair. It was a pathetic sight as the three of us were grunting and sweating in the now nearly 100 degrees. Talk about starting a party badly! My other constant fear is that he is going to choke while eating in front of other people. Fortunately, this didn't happen, but he did drop his plate of cheese crackers and chips on the floor giving their big black Labrador a tasty treat. I had to feed him his ice cream when I could see he had no strength to get the spoon up to his mouth. At that point I pulled my son-in-law aside and asked him if he would follow us home and help me get him upstairs, carry the wheelchair, etc. He and our teenage grandson did follow us, and I really don't know what I would have done without them. Paul was so wiped out I didn't even try to get him out of the wheelchair until he went to bed, which was at eight forty-five! He didn't make a sound all night; even his usually loud breathing didn't occur. At one point I got up and looked to see if he was still alive. The nurse aide had told me the last time she was there that he told her he thought he was dying! I finally had to wake him up at eight fifteen the next morning. He had never slept nearly 12 hours before. However, the rest must have been what he needed, and he was a little more mobile that day.

The following day was Sunday, July 23, and I had already made the decision to forego church. I thought both of us could do with a day to do nothing. He still used the wheelchair in the house, and I had a little less trouble transferring him from recliner to wheelchair and from commode to wheelchair. It really was both mentally and physically exhausting for both of us to make these transitions since his feet just didn't want to move.

Months before when Tracy gave me some end of life reading to prepare me for the signs that things were escalating, I told her I didn't think he was anywhere near that point, but I remembered every sign I read. Now, only a few months later, I was seeing many of those signs. His appetite was decreasing; he needed more sleep;

he had more trouble walking; he was very weak. He only had his eyes open for a short time, and then he would have to close them for longer and longer periods. The dementia was getting worse. He seemed more confused. The nurse had predicted that autumn might be difficult. This was only July. I couldn't believe this was happening so fast.

When Tracy came on Monday, July 24, I told her he had not walked since Thursday since I was too afraid he would fall again, and I wouldn't be able to get him up. But I asked her if she would try to see if he could? She got him to walk from the bedroom and down the hall to the family room door, but then he said he was too tired to go any farther. That was the last time he walked at all.

I knew my patron saint's feast day was coming up on Wednesday, July 26, and I had a strong faith in her intercession on my behalf. She had shown me her friendship several miraculous times in the past so I began a novena to her on July 16, ten days before her feast. I sat alone in an empty church and I begged her to intercede on behalf of my dear, tired husband since he needed to be released from his exhausting health journey. I finished the novena on the twenty-fifth of July. It was the following day that he finally said to me, "I think I am checking out!" I knew what he meant, but this was significant since only a week before he had told three caregivers he knew he was dying but didn't want me to know. I knew this was the turning point if he decided to share that with me, and it was. He said he wanted to tell me some things. He wanted to talk about our finances even though I had been handling all the money issues for eight years. But even at the end, he had still wanted to take care of me.

The following day, Wednesday, St. Anne's feast day, he took a serious turn for the worse and was incapable of walking to the shower with the nurse aide. That morning he didn't finish his breakfast, didn't want lunch and was pretty much out of it for the day. I got him to agree to play our favorite board game, Sequence, but he couldn't seem to remember what to do. After his nap, I came into the bedroom to get him up for dinner. I needed a shower and shampoo badly, wore no make-up and had on baggy clothes since by then I had lost twenty-eight pounds, and everything hung on me. He looked at me, smiled and said, "You sure do look pretty today." Those were some of his last words to me.

On Thursday, July 27, he was totally bedridden, and I had a very difficult time trying to care for a 200 lb. man in bed especially with regard to hygiene needs. Hospice came a few times to check on him but never stayed long. Now his incontinence was presenting a real hardship for me since I didn't have the kind of diapers that hospitals use on bedridden patients. He kept asking if Julie, our daughter, was home from vacation yet. He wanted to see Julie. I knew she was in Louisville for the night and coming home on Saturday, but I finally had to call her and tell her dad was asking for her. They left Louisville immediately, and she came right to the house and told him she was there. That night she stayed the night with me because I was honestly afraid to be alone with my own husband. I knew we were going to have to change his diaper. Hospice had provided the style with the tabs rather than the pull-up briefs, and the demo on how to do it in bed looked hard. But we gave it a shot. It wasn't just difficult; it was awful and he was in pain as we tried to work through it, and to make it worse he was still in the process of defecating after we began. Dear Julie just kept repeating, "It's alright, Dad; it's just poop!" We finally got it done, and a sloppy finished product it was.

Thursday during the night he needed three breathing treatments. Once again I was treating asthma, I thought, since his feet and ankles were not swollen at all like they had been in December. Every time he would cough, he would get wide-eyed with a look of terror on his face. It was like fear, but mixed with love, goodbye, all kinds of non-verbal messages, and a look I wish I could forget but never will, I'm afraid.

Friday, July 28, Tracy returned and was shocked at how quickly he had declined in such a short time. After examining him, she took Julie and me to the kitchen and said, "It's time to start the twenty-four hour care program right this minute. Death is imminent." It was like a one-two punch in the gut. It had been what we were all praying for, his release from all the pain, humiliation, fear and hard work. But it was still difficult to hear those words. Death is imminent. Earlier that morning, I had called Paul's long term health insurance company to see how much they would pay for in home nursing since just the day before one of the nurses had said he could linger for maybe six more weeks. I was floored when they told me the insurance wouldn't kick in at all until I had paid out of pocket for thirty days. I knew in my heart he didn't have thirty days, and the cost out of pocket would be $576.00 per day! We had been paying this company for seventeen years to the tune of $21,000, and it was all for nothing. But then Tracy said the words, "Death is imminent". He would die at home surrounded by family with professional care. I nearly collapsed in relief, but Friday was the longest full day of his life and the longest day of mine. The kids and grandkids came to see him in waves to tell him they loved him and to say goodbye except for our nine year old grandson who hugged him and said, "See ya, Papa." It was a gut wrenching day.

Our three kids came to be with their dad and stayed with me until he breathed his last. At around eleven thirty, he coughed, opened his eyes wider than they had been for years, stared first at me, then straight ahead and up. He just stared, a peaceful, calm look on his face, and Tracy said, "He's seeing something or someone right now. He's got one foot crossed over." What a comforting thought. Was it God? Was it his mom? My dad, whom he really missed? I'd have given anything to know. He closed his eyes again, and his breathing became very gurgled and audible. Then Tracy explained that his lungs had been filling, and he did in fact have congestive heart failure again. The symptoms had just not begun in his feet this time, but instead his belly had looked a bit distended, and then it went to his lungs. It sounded like he was drowning, but they kept giving him medications to keep any discomfort from him.

By this time, it was two o'clock in the morning, Saturday, July 29. The one nurse who had just arrived had blocked the car of the nurse who had just left. She came back in and told the second nurse she had to move her car. They left the room together, and then Julie, who was lying down in bed with me, sat up and said, "Do you hear the change in his breathing? It's so slow." She ran over to him, saw the final signs of congestive heart failure and yelled for me to wake her brother, who was asleep on the floor and her sister asleep on our couch. I kicked him in the butt and ran to the couch just as the nurse returned. I think I said, "Run!" At two twenty-two in the morning, he died with all of us there to see the moment he left us. He looked awful; his pallor was frightening to see, and his mouth hung open as all seem to do in death. I could hardly look at him; this wasn't him; this wasn't him. I lay my head on his chest and cried, and Julie began to finally wail in body wracking sobs. She ran out of the room and went outside, and I heard her sobbing by the mailbox. She could not get a breath, and I was very concerned for her. Both her brother and sister had been crying, too, but Julie had been with her dad constantly from Thursday till the last moment, helping to give him his meds, cleaning him up. "It's alright, dad, it's just poop!" Those words will always stay with me.

Jamie and I went to her to try to help her breathe again. He was wonderful with her, calmly talking and modeling deep breaths for her to follow to keep her from hyperventilating. I was literally holding her up as we walked to the front porch chairs and sat down. When she could talk she said, "He was trying to sneak out on us. The two nurses were out of the room and he thought we were asleep!" she said with a tinge of anger in her voice. "He thought he could sneak out on us." That wouldn't have surprised me a bit. For the fifty plus years he had been in my life, he had never sought attention. But it didn't work this time. The 'till death do us part' had finally come and gone with much loving attention.

Jennie went home to be with her family and Jamie and Julie stayed with me. We uncorked a bottle of wine at three in the morning and talked in the kitchen. They felt that when he had opened his eyes seeing something, when Tracy said he was crossing over to the other side, that was when his spirit left, the moment we felt he died. It was only Hospice's compassionate care, the oxygen, the liquid morphine and other relaxant meds that kept his body going for three more hours.

I had to stay up till the funeral home people came at four in the morning to take his body. I hadn't wanted to even go back into the bedroom so I wouldn't have to see that face that no longer looked like the man I had married. The man whose eyes I had gazed at with love at the altar was gone. The kids kept saying, "He's not in there anymore, Mom. That's not him." Of course I knew in my head that was true, but I couldn't look at him like that. The funeral directors wrapped him in a lovely quilt, and I needed to see him leave our home for the past thirty years for the last time. I thought I was prepared for that, but I wasn't. They had not covered his face in case I wanted any last minutes with him. I declined. They lifted the gurney down the stairs and wheeled him out into the dark night as I said my final goodbye. And then I sank to my knees.

Our wedding day remains with me still as I calculated then how many years I would have with him until he reached the age of fifty eight when I was sure he would follow in his father and grandfather's footsteps with a massive heart attack. But God gave me nineteen more years than I thought I would have. He had lived to welcome eight grandchildren into the family and loved them all dearly. Julie shared with me a conversation she had had with him months before and asked him if he was afraid to die. He said, "No. I have lived a long life and it has been a really good life."

Later that last day of his life, I was searching for something on my desk shelf, and a card fell out from a place where I kept meaningful greeting cards I had received over the years. It was postcard size with a photograph of a full moon I think our daughter had taken. On the back was a handwritten message from him that I could hardly decipher since his handwriting had become pinched, tiny and nearly illegible. It had to be two or three years old because he hadn't been able to write at all his last few years. But the message read, "The moon and stars belong to you. Thank you for all the adventures. Love on this Valentine's Day." I had forgotten all about that card that I had stuck away, and on the day he died it fell onto my desk!

Valentine's Day, 1963, I had mentally committed myself to him alone. How grateful I was to know he felt he had had a good life, and that he valued the adventures we had shared for fifty years. How blessed I was to have been a part of it for better for worse, for richer or poorer, in sickness and in health, till death do us part.

EPILOGUE

As I write this epilogue, it has been eight weeks since my husband left me. In rereading all the previous chapters, it seemed to me that his chapters were indeed complete but mine were not. As I mentioned elsewhere in this memoire, we can learn how to handle the better and the worse, the richer and the poorer, the sickness and the health if we remain in a marriage long enough to experience all those aspects of living together with another human being. But nothing really prepares us for the 'death till us part' scenario. Nothing can teach us how to handle that until it hits us smack in the face, and when it does, we are pretty much on our own writing the lesson plan. And so, eight weeks into this new journey, I am beginning to write the new chapter of my life, the widow chapter, the re-invention of myself chapter, and it is harder to write than most of the previous ones.

I am one of the fortunate ones to have all my children and grandchildren living within ten minutes from me. Their presence has been lifesaving, but they can only be present for small windows of time. They have their lives to live, and they have busy lives. In some of my weaker moments, I recognized how easy it could be to rely on them for my happiness, my sanity, my reason to get up in the morning. But after a good cry, I say out loud something my son told me to say. "Feed the good wolf, Dee, feed the good wolf." I can have my five minute pity party (the bad wolf) when I am alone at home and then pull myself together and attempt to feed the good wolf with more positive energy. Not that there's always a lot left, but it's a goal to try to achieve.

I knew logically that there would be many "punch in the gut" moments that would come with no warning, those indescribable jolts of reality and sadness that couldn't be stuffed down no matter how hard I would try. And there have been several of those these last eight weeks. And in retrospect, there was no way to prepare for them. The first came the weekend I had to go back to Mass without pushing Paul in the wheelchair. We had gone to the same Mass every Sunday, saw the same friendly, welcoming people, thanked the same man who opened the door for me as I pushed the wheelchair through, and sat in the same pew reserved for the handicapped. That first Sunday without Paul, I felt like I had a bull's eye on my back with the word "WIDOW" in the center. I felt I was missing a limb; I couldn't decide where to sit; I got terribly choked trying to sing. All I could think about was how I used to cherish the infrequent times when Paul would try to sing. That was an awful morning and not a very good spiritual experience. I couldn't wait to leave the church, and I cried all the way home.

The following week, I decided to get smart and go to the Saturday evening Mass where no one would even recognize me. It is commonplace in our parish to have a baby baptized right after the homily, and the entire congregation then welcomes this new little Christian into the fold. But never have I witnessed a marriage in the middle of a weekend Mass. Unfortunately for me, there was going to be a wedding ceremony taking place after the homily. At the entrance hymn, the priest, servers and lectors processed in as always, but they were followed by the wedding attendants and the beautiful bride in her long white dress and flowing veil and looking as radiant as only a bride can look. My immediate reaction was to think, "I remember how I felt walking down the aisle fifty years ago. You're just beginning your marriage, and I just ended mine." I got up and practically ran out of the church and barely made it to the door before the tears came in torrents. I couldn't get to my car fast enough, and then came the ugly cry, the moments of feeding the bad wolf until there were no more tears to give him. My daughters invited me to go to Mass with them the following week, and for a brief moment I considered it. But then, I thought, I would be relying on them to keep me together. This was something I had to do alone. And now after eight weeks, I have finally accomplished it.

After a month passed, the cemetery director called to say the headstone was finished if I wanted to come and see it. I knew what it was supposed to look like; I had designed it shortly after Paul's death. But as much as I didn't want to go and see it, I knew it was something else that had to be done. My daughter offered to go with me, and I was very tempted to say yes. Just as I was going to turn down her offer because I knew how much she hated going to cemeteries, too, and before I could think about it too long, I said yes. This was one time I really thought I needed some moral support. We parked the car, walked past the graves of my parents and grandmother and down a slope to where our plot was. I thought I knew what I was going to see, but when I saw his name in big letters with his birth and death dates and my name right under it, I wasn't ready for it, not even a little bit. All I could say was, "OH!" It was like having the wind knocked out of me for a moment. I don't know what I thought it was going to feel like, but the reality of that moment, the finality of his life, engraved into a stone for all eternity made my knees weak. I tried to talk to him; I needed to tell him how much I missed him, but that I knew I could not come back, would not come back because I didn't feel like I wanted to spend time with his ashes. That was not him. I told him that I was so sorry, but I just couldn't return. Then as we walked to the car, the bad wolf came to get me again. I didn't just cry; I wailed like Julie had done the night he died. It was worse than the first church experience, worse than the new bride experience. It came from inside a part of me I didn't even know existed, and I was helpless to contain it. I don't remember much of what I said, but I do remember when I could finally get a breath saying, "Why would anyone want to marry a second time and have to possibly experience a loss so profound again?"

Since his death, I had begun de-cluttering the house, throwing things away, giving things away knowing I was going to try and sell the house in the spring. Getting rid of Paul's clothes took a big chunk of time, and that was difficult. I looked at the neckties I had bought him in Paris and the tee shirts and sweatshirts he had bought on so many vacations. I couldn't part with some of those. Then I started on his office downstairs. It was a daunting task, and I hardly knew where to begin. Since our daughter was going to take his desk, I began there emptying everything in the drawers, on the desk and in the hutch. It was a start but hardly made a dent in the room. There were fourteen book shelves in this office as well as another built in desk on the opposite side of the room. There was also a small closet filled with miscellaneous "stuff". After two weeks of daily de-cluttering, throwing out, shredding and setting aside things to keep, I had to begin tackling the 14 book shelves, six of which were filled with heavy medical tomes and old college texts. I had also found hundreds of catalogued Kodachrome slides of lab specimens he had prepared for the many lectures given to medical students over his thirty year career. I had no idea what to do with any of this. I phoned his best friend and former colleague who commiserated with me. He said he had done the same thing with all his old lab paraphernalia the previous year. Unfortunately, there was not a library anywhere that wanted any old medical books, and he told me he had to throw them all out! To me, throwing any book in the garbage is tantamount to a mortal sin, but what else could I do? He also told me to do the same with the slides. "No one uses old Kodochrome any longer," he said. I couldn't even imagine at that moment doing this. It felt like I was tossing a thirty year career in the trash can. I thought of all the hours it must have taken him to prepare all those slides, all those lectures he had given and for which he had won "Teacher of the Year" three times, and it broke my heart to get rid of them. But I had no choice. What did I want with them? I didn't even understand what I was looking at. I cleared the book shelves and stacked his books in the little closet and decided I would have 1-800-got-junk come later to haul them away. The three kids came to take other books that remained and some of the other memorabilia like the framed Who's Who in American Colleges and Universities and other awards he had been given at various times. Finally, after five weeks of daily work, I boxed up what I wanted to keep and looked at a very sad, empty room. I cried as I closed the door and knew I would not look in there again until it was time to put the house on the market. After feeding the bad wolf a bit more, I talked myself into holding on to the idea that his legacy was not the old, heavy tomes on the closet floor or the ancient lab slides in the garbage can but rather it lived on in the minds of all the scientists who are using the knowledge they gained from him. It was the best I could do, and it did help somewhat to keep the wolf at bay.

Six weeks after his death, I began the fall quarter at the University of Cincinnati moderating my French Conversation Class for retirees. I had been doing this ever since I retired thirteen years earlier and had made wonderful friends in the process. During the previous three years when Paul needed constant care, preparing to go to the class had been most stressful. I had to get up early enough to get myself ready, get him ready for someone else to be with him, drive thirty minutes to the campus and keep my phone handy during the class in case something happened while I was away and then race out immediately when the class ended to get home in time to relieve my helper. Add to that the fact that mornings were always the most labor intensive care-giving time. There were some days I questioned whether it was all worth it. So beginning the new term after Paul died was a totally different situation. I slept later, only had to take care of myself and the dog, had a relaxing breakfast and drive to campus. Everyone there knew Paul had died, many had sent sympathy cards, and even people I only recognized but whose names I didn't know greeted me with sincere compassion. I felt all the love and warmth of people who genuinely cared envelope me, and it was so heartwarming. I didn't take my phone out of my purse, enjoyed seventy-five minutes of great French conversation and even stayed after to have lunch with a friend. Then on the way home, it came crashing down on me that the reason I had been able to enjoy such a great time was because Paul was no longer here. The guilt was overwhelming, and the bad wolf returned. Elation, guilt and grief... so many different emotions in a matter of a few hours made me question my own mental stability, and it scared me. I cried off and on the rest of the day and wondered if I could ever really be happy and enjoy this new life I was living. I tried talking to the kids about it, but I couldn't even talk to them without crying. They convinced me that Paul wouldn't want me to feel guilty for enjoying this new experience. It was a new chapter, and only I could make it an interesting one. It just seemed like there were so many mental hoops to jump through to get through a day, and it was exhausting. I could only hope that these feelings would be temporary, but only time would tell.

There have also been moments of reflection that have been unsettling. In looking back over the last eighteen years when I became a grandmother, I realized that I had always been a caregiver of one sort or another. When I retired from teaching I couldn't wait to give our three kids one day a week to babysit. It gave them a break, and I had precious time to forge bonds with these eight little ones God blessed me with. It was quality time I relished and care I loved to give. Just about the time they were all in school and my babysitting job was not needed on a regular basis, Paul began needing more care. I am convinced this was all a part of a greater plan for my life. But the grandkids are old enough now to either be alone or babysit others themselves; Paul is no longer here to need my constant care, and it feels like everything I do to fill my days is self-centered. It's a feeling that leaves me unfulfilled, like there has to be something more important than taking care of myself and the dog! But in more rational moments I recognize that it has only been eight weeks, and I have not taken care of myself for a very long time. Now I have an obligation to myself to be active, healthy, both physically and mentally, and if that is all I am capable of at the moment, maybe that's okay.

Something that came to light after the first few weeks while talking with my kids was somewhat mystical. Paul and I had been enjoying our patio over the course of his last spring and summer and wondering why we hadn't seen any hummingbirds at the feeder. He had commented that he hadn't seen even one. I, too, found it odd since we had enjoyed seeing them the previous year. Several days after he died, as I was in the TV room, I heard a tap on the picture window, and there was a hummingbird just hovering there, not flying away but just looking in the window. It seemed odd, but I thought no more about it after it left. Then the same thing happened three evenings in a row, a hummingbird tapping the window and hovering there for a while! I couldn't believe my eyes. When I mentioned this to my daughter, she said something that gave me chills. "Mom, when the priest came to give dad the sacrament of the sick on his last day, he was standing by the bedroom window. I saw a hummingbird over his shoulder outside." There had never been a hummingbird in the front of the house since in that spot there is nothing to attract one. Several days later, my other daughter said that the day her dad died, she went home and needing to be alone for a bit, she went out to her vegetable garden. Suddenly, she looked up and a hummingbird hovered right in front of her face not more than six inches away. She was so startled but was frozen on the spot. She couldn't believe how close it stayed and how long it stayed before it flew away. The following week, my older daughter had the same experience while sitting on her deck, a hummingbird hovering so close to her face that she was afraid to move. All this seemed most atypical since these tiny creatures are not usually people friendly. Later, my daughter heard a lecture given by a neurosurgeon who had written a book called <u>Proof of Heaven</u> in which he described his own "life after death" experience. He said that he saw hummingbirds everywhere, and that they were messengers from beyond. I had to know what was going on. I looked online "symbolism of hummingbirds" and found that in many cultures they are a religious symbol of resurrection and hope! This could no longer be a coincidence!

As the longest eight weeks of my life were coming to an end, Paul's wonderful nurse, Tracy, came to visit me. I was very happy to see her again, and what was supposed to be a short visit after work became a three hour conversation. It was important for me to get a few things off my mind, and, as always, she said all the right words of reassurance. But it was something else that she said that will stay with me forever.

She told me that on July 20, the day he collapsed in the hall and I had to call 911, he probably did have a cardiac event, just as the EMT's had said. They had wanted to take him to the hospital, but he refused. When she came over an hour later at my urgent request, she read the EKG and said then that it looked normal to her given his history. But in fact, she knew it wasn't, but she also knew he didn't want to die in a hospital; besides, there was nothing they could have done for him then. Then on July 24, at her last Monday morning check up with Paul, the morning I had asked her to see if he could walk, he told her he couldn't make it to the family room. She had put him in the wheel chair and over to the recliner where they had a talk. He told her that he knew he was dying. She told him that she knew it also. He still didn't want her to tell me, and she honored the wishes of her patient. If he had hung on until the following Monday, she had decided to pull me aside and tell me. But of course, he didn't live that long. They discussed how he felt about it, and she wanted me to know that he was not afraid of dying, he was at peace with it and he knew it was time. His body was getting weaker, and he was too tired to keep up the fight. It was only two days later, when he did finally choose to tell me he "was checking out". Somehow he knew; he was well aware that death was coming soon, and that's why he decided to finally tell me. She was convinced that he had been hanging on until our fiftieth anniversary, his birthday, my birthday and Father's Day in June were over, and that he could let go. And in retrospect it was after that, late June, early July that his decline was more rapid. After he shared his imminent death with me on Wednesday, July 26, St. Anne's feast day, he lived only two more days. He died doing it his way, at home with the entire family present. Tracy also believed what I had thought regarding the vision he apparently had. That was the moment he crossed over, his spirit no longer with us, and it just took his body a couple of hours to catch up. What a blessing that all of his family witnessed that moment. I will always consider that beautiful moment as the time he died, not the moment he finally drowned with congestive heart failure.

So as I conclude this epilogue, I am still working hard with house preparations, enjoying more time with my grandchildren without guilt, writing my children's books and teaching the French class. I am trying to get back into a fitness routine, and when the house projects wind down, I hope to do some volunteering at church and maybe even take a few courses at U.C. all in good time. I have come to appreciate more than ever my women friends who call, text, email and plan get-togethers. Their moral support has been most appreciated. And I know that when any of them will be facing this time in their lives, I will be there for them. When I mentioned to Julie that I had not exercised my social, people skills in a long time, she said they were still there; they had just been dormant. How insightful of her.

There was, however, one more thing that still haunted me. For several years, Paul had mentioned that he missed hearing me sing in church. Thirty years ago, when I was young, had a pretty good voice and mediocre guitar playing skills I organized a guitar Mass at our parish, a group that continues there to this day. When we moved from that parish, I sang my last Mass and began enjoying anonymity in a new parish. Over the course of those thirty years, I sang now and then, at Christmas with my family at home, but no longer publicly. And apparently, Paul had missed it.

For the last five years, I had contributed to our parish multi-lingual, multi-cultural Mass on Mission Sunday in October by reading several petitions in French. The thought always crept into my mind to try to sing something after communion in French, but after not using my voice or my guitar skills in such a long time, I always lost my nerve. I never got around to singing for my husband in church before he died, and I regretted it terribly. When my granddaughter agreed to accompany me on violin, I decided I had to try and hoped that he would still be able to hear it. I got out my guitar and discovered that the arthritis in my hands compromised my ability to play a bit, but with daily practice and newly formed callouses on my fingers, I found I could still get through a song. The problem was my voice! Being of *une certaine age,* my singing range was considerably lower and, like any other part of one's body that doesn't get used enough, my vocal cords needed lots of exercise! And so I sang every day and played guitar every day until I could feel the strength and confidence return little by little. I practiced every week with my granddaughter who composed her own accompaniment for my French song.

Finally the moment arrived when I had to pull myself together and prove that I could still do this. My three children and all eight grandchildren were sitting in the pew sending me positive energy and moral support. Eleven weeks after Paul's death, my granddaughter and I performed at Mass in what I can only describe as a graced moment. My heart soared with every note in a way that is difficult to really put into words. It truly was a love song, to God and to Paul.

My new chapter is a work in progress and will be for a long time. I did eventually have the procedures to diagnose my stomach issues and found that I never really had irritable bowel syndrome at all but rather microscopic colitis. Its cause is unknown but stress, caffeine, alcohol and some foods that I loved exacerbated the condition, and there is no cure. A few Pepto Bismal tablets twice a day and making some easy dietary changes was all I needed. The three month checkup was a success story! My own health is now a priority.

Recently I heard a homily by my Pastor that discussed the "givens of life". It seemed like an appropriate way to finish this memoire.

The first given is: "Nothing stays the same; change is inevitable." Anyone who has lost a spouse can identify with that one! Marital status changes; finances change; friendships may change; emotional stability changes at least for a while; the reason for getting up in the morning changes.

The second given is: "God's timetable is not necessarily my timetable." Well, that's for sure! My timetable for a marriage that would last more than fifty years wasn't His timetable. My need to have a buyer for my house quickly was not His timetable though it did eventually sell.

The third given is: "Life isn't always fair." It certainly wasn't fair that my sweet, intelligent professor husband lost his ability to think clearly or speak audibly. It certainly wasn't fair that all the plans we made for our retirement and golden years became impossible for us to achieve.

The fourth given is: "There will be pain and suffering." Any family that says they have not experienced pain and suffering is living in a dream world of delusions. Paul's pain before and after his open heart surgery, my hip pain and recovery after total hip replacement, Paul's physical and emotional pain after the brain surgery, his continued decline and the emotional pain my entire family experienced watching Paul's physical and cognitive decline are just a few of the examples of this given.

The fifth given is: "People are not always loving and caring." Unfortunately I know that during my years of caregiving, I was not always as loving as I should have been when I was exhausted, afraid, angry, or filled with self-pity. Former friends were not always as caring as I thought they would be as they fell by the wayside. Some of the medical community wasn't always as compassionate as I felt they should have been when I would fall apart with fear and sadness.

This all sounded so grim, but the homily ended with the reassurance that if we live our lives with love, accepting and making the best of these givens as they come along as a part of God's greater plan for us, we can sustain almost anything. This homily hit me like a lightning bolt because just moments before hearing it I was feeling very sad and sorry for myself that Paul was not there with me. I had to smile as I thought, "Okay, Lord, message received."

There are still moments every day when I miss my husband terribly, especially the weekends when the feelings of loneliness creep in, the moments when I look in the mirror and see the evidence of sadness in my eyes that no amount of makeup can seem to cover. I realize that will continue to happen, maybe for a long time. But friends and family aside, only I can choose to live this new chapter of my life as I think Paul would want me to, with love, acceptance and gratitude. And with God's help, I will do my best.

Printed in the United States
By Bookmasters